Social Marketing to Protect the Environment

Social Marketing to Protect the Environment

What Works

Doug McKenzie-Mohr

McKenzie-Mohr & Associates Inc.

Nancy R. Lee

Social Marketing Services, Inc.

P. Wesley Schultz

California State University, San Marcos

Philip Kotler

Northwestern University

Los Angeles | London | New Delhi
Singapore | Washington DC

Los Angeles | London | New Delhi
Singapore | Washington DC

FOR INFORMATION:

SAGE Publications, Inc.
2455 Teller Road
Thousand Oaks, California 91320
E-mail: order@sagepub.com

SAGE Publications Ltd.
1 Oliver's Yard
55 City Road
London EC1Y 1SP
United Kingdom

SAGE Publications India Pvt. Ltd.
B 1/I 1 Mohan Cooperative Industrial Area
Mathura Road, New Delhi 110 044
India

SAGE Publications Asia-Pacific Pte. Ltd.
33 Pekin Street #02-01
Far East Square
Singapore 048763

Senior Executive Editor: Lisa Cuevas Shaw
Editorial Assistant: Megan Krattli
Production Editor: Libby Larson
Copy Editor: Megan Markanich
Typesetter: C&M Digitals (P) Ltd.
Proofreader: Susan Schon
Indexer: Terri Corry
Cover Designer: Bryan Fishman
Marketing Manager: Helen Salmon
Permissions Editor: Adele Hutchinson

Copyright © 2012 by SAGE Publications, Inc.

Printed in the United States of America

Library of Congress Cataloging-in-Publication Data

Social marketing to protect the environment: what works/ Doug McKenzie-Mohr . . . [et al.].

p. cm.
Includes bibliographical references and index.

ISBN 978-1-4129-9129-2 (pbk.)

1. Social marketing. 2. Green marketing.
I. McKenzie-Mohr, Doug, 1959-

HF5414.S664 2012 658.8′02—dc22 2010053364

This book is printed on acid-free paper.

11 12 13 14 15 10 9 8 7 6 5 4 3 2 1

Brief Contents

Detailed Contents

Foreword

As the size of our global society climbs rapidly toward 7 billion, there is an ever more pressing need to help people, communities, and nations live more sustainable lifestyles. Many of us have high hopes that technological innovation will eventually provide the world with vast quantities of cheap, clean renewable energy; dramatically improved agricultural yields; and the means to keep the earth's waters clean, but this currently appears to be more of a long-term vision than a near-term reality.

Technologist and philanthropist Bill Gates—in his 2007 commencement speech at Harvard University—said that the process of finding solutions to wicked problems such as those posed by human civilization's currently unsustainable lifestyles runs through four predictable stages: (1) determine the goal; (2) find the highest-leverage approach to achieve the goal; (3) discover the ideal technology for that approach; and (4) in the meantime, "make the smartest application of the technology that you already have—whether it's something sophisticated, like a drug, or something simpler, like a bednet." This book—*Social Marketing to Protect the Environment: What Works*—represents the best available thinking about how to make the smartest use of the technologies that we already have to address the challenges of sustainability.

Social marketing has been around—at least in concept—for 40 years now, since two young marketing professors named Philip Kotler and Gerald Zaltman first proposed it in 1971. Regrettably, four decades later, it remains a poorly understood and highly underutilized method for helping people embrace behaviors that are in their and society's best interest, including behaviors that can move us toward more sustainable lifestyles. I have high hopes that *Social Marketing to Protect the Environment* will prove pivotal in advancing a more widespread application of social marketing, at least with regard to influencing more sustainable lifestyles.

Chip and Dan Heath—in their terrific book called *Made to Stick*—made the case that useful ideas can be made "stickier." Specifically, they suggested that stickier ideas are better remembered and are more likely to be used when it is useful to do so. The means by which ideas can be made stickier is to explain them in SUCCESsful ways: *simple, unexpected, concrete, credible, emotional,* and based in a good *story*. In *Social Marketing to Protect the Environment*, Doug McKenzie-Mohr, Nancy Lee, Wesley Schultz, and Philip Kotler have rendered the concepts of environmental social marketing in a manner that is indeed SUCCESsful. They have described the principles of community-based social marketing (CBSM)—Doug McKenzie-Mohr's uniquely insightful adaptation of social marketing techniques to the task of fostering sustainable behaviors—simply and clearly, laying bare the essential steps of the process so that others can understand and apply them. Through a range of concrete case studies—each a compelling story unto itself—they have shown us how others have applied these principles to identify unexpected and effective ways of fostering sustainable behaviors at home and in our businesses. The unrivaled credibility of these authors—all of whom are veritable rock stars of social marketing and/or social influence—has produced a book that does not merely have an aura of authority but rather possesses genuine expertise, experience, and wisdom. And lastly, it is a book that evokes an important emotion—hope. Specifically, it gives me a sense of hope that by applying methods described in this book we can turn many of our sustainability challenges into opportunities.

This book is likely to become a favorite of both the current generation and next generation of sustainability program developers. Its greatest gift to the field of sustainability may, however, go beyond its direct instructional value for practitioners. The book closes with a set of recommendations to federal, state, and provincial governments and philanthropic funders who have the potential to create important economies of scale for environmental social marketers. If implemented, these recommended investments in audience research, materials development, and program pilot testing can change the social ecology of sustainability programs, such that it will become easier, less costly, and less risky for program managers to implement effective sustainability behavior change programs. In short, McKenzie-Mohr and his coauthors have proposed a promising "upstream" social marketing initiative that may enable social marketing to finally live up to its fullest potential with regard to promoting more sustainable communities.

Edward Maibach, MPH, PhD
Director, Center for Climate Change Communication
George Mason University
Fairfax, Virginia, USA

Preface

At a small cafe in a hotel in Brighton, England, on September 29, 2008, three of the authors of this book (Doug McKenzie-Mohr, Nancy Lee, and Philip Kotler), as well as the author of the Foreword (Ed Maibach) met to discuss a common passion and shared vision. We were attending the first World Social Marketing Conference and were struck by two major "missings." First, relatively few of the presentations for the 2-day event related to influencing behaviors to protect the environment. As with most social marketing conferences and publications to date, public health topics and cases dominated the agenda. Secondly, we had each heard the call from colleagues at the conference, as well as "back home," for references to find a variety of soli d case examples using social marketing to influence environmental protection behaviors—especially ones that involved audience research, utilized more than communications and advertising, and included rigorous evaluations confirming success. We have written this book to fill this void and address this need. Subsequently we included P. Wesley Schultz on the writing team, who has expertise in CBSM, social psychology, and program evaluation.

We believe this book is a first of its kind. Many readers may be familiar with CBSM and others may be more familiar with the traditional social marketing approach. We have blended these two models and point out where they complement, as well as enhance, each other. We have included success stories from around the world. We selected them based on their focus on influencing a behavior, versus awareness and attitude change. We looked for cases that included insights into target audience barriers and benefits and then developed strategies using a variety of tools to address them. We wanted cases where a pilot had been tried before full-scale implementation and where a formal evaluation had been conducted.

A quick glance at the table of contents indicates we have the following cases: Reducing Waste (Chapters 2 and 8), Protecting Water Quality (Chapters 3 and 9), Reducing Emissions (Chapters 4 and 10), Reducing Water Use (Chapters 5 and 11), Reducing Energy Use (Chapters 6 and 12), and Protecting Fish and Wildlife Habitats (Chapter 7). About half of the cases involve influencing behaviors in the residential sector, while the remaining cases target the commercial sector. Global examples include cases from Australia, Canada, Western Europe, Ireland, Jordan, the Netherlands, New Zealand, Spain, the United Kingdom, the United States, and Vietnam.

The cases explored in this text may span the globe and the commercial and residential sectors, but as authors, we endeavored to present each chapter in a uniform and accessible format.

- Every chapter begins by presenting an environmental challenge and exploring the nature of the problem and relevant environmental trends.
- Each chapter then explores potential behavior solutions that could be used to address the problem.
- Two to three case studies are included in each chapter to highlight examples of "what works" in addressing the particular environmental challenge under consideration. Within each case study, readers are provided with
  - background information on the organization being examined and its social marketing endeavors,
  - an account of the target audience and its desired behaviors,
  - an explanation of the barriers and benefits unique to the environmental problem being addressed,
  - a description of the program that was implemented, and
  - a critical review of the program's outcomes.
- All chapters include a discussion of other notable programs to illustrate how the principles explored in the chapter extend beyond the specific cases examined.
- A summary at the end of each chapter helps readers to make connections between the cases explored in the chapter.
- Questions for Discussion engage readers in examining the cases and investigating how their principles apply to other environmental scenarios.

Our intention is that current and future practitioners charged with influencing behaviors to protect the environment will find these cases and their critical reviews informative, instructional, and inspiring. Our hope is that the next time we compile a list of potential success stories, it is "a mile long."

We would like to acknowledge and thank the reviewers who assisted in reviewing our manuscript: Nancy Artz, *University of Southern Maine*; Ken Donnelly, *Lura Consulting*; Darrin C. Duber-Smith, *The Metropolitan State College of Denver*; Gail H. Kirby, *Santa Clara University*; Thomas A. Klein, *The University of Toledo*; Jennifer Lynes, *University of Waterloo*; Christie Manning, *Macalester College*; Keith McDade, *Green Mountain College*; Catherine Ray, *Natural Resources Canada*; Doug Rice, *King County, Department of Natural Resources and Parks, Water and Land Resources Division*; Marsha L. Walton, *NYSERDA*; Dave Ward, *Snohomish County Public Works*; Don Waye, *U.S. Environmental Protection Agency (EPA)*; Tina Woolston, *Tufts University.*

We would also like to thank the many who shaped this book by providing information for the case studies, sharing their research, or offering suggestions for the chapters.

And finally, our deep gratitude goes to those who supported our efforts during the writing of this book: Amanda Kilburn, Nancy Kotler, Terry Lee, Sue McKenzie-Mohr, Lori Schultz, and Sunshine.

Doug McKenzie-Mohr

Nancy R. Lee

P. Wesley Schultz

Philip Kotler

SECTION I

Introduction

CHAPTER 1

Fostering Sustainable Behavior[1]

The cornerstone of sustainability is behavior change. Sustainability requires that we tackle diverse goals, such as increasing water and energy efficiency, protecting water quality and biodiversity, reducing waste, and altering transportation choices. If we are to hasten the transition to a sustainable future, we must encourage the adoption of a wide array of behaviors that support these goals. To date, most initiatives to foster sustainable behavior have relied primarily upon large-scale information campaigns that utilize education and/or advertising to encourage the adoption of sustainable actions. While education and advertising can be effective in creating awareness and in changing attitudes, numerous studies document that behavior change rarely occurs as a result of simply providing information as information alone cannot address the diversity of barriers that exist for most sustainable behaviors (Environment Canada, 2006; Geller, 1981; Geller, Erickson, & Buttram, 1983; Jordan, Hungerford, & Tomera, 1986; Midden, Meter, Weenig, & Zieverink, 1983; Schultz, 2002; Tedeschi, Cann, & Siegfried, 1982). In contrast, community-based social marketing (CBSM) has been demonstrated to be an attractive alternative to information-intensive campaigns for the design of programs to foster sustainable behavior (McKenzie-Mohr, 2011). Thousands of programs are now utilizing this methodology—often with remarkable results. To learn more about CBSM, read *Fostering Sustainable Behavior: An Introduction to Community-Based Social Marketing* (McKenzie-Mohr, 2011; McKenzie-Mohr & Smith, 1999). Also visit the CBSM website (www.cbsm.com), where you can find articles, case studies, and discussion forums related to fostering sustainable behavior.

CBSM is based upon research in the social sciences that demonstrates that behavior change is often most effectively achieved through initiatives delivered at the community level that focus on removing barriers to an activity while simultaneously enhancing the activity's benefits. CBSM merges knowledge from the social sciences with knowledge from the field of social marketing (see, for example, Andreasen, 2006; Kotler & Lee, 2008). Social marketing has been utilized for several decades primarily to influence behavioral changes that improve public health and prevent injuries. Social marketing has been defined as "a process that applies marketing principles and techniques to create, communicate, and deliver value in order to influence target audience behaviors that benefit society (public health, safety, the environment, and communities) as well as the target audience" (P. Kotler, N. R. Lee, & M. Rothschild, personal communication, 2006). CBSM borrows from social marketing an emphasis on understanding what impedes and motivates a target audience to act as well as the importance of piloting programs prior to their broadscale implementation. From the social sciences, and particularly social and environmental psychology, CBSM inherits a variety of behavior-change "tools" that can be utilized to foster changes in behavior.

CBSM involves five steps:

1. Selecting which behavior to target

2. Identifying the barriers and benefits to the selected behavior

3. Developing a strategy that reduces barriers to the behavior to be promoted, while simultaneously increasing the behavior's perceived benefits

4. Piloting the strategy

5. Evaluating broadscale implementation and ongoing evaluation once the strategy has been broadly implemented

In this overview of CBSM, each of these steps will be described.

Step 1: Selecting Behaviors

Prior to selecting which behavior(s) to promote, consider first which audiences are relevant to target. For example, imagine that a program is being developed to promote energy efficiency in order to reduce CO_2 emissions. To gauge which audience should be targeted, program development should begin by comparing energy use by sector. In Canada, energy use differs markedly by sector, with industrial, transportation, and residential sectors responsible for the greatest energy use (Natural Resources Canada, 2010).[2] Of these, further imagine that the residential sector has been selected as it provides the opportunity to address both residential energy use and transportation choices (in this example, however, we will focus only on residential energy use).

It is nearly always the case that organizations working to promote sustainability have a plethora of behaviors from which to choose, and residential energy use is no different. For example, in delivering a program to enhance the energy efficiency of residential homes, we could promote the installation of low-flow showerheads or programmable thermostats, the addition of insulation to an attic, or the turning off of lights. Indeed, in a program in Queensland, Australia, over 200 actions were identified that a homeowner can take to increase residential energy efficiency (C. Hargroves, C. Desha, & D. McKenzie-Mohr, personal communication, 2009). Other areas, such as waste reduction, watershed protection, biodiversity protection, and water efficiency have similarly long lists of potential behaviors that could be fostered. Clearly not all behaviors are of equal importance, so how do we determine which to promote? Begin by assessing how your issue (e.g., landfill waste, water, biodiversity loss, air pollution) is affected by a particular sector. In the case of residential energy use, this would involve beginning by exploring how energy is utilized within a home.

As shown in Figure 1.1, space heating makes up the majority of Canadian residential energy use (60%), while space cooling contributes only 2%. Clearly, far larger reductions in residential energy use and associated CO_2 emissions can be gained by focusing on space heating rather than cooling. The chart also reveals that water heating contributes 18% of energy use, which is intriguing as numerous energy-efficiency campaigns in Canada focus on space heating and the purchase of energy-efficient appliances (the third most important category at 10%) while largely ignoring water heating.

This type of analysis provides useful guidance regarding which behaviors are potential candidates for programs you might deliver. Based on the figure, we should

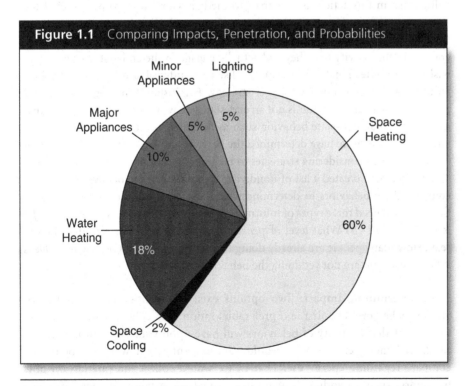

Figure 1.1   Comparing Impacts, Penetration, and Probabilities

Source: Natural Resources Canada (2010). Canada's secondary energy use by sector, end-use and sub-sector. Available online at: http://oee.nrcan-rncan.gc.ca/corporate/statistics/neud/dpa/tables handbook2/aaa_ca_2_e_4.cfm?attr=0

gravitate toward behaviors related to reducing energy use for space heating, water heating, and major appliances. How do we select behaviors within each of these areas? In creating our list of behaviors, we should be guided by two criteria: (1) no behavior should be *divisible* and (2) each behavior should be *end state*. As the name suggests, divisible behaviors are those actions that can be divided further into more specific behaviors. For example, adding additional insulation to a home is a divisible behavior. A homeowner might add insulation to their attic, their basement, or to the external shell of their dwelling. Each of these behaviors is distinct and will have their own set of barriers and benefits. Since the barriers to sustainable behaviors are often behavior specific, it is critical to begin by listing behaviors that are nondivisible. Failing to do so will leave a program planner with *categories* of behaviors that often differ dramatically in their associated barriers and benefits.

In addition to ensuring that a behavior is not divisible, we also want to ensure that it is end state. For instance, our principal interest is not in having people purchase high-efficiency showerheads but rather in having them installed. In contrast, in the case of programmable thermostats, our principal interest is not in having homeowners install a setback thermostat but rather in them programming it. Too frequently, initiatives to promote sustainable behavior focus on prior behaviors and never achieve the end-state behavioral change that matters. In determining whether a behavior is end state, simply ask, Am I hoping that someone will engage in this action as precursor to the behavior I wish to promote? If the answer is "yes," you have not selected an end-state behavior. It is important to not list actions that precede end-state behaviors as there is no guarantee that if someone engages in the activity that they will actually engage in the end-state behavior you wish to promote. Finally, in creating a list of nondivisible end-state behaviors, ensure that no item on the list is a strategy. For instance, having a household participate in an energy audit is not an end-state behavior but rather a strategy that might lead to an end-state behavior, such as installing additional insulation in an attic. It is not until we have determined the barriers and benefits to a behavior that we should begin considering strategies to facilitate the adoption of that behavior.

Once we have created a list of nondivisible end-state behaviors, we will want to compare these behaviors to determine which are worth promoting. To compare them, we will need three types of information for each behavior: (A) How *impactful* is the behavior? (B) What level of *penetration* has the behavior already achieved (e.g., How many people are already doing the behavior?)? and (C) How *probable* is it that those who are not yet doing the behavior will adopt it?

A. Determining Impact: Two options exist for identifying the impact of various behaviors. The first and preferable option is to collect rigorous data on the impact that a variety of behaviors will have upon your issue. In the case of residential energy efficiency, we would want to scrutinize how various behaviors compare regarding energy use. That is, we would collect information on how behaviors, such as adding insulation to an attic, installing a high-efficiency showerhead, and turning down the temperature on the hot water heater, compare to one another related to energy use. Frequently, this information is available from federal and state/provincial agencies. When such data does not exist, we will need to employ the second option, which involves surveying individuals who have technical expertise in the area of interest. It is suggested that these experts be asked to rate each behavior on a scale of 0 to 4, where 0 equals "no impact" and 4 equals "high impact." Ratings from experts should be sought independently and then averaged. That is, do not bring together a group of experts, have them discuss residential energy use associated with the list of behaviors, and then have them rate the actions. Independent ratings have superior psychometric properties and are less prone to errors that can occur with group-based ratings (McKenzie-Mohr, 2011).

B. Determining Penetration: Two options also exist for determining penetration. The first, and most reliable, is to unobtrusively observe the target audience to gauge their present level of engagement in various behaviors. This approach works well for such behaviors as curbside recycling, bicycling, and carpooling, which are easily observed, but is not useful for behaviors that are not easily observed, such as the installation of high-efficiency showerheads. When behaviors are not easily observed, utilize the second option which involves surveying the target audience and asking them how often, if at all, they engage in each of the behaviors on the list. If the behavior is a one-time action, such as installing a water-efficient showerhead, simply ask if they have done the action. In contrast, if the behavior is repetitive, such as washing clothes in cold water, ask what percentage of the time they engage in the action. As with ratings of probability, these numbers are likely to be unreliable. As a consequence, it is not the absolute numbers that we should attend to but rather the range of values. For example, if 50% of households indicate that they have installed high-efficiency showerheads and 20% note that they have insulated their hot water heater, it is not the absolute numbers (50% versus 20%) but rather the range between these numbers that we should attend to. That is, we can't say with confidence that 50% of households have installed high-efficiency showerheads as there is a tendency for positive environmental behaviors to be overreported, but we can say with confidence that high-efficiency showerheads are more likely to have been installed than hot water heater insulation. Finally, remember that we are looking for behaviors that have low penetration associated with them. That is, we are looking for those behaviors that fewer people have engaged in as they provide more potential for change.

C. Determining Probability: Two options also exist for determining probability. The most rigorous and desirable option is to look for carefully evaluated programs that have been delivered to facilitate each of the behaviors on your list. It is important to note several issues regarding such programs. First, the generalizability of the programs needs to be considered. Only those programs that closely match the circumstances and context under which we would be delivering a program should be considered. For instance, water shortages in Australia are a more pressing problem and have received far more national attention than water shortages have in Canada. Further, information regarding the per capita costs to deliver each program should be obtained so that return on investment (ROI) for each program can be calculated. Collecting detailed case study information for a long list of behaviors is cost and time prohibitive. If the list of behaviors is large, we may wish to first survey the target audience regarding the probability of them engaging in each behavior (this survey would also include the penetration ratings previously described). In the case of residential energy efficiency, householders should be asked to rate the probability of engaging in each of the behaviors on a scale of 0 to 4, where 0 equals "no likelihood" and 4 equals "high likelihood." You will need to provide some context in order for the responses to be meaningful (e.g., What is the likelihood that you would install a high-efficiency showerhead if you had to purchase and install the showerhead yourself? versus What is the likelihood that you would install a high-efficiency showerhead if we provided you with a showerhead and you had to install it yourself?). Note that as with ratings for penetrations, values obtained from this survey will not be representative of the *actual* likelihood of householders engaging in these behaviors, as there is a strong tendency for respondents to "inflate" the likelihood of engaging in a behavior. Nonetheless, the range of the values obtained is a good indicator of the *relative* likelihood of a target audience engaging in these behaviors. When the list of nondivisible end-state behaviors is large, it is worthwhile to begin with this survey in order to cull the list down to a more manageable number for which case study information (e.g., option 1) can be collected. Note that we can often also substantially reduce the length of the list by focusing on those categories that will lead to the greatest impacts. In the case of reducing residential energy use in Canada that would involve behaviors related to space heating, water heating, and major appliances.

Use a table such as Table 1.1 to compare your list of behaviors. Ideally, we are looking for those behaviors that have high impact and probability but low levels of penetration. We can compare various behaviors by multiplying the impact that a behavior has by the current level of penetration by the probability of a target audience engaging in the behavior to obtain a behavior's weight (we are looking for those behaviors that have the largest weights). Since we are looking for behaviors that presently have low levels of adoption, we need to invert penetration values before multiplying the three numbers. To do this, simply subtract the present level of adoption from one (e.g., if 60% of households have installed high-efficiency showerheads subtract .60 from 1) to obtain the number of people (40%) who we could realistically encourage to install high-efficiency showerheads. The following table provides some fictitious values to demonstrate how two residential energy-efficiency behaviors might compare to one another. As is shown in the table, even though the probability of installing compact fluorescent lightbulbs (CFLs) is significantly higher than the probability of installing high-efficiency showerheads, the higher impact and lower level of penetration for showerheads makes their promotion more worthwhile than that of CFLs.

Formula: Weight = Impact $\times$ (1 − Penetration) $\times$ Probability

Table 1.1 Comparing Impacts, Penetration, and Probabilities				
Behavior	Impact (pounds of CO_2/household/year)	Penetration	Probability	Weight
High-efficiency showerhead	400	.40	2.2	352
Install five compact fluorescent lightbulbs (CFLs)	100	.20	3.4	68

In determining which behaviors to select for your program, you should gravitate toward two types of behaviors. If you are interested in encouraging only one action, then you will want to choose the behavior that has the largest weight as it represents the best interaction among impact, penetration, and probability. In contrast, if you are interested in encouraging a variety of actions over time, you may wish to select a behavior that is less impactful but has a very high probability of your target audience engaging in the action and for which there are currently low levels of adoption. In well-designed programs, such catalytic behaviors may be used as stepping-stones to more substantive actions being taken at a later time.

In summary, begin by determining the relative importance of various sectors for the issue of concern (e.g., watershed contamination, airshed pollutants, water use). Second, for the most important sectors, determine how they contribute to your issue (e.g., What percentage of residential water use is for using toilets, showering, washing dishes, washing clothes, and watering lawns and gardens?). Third, determine the behaviors that are associated with each of these areas (e.g., reducing water used for showering could involve taking shorter showers or installing high-efficiency showerheads). Fourth, compare these behaviors regarding impacts, penetration, and probability to determine the most important behaviors to target in your program. This process can be used for a wide diversity of environmental issues and will significantly enhance your confidence that you have selected the most appropriate behaviors to target.

Step 2: Identifying Barriers and Benefits

Research indicates that each form of sustainable behavior has its own set of perceived barriers and benefits (Oskamp et al., 1991; McKenzie-Mohr, Nemiroff, Beers, & Desmarais, 1995; Tracy & Oskamp, 1983/1984). For example, the factors that impede individuals from composting are quite different from those that preclude more sustainable forms of transportation. Even with apparently closely associated behaviors such as recycling, composting, and source reduction, different sets of barriers and benefits have been found to be important. Further, barriers and benefits also differ by groupings of individuals or "segments." Identifying these segments occurs during both the first and second steps of CBSM. When selecting behaviors, determining which sectors are most important (e.g., residential, commercial) broadly defines target audiences. During the second step, uncovering how barriers and benefits differ for different segments within a sector will allow you to more effectively target different audiences. For instance, low-income households will be less able to afford the purchase of a high-efficiency showerhead than households that are more affluent. Consequently, a strategy to encourage the installation of high-efficiency showerheads for low-income households would differ from a strategy that was promoting the same behavior for more affluent households.

Barriers to a sustainable behavior may be internal to an individual, such as one's lack of knowledge, nonsupportive attitudes, or an absence of motivation (Stern & Oskamp, 1987). On the other hand, barriers may reside outside the individual, as in changes that need to be made in order for the behavior to be more convenient (e.g., providing curbside organic collection) or affordable (e.g., subsidizing public transit or compost units). Multiple barriers may exist for any form of sustainable behavior. As a result, once we have selected which behavior has the best combination of impact, penetration, and probability, we next need to identify its barriers and benefits.

Uncovering barriers and benefits involves four steps. Begin by reviewing relevant articles and reports. Next, obtain qualitative information through observations and focus groups: methodologies that are intended to help you identify "a list" of potential barriers and benefits. Finally, conduct a survey with a random sample of your target audience. The use of several different methodologies to uncover and rank barriers and benefits is called triangulation. Triangulation allows the weaknesses of one approach (e.g., focus groups have poor generalizability due to the small number of participants and low participation rates) to be addressed by the strength of another approach (e.g., survey results can be more easily generalized to your target audience but don't often provide the rich detail that focus groups do).

Literature Review

In conducting the literature review, consult five sources: (1) trade magazines and newsletters, (2) reports, (3) academic articles, (4) authors of reports and articles that you found particularly useful, and (5) list serves to identify colleagues who can assist you.

Observations

Observational studies of specific behaviors are another valuable tool. By directly observing people, we can more easily identify skill deficits and sequences and incentives that are already at work to reward existing behaviors. Observational studies help reduce the problems of self-report data and get the researcher much closer to the community and the behavior. Observation is also useful in evaluating behavioral compliance, particularly for behaviors where people are being asked to learn and maintain new skills.

Focus Groups

The literature review and observations will assist you in identifying issues to further explore with your target audience through focus groups and a survey. Limit the size of each focus groups to 6 to 8 people, and divide participants into different groups based on whether they have previously engaged in the behavior (e.g., installed a programmable thermostat) or not. Further, make it easy for people to participate by providing services such as child care and transportation. Come to the focus groups with a set of clearly defined questions that have been informed by the literature review and observations. The facilitator of the focus groups must clearly steer the discussion and ensure that all participants feel comfortable in participating. Record the session, or have an assistant take notes during the group meeting. Don't provide information about your program prior to the focus groups, as this information will influence the information received from participants. When the focus groups are completed, tabulate the responses and identify barriers and benefits that are mentioned by significant numbers of participants (see the *Focus Group Kit* by Morgan & Krueger, 1998, for further information).

Focus groups are useful in obtaining in-depth information but are limited by the small number of participants and the influence that the group itself has upon what each member feels comfortable saying. Surveys overcome these two limitations.

Surveys

Conducting a survey consists of seven steps. First, begin by clarifying the objective of the survey. Do this by creating a survey objective statement, which indicates the purpose of the survey. A good question to help facilitate this is to ask, What decisions am I trying to make that I need this research to help answer? This statement can be used to ensure the support of colleagues before proceeding. This statement can also act as a reference when later deciding upon the relevance of potential survey items. Second, list the items that are to be measured. Note that at this point we are not concerned with writing the questions but rather with identifying the "themes" or "topics" that will be covered in the questionnaire. Third, have someone skilled in survey development write the survey. Fourth, when the survey is completed, take the time to pilot it with 10 to 15 people. Piloting the survey allows you to scrutinize the wording of the questions and the length of the survey. Don't include the data obtained from the pilot with the data obtained from the actual survey. Fifth, select the sample. Surveys are most useful when the respondents are randomly selected from the target audience. A sample has been randomly selected when each adult in the target audience has an equal chance of being asked to participate. When this criterion is met, we can generalize results back to the whole community with greater confidence. As with the focus groups, survey samples should be comprised of two subgroups—those who have engaged in the behavior already and those who have not yet done so, sometimes referred to as a "doer versus nondoer" analysis. Sixth, conduct the survey. Strive to conduct the survey as quickly as possible to reduce the likelihood of an event in the real world impacting upon your survey results (e.g., British Petroleum [BP] and the Gulf of Mexico). Seventh, analyze the data. Unless you have someone on staff with a statistical background, you will want to have the survey data analyzed for you. In having the data analyzed, ask for a thorough description of those individuals who are engaging in the activity, as well as for those that are not (descriptive statistics). Also, ask for the factors that distinguish people who are doing the behavior, such as composting, from those who are not and the relative importance of these factors (multivariate statistics).

Significant pressures, such as time and staffing constraints, and increased project costs often result in this second step—the identification of barriers and benefits—being skipped. While these pressures are real and important, failure to identify barriers will often result in a program that either has a diminished impact or no impact at all. The identification of barriers and benefits is an essential step in the development of a sound CBSM strategy. By conducting a literature review, focus groups, observations, and a survey, you will be well positioned to develop an effective strategy.

Step 3: Developing a Strategy

CBSM involves developing a strategy that addresses both the behavior we wish to promote and the behavior we wish to discourage. For the behavior we wish to promote, we want to reduce its barriers while simultaneously increasing its benefits. In contrast, we wish to do the opposite for the behavior we wish to discourage—we wish to increase its barriers while also reducing its benefits (the introduction of carpooling lanes both increases barriers to single occupant driving and reduces its benefits). A variety of behavior change tools can assist with this task. There are the traditional 4Ps in the commercial marketing toolbox (e.g., product, price, place, and promotion), three of which are similar to CBSM tools where incentives = price; convenience = place; and communications = promotion). New to the traditional toolbox are commitments, prompts, norms, and social diffusion. Additional information on these tools can be found in *Fostering Sustainable Behavior: An Introduction to Community-Based Social Marketing* (3rd ed.) (McKenzie-Mohr, 2011).

Commitment

In a wide variety of settings, people who have initially agreed to a small request, such as to wear a button saying they support the purchase of products with recycled content, have subsequently been found to be far more likely to agree to a larger request, such as actually purchasing these products (McKenzie-Mohr, 2011).

Why does seeking commitment to an initial small request work? There are likely two reasons (Cialdini, 1993). First, when people go along with an initial request, it often alters the way they perceive themselves. That is, they come to see themselves, for example, as the type of person who believes it is important to purchase products that have recycled content. Second, we have a strong desire to be seen as consistent by others. Indeed, our society emphasizes consistency, and people who are inconsistent are often viewed negatively. As a result, if we agree to wear a button supporting the purchase of recycled-content products, it would be inconsistent not to purchase these products when we shop.

Commitment has been utilized as a behavior change tool in a variety of studies with often dramatic results. In considering using commitment, follow these guidelines:

- Emphasize public over written or verbal commitments. Public commitments (e.g., having a sign placed on lawns indicating that the lawn is pesticide free) have been found to be more effective in bringing about long-term behavioral changes (Pallak, Cook, & Sullivan, 1980).
- Seek commitments in groups. If possible, seek commitments from groups of people who are highly cohesive, such as a church group. The close ties of these individuals, coupled with the importance of being consistent, make it more likely that people will follow through with their commitment (Wang & Katzev, 1990).
- Actively involve the person. When people are actively involved, such as being asked to peer into an attic to view the amount of insulation or hold a container to measure the flow rate of a shower, they are more likely to see themselves as committed to the activity (Gonzales, Aronson, & Costanzo, 1988).
- Use existing points of contact to obtain commitments. Wherever natural contact occurs, look for opportunities to seek a commitment. For example, when people purchase paint, ask them to sign a commitment that they will dispose of any leftover paint properly or, better yet, take it to a paint exchange if one exists.
- Help people to view themselves as environmentally concerned. We can help people to see themselves as environmentally concerned and therefore more committed to other sustainable activities, by commenting on their past actions (McKenzie-Mohr, 2011). For example, when someone comes to pick up a composter, ask if they recycle. If they do, note that their recycling is evidence of their concern for the environment and that beginning composting is a natural way to reduce waste even more.
- Don't use coercion. In order for this behavior change tool to be effective, the commitment has to be freely volunteered—that is, only ask for commitments when people appear to be interested in an activity (McKenzie-Mohr, 2011).

Prompts

Numerous behaviors that support sustainability are susceptible to the most human of traits: forgetting. People have to remember to turn off lights, check the air pressure in car tires, turn off the engine when waiting to pick someone up, turn down the thermostat, select items that have recycled content, etc. Fortunately, prompts can be very effective in reminding us to perform these activities. Prompts are visual or auditory aids that remind us to carry out an activity that we might otherwise forget. In using prompts, you will want to ensure that you follow these guidelines (McKenzie-Mohr, 2011):

- Make the prompt noticeable. In order for a prompt to be effective, it has to first be noticed. Make sure that your prompt is vivid (a bright color) and eye catching.
- Make the prompt self-explanatory. All the information that is needed for someone to take the appropriate action should be conveyed in the prompt. For example, if we were using a prompt to increase the likelihood that people with odd numbered street addresses would only water their lawns on odd numbered calendar days (and vice versa), the prompt that we attach to an outside faucet could read (water your lawn only on odd numbered calendar days).
- Present the prompt in as close proximity as is possible to where the action is to be taken. If we wanted to encourage people to turn off lights upon leaving a room, for example, we would affix the prompt beside or directly on the light switch plate.
- Use prompts to encourage people to engage in positive behaviors. It is important, when possible, to encourage positive behaviors. If you want people to purchase environmentally friendly products when shopping, place prompts throughout a store that bring attention to those items rather than bringing attention to items that should be avoided. Not only is the encouragement of positive behaviors more likely to be supported by retail outlets (few would let negative prompts be posted) but positive behaviors also make people feel good about their actions, which increases the likelihood that the actions will be carried out in the future.

Norms

To date, few programs have emphasized the development of community norms, which support people engaging in sustainable behavior. This lack of attention to norms is unfortunate given the impact they can have upon behavior. Norms guide how we should behave (McKenzie-Mohr, 2011). If we observe others acting unsustainably, such as using water inefficiently, we are more likely to act similarly. In contrast, if we observe members of our community acting sustainably, we are more likely to do the same. When considering including norms in programs you develop, keep the following guidelines in mind (McKenzie-Mohr, 2011):

- Make the norm visible. For norms to influence the behavior of others, they have to be aware of the norm. The very act of taking recyclables to the curbside, for instance, communicates a community norm about the importance of recycling. Most sustainable activities, however, do not have the community visibility that recycling has, and norms that support the activity, therefore, have to be promoted more actively. Find ways to publicize involvement in sustainable activities, such as providing ongoing community feedback on the amount of water that has been saved by homes using water efficiently.

- Use personal contact to reinforce norms. Research suggests that internalization of norms is more likely to occur as a result of personal contact. As a consequence, use personal contact as an opportunity to reinforce norms that support sustainable behavior.

Social Diffusion

New behaviors are frequently adopted because friends, colleagues, or family members have adopted the behavior—a process known as social diffusion (Rogers, 1993). Social diffusion has been found to be relevant to the adoption of a wide variety of sustainable actions, including, for instance, the installation or programmable thermostats and solar hot water heaters (Darley & Beniger, 1981). There are two ways to facilitate the adoption of new behaviors through social diffusion:

- Make commitments public and durable. Many of the sustainable actions that we would like people to adopt have no visibility in the community (McKenzie-Mohr, 2011). For example, if a household installs a high-efficiency shower-head, no one in the community is aware that this behavior has taken place. Contrast the installation of high-efficiency showerheads with curbside recycling, in which the placement of a container at the curbside clearly communicates engagement in the behavior. An effective way to increase the visibility of *invisible* behaviors is to ask for public commitments, such as the placement of a sticker on the side of recycling container indicating that a household has installed a high-efficiency showerhead. Whenever possible, these public commitments should be durable. That is, favor attaching a sticker to the side of a recycling container versus asking someone to put up a sign on their lawn. The sign is likely to last only a few weeks while the sticker might last for several years. Public and durable commitments enhance social diffusion by encourage conversations regarding the behavior.
- Recruit well-known and well-respected people. Individuals who are well known and well respected have an inordinate impact upon the adoption of new behaviors. For example, well-known and well-respected farmers are more likely to affect the practices of other farmers than those who are less well known and less respected (Rogers, 1993). To identify these individuals, simply ask a number of members of your target audience who are well known and well respected.

Goods and Services (Products)[3]

Effective programs often involve providing our target audience with a service (household energy audit) or a new product (high-efficiency showerhead). Note that barriers exist to the provision of services (e.g., cost of an audit, when they are available) and products (e.g., cost to purchase the product, knowledge of product, availability of product) that a program needs to address if it is to be effective. The delivery of a new service (curbside collection of recyclables) and the provision of a new product (curbside recycling cart) can often dramatically affect the barriers to a behavior and encourage its rapid adoption.

Communication (Promotion)

Most programs to foster sustainable behavior include a communication component. The impact of communications upon behavior can vary dramatically based upon how the communications are developed. To develop effective communications, consider the following elements:

- Use captivating information. All persuasion depends upon capturing attention (Stern & Aronson, 1984). Without attention, persuasion is impossible. Communications can be made more effective by ensuring that they are vivid, personal, and concrete (Gonzales et al., 1988).
- Know your audience. All communications should be developed with your audience in mind. Before developing communications, you should have a firm sense of the attitudes, beliefs, and behavior of your intended audience(s).
- Use a credible source. The individual or organization that presents your message can have a dramatic impact upon how it is received and subsequent behavior (Eagly & Chaiken, 1975). Ensure that whoever delivers your message is seen as credible. Individuals or organizations tend to be viewed as credible when they have expertise or are seen as trustworthy.
- Frame your message. How you present, or "frame," your activity can impact upon the likelihood that people will engage in it (Davis, 1995). In general, you should emphasize the losses that occur as a result of inaction (e.g., from not insulating) rather than the savings that occur from action (e.g., insulating).
- Carefully consider threatening messages. While environmental issues lend themselves easily to the use of threatening messages, do so with caution. While the public needs to understand the implications of such serious issues as global warming, toxic waste, or ozone depletion, they also need to be told what positive action they can take if threatening information is to be useful. In short, whenever you contemplate using a threatening message consider whether you can at the same time present concrete actions that individuals can take to reduce the threat (Lazarus & Folkman, 1984).
- Make your message easy to remember. All sustainable activities depend upon memory. People have to remember what to do, when to do it, and how to do it (Heckler, 1994). Use prompts to assist people in remembering. Also develop messages that are clear and specific.
- Provide personal or community goals. Providing targets for a household or community to achieve can help to provide motivation for sustainable behavior (Folz, 1991).
- Emphasize personal contact. Research on persuasion documents that the major influence upon our attitudes and behavior is the people we interact with rather than the media (Aronson & Gonzales, 1990). Create opportunities for people to talk to one another through programs such as block leaders—individuals from a neighborhood who already have experience in a sustainable activity such as composting—speak to others who live close by. Through personal contact, provide opportunities for people to model sustainable behavior for one

another, such as installing weather stripping, and facilitate ongoing discussions in your community to allow social diffusion of new behaviors to occur.

- Choose communication channels that will reach your target audience in an effective and efficient way. Additional information on communication channel techniques can be found in *Social Marketing: Influencing Behaviors for Good* (4th ed.) (Kotler & Lee, 2011).

- Provide feedback. Remember to provide members of your community with feedback about the effectiveness of their actions. Feedback has been found to have a positive impact upon the adoption and maintenance of sustainable behaviors.

Incentives/Disincentives (Price)

Incentives and disincentives have been shown to have a substantial impact on a variety of sustainable activities including waste reduction, energy efficiency, and transportation. They are particularly useful when motivation to engage in action is low or people are not doing the activity as effectively as they could. Gardner and Stern (1996) suggested the following guidelines in using incentives/disincentives:

- Closely pair the incentive and the behavior. The closer in time the incentive is presented to the behavior it is meant to affect, the more likely that it will be effective.

- Use incentives to reward positive behavior. Where possible, use incentives to reward people for taking positive actions, such as returning beverage containers, rather than fine them for engaging in negative actions, such as littering.

- Make the incentive visible. For incentives to be effective, you need to draw people's attention to them. Consider using vivid techniques to make incentives noticeable. Also, incentives can be made more visible by closely associating them with the behavior they are meant to affect, such as having people attach tags to their garbage bags in order to have them picked up in a user pay garbage disposal program.

- Be cautious about removing incentives. Incentives can be powerful levers to motivate behavior, but they can also undermine internal motivations that people have for engaging in an activity. If you plan to use an incentive to encourage a sustainable behavior, remember that if you elect to remove the incentive at a later time the level of motivation that existed prior to the introduction of the incentive may no longer exist.

- Prepare for people's attempts to avoid the incentive. Incentives such as separate laneways for multiple occupant vehicles can have a significant impact upon behavior. However, because these incentives powerfully reward one behavior (carpooling) and strongly punish another (single occupant driving), there is strong motivation to try to "beat" the incentive and not engage in the desired sustainable behavior (e.g., having a mannequin as a passenger rather than a real person in order to drive in carpooling lanes). In preparing incentives, give careful consideration to how people may try to avoid the incentive and plan accordingly.

- Carefully consider the size of the incentive. In arriving at what size of incentive to use, study the experience of other communities in applying incentives to motivate the same behavior.
- Use nonmonetary incentives. While most incentives are monetary, nonmonetary incentives, such as social approval, can also exert a strong influence upon behavior. Consider ways that social approval and other nonmonetary incentives can be integrated into your program.

Convenience (Place)

The behavior change strategies previously presented can have a significant influence upon the adoption and maintenance of sustainable behaviors. However, they will be ineffectual if significant external barriers exist to the behavior you wish to promote (McKenzie-Mohr, 2011). It is important to identify these external barriers and plan for how you will overcome them. Study other communities to see how they have managed to overcome similar obstacles. For example, some communities now provide curbside pickup of used motor oil, dramatically enhancing the convenience of proper disposal. Assess whether you have the resources to overcome the external barriers you identify. If you do not, carefully consider whether you wish to implement a program until you are able to address these barriers effectively.

Step 4: Conducting a Pilot

As noted previously, the design of a CBSM strategy begins with carefully selecting a behavior, identifying a target audience, and then identifying the perceived barriers and benefits to the activity you wish to influence. Knowledge of these barriers and benefits is particularly important. Without this information, it is impossible to design an effective program. In identifying barriers, be sure to conduct statistical analysis that allows you to prioritize the barriers and benefits. Knowing their relative importance allows limited resources to be used to their greatest benefit. Once you have identified and prioritized the barriers and benefits of your target audience, select behavior change tools that match the barriers you are trying to overcome and create or highlight perceived benefits. When you have arrived at a design for your program, obtain feedback on your plans from several focus groups. Look for recurring themes in their comments as they may indicate areas in which your planned program needs to be redesigned.

Once you are confident that you have a program that should affect behavior, pilot the program. The most common pilot involves collecting baseline measurements, implementing a strategy, and then collecting follow-up measurements. While this is the most common form of pilot, avoid using this method. Imagine that we are developing a program to encourage bus ridership. We collect data on the number of people riding the bus prior to implementing our strategy and then again afterward and notice a marked increase. However, at the very same time that we implemented our strategy the cost of gasoline rose sharply. As a consequence, we do not know whether it was our strategy, the cost of gasoline, or a combination of the two that led to the observed increase in ridership. To avoid this problem, in conducting the pilot, ensure that you have at least two groups: one that receives the strategy that you developed and another that serves as a comparison or control group. You may have more than one strategy group if you have developed more than one strategy. Testing several strategies against each other on a small scale is an effective way of identifying the most cost effective way of affecting behavior change. When possible, randomly assign your target audience into each of your groups. Using random assignment ensures that the only difference between your groups is whether they received a strategy or were in a control group. In evaluating the effectiveness of a pilot, focus on behavior change rather than measures of awareness or attitude change. Further, try to measure behavior change directly rather than rely on self-reports as these reports are prone to exaggeration. If a pilot is not successful in altering behavior, revise the strategy and pilot it again. Assuming that we know why a pilot did not work and that we now have the information needed to go straight to community-wide implementation can be a very expensive mistake.

Finally, when conducting a pilot, only include those program elements that you can afford to deliver in a broadscale implementation. If you deliver a pilot in which you violate this rule and then strip away program elements for your broadscale implementation, your broadscale rollout may be unsuccessful.

Step 5: Evaluating Broadscale Implementation

When a pilot is effective at changing behavior, we are ready to implement the strategy across the community. Evaluate community-wide implementation by obtaining information on baseline involvement in the activity prior to implementation—and at several points afterward. This information can be used to retool a strategy as well as to provide a basis for continued funding and provision of important feedback to the community.

Summary

The process of CBSM (carefully selecting behaviors, identifying the barriers and benefits for the selected activity, developing strategies to target these barriers and benefits, pilot testing the strategy, and finally broadly implementing it once it has been shown to be effective) is transforming the way that environmental behavioral change programs are delivered. The following chapters describe a wide array of programs to foster sustainable behavior that are either based directly on CBSM or use aspects of this approach. Each chapter begins by describing a particular issue (such as pollution of watersheds) and the end-state, nondivisible behaviors that can be promoted to address the issue. Several programs are then reviewed and critically evaluated from a CBSM perspective. Finally, more general comments are provided at the end of each chapter regarding how to utilize CBSM in addressing the particular issue.

Notes

1. This overview of CBSM first appeared as a "Quick Reference" addendum in *Fostering Sustainable Behavior: An Introduction to Community-Based Social Marketing* (2nd ed.) (McKenzie-Mohr & Smith, 1999). A revised version appeared in the *International Journal of Sustainability* (McKenzie-Mohr, 2008). It has been further updated for this book. © Doug McKenzie-Mohr

2. Note that you cannot simply look at energy use, as various forms of energy production differ dramatically in their output of CO_2 (e.g., coal versus hydroelectric).

3. For clarity, the terms used by conventional marketing and some social marketers are shown in brackets after the behavior change tool. See Kotler and Lee (2008) for more information on the Ps.

References

Andreasen, A. (2006). *Social marketing in the 21st century*. Thousand Oaks, CA: Sage.

Aronson, E., & Gonzales, M. H. (1990). Alternative social influence processes applied to energy conservation. In J. Edwards, R. S. Tindale, L. Heath, & E. J. Posaval (Eds.), *Social influences, processes and prevention* (pp. 301–325). New York: Plenum.

Cialdini, R. B. (1993). *Influence: Science and practice*. New York, NY: HarperCollins College Publishers.

Darley, J. M., & Beniger, J. R. (1981). Diffusion of energy-conserving innovations. *Journal of Social Issues, 37*, 150–171.

Davis, J. J. (1995). The effects of message framing on response to environmental communications. *Journalism and Mass Communication Quarterly, 72*, 285–299.

Eagly, A. H., & Chaiken, S. (1975). An attributional analysis of the effect of communicator characteristics on opinion change: The case of communicator attractiveness. *Journal of Personality and Social Psychology, 32*, 136–144.

Environment Canada. (2006). *Evaluation of the one-tonne challenge program*. Retrieved from http://www.ec.gc.ca/ae-ve/F2F5FD59-3DDA-46BC-A62E-C29FDD61E2C5/Evaluation Report-OTC-Eng.doc

Folz, D. H. (1991). Recycling program design, management, and participation: A national survey of municipal experience. *Public Administration Review, 51*, 222–231.

Gardner, G. T., & Stern, P. C. (1996). *Environmental problems and human behavior*. Boston: Allyn & Bacon.

Geller, E. S. (1981). Evaluating energy conservation programs: Is verbal report enough? *Journal of Consumer Research, 8*, 331–335.

Geller, E. S., Erickson, J. B., & Buttram, B. A. (1983). Attempts to promote residential water conservation with educational, behavioral and engineering strategies. *Population and Environment Behavioral and Social Issues, 6*(2), 96–112.

Gonzales, M. H., Aronson, E., & Costanzo, M. A. (1988). Using social cognition and persuasion to promote energy conservation: A quasi-experiment. *Journal of Applied Social Psychology, 18*(12), 1049–1066.

Heckler, S. E. (1994). The role of memory in understanding and encouraging recycling behavior. Special issue: Psychology, marketing, and recycling. *Psychology and Marketing, 11,* 375–392.

Jordan, J. R., Hungerford, H. R., & Tomera, A. N. (1986). Effects of two residential environmental workshops on high school students. *Journal of Environmental Education, 18*(1), 15–22.

Kotler, P., & Lee, N. R. (2008). *Social marketing: Influencing behaviors for good* (3rd ed.). Thousand Oaks, CA: Sage.

Kotler, P., & Lee, N. R. (2011). *Social marketing: Influencing behaviors for good* (4th ed.). Thousand Oaks, CA: Sage.

Lazarus, R., & Folkman, S. (1984). *Stress, appraisal, and coping.* New York: Springer.

McKenzie-Mohr, D. (2008). Fostering sustainable behavior: Beyond brochures. *International Journal of Sustainability Communication, 3,* 108–118.

McKenzie-Mohr, D. (2011). *Fostering sustainable behavior: An introduction to community-based social marketing* (3rd ed.). Gabriola Island, BC: New Society.

McKenzie-Mohr, D., Nemiroff, L. S., Beers, L., & Desmarais, S. (1995). Determinants of responsible environmental behavior. *Journal of Social Issues, 51,* 139–156.

McKenzie-Mohr, D., & Smith, W. (1999). *Fostering sustainable behavior: An introduction to community-based social marketing* (2nd ed.). Gabriola Island, BC: New Society.

Midden, C. J., Meter, J. E., Weenig, M. H., & Zieverink, H. J. (1983). Using feedback, reinforcement and information to reduce energy consumption in households: A field-experiment. *Journal of Economic Psychology, 3,* 65–86.

Morgan, D. L., & Krueger, R. A. (1998). *The focus group kit.* Thousand Oaks, CA: Sage.

Natural Resources Canada. (2010). *Total end-use sector. Energy use analysis.* Retrieved from http://oee.nrcan-rncan.gc.ca/corporate/statistics/neud/dpa/tablesanalysis2/aaa_ca_1_e_4.cfm?attr=0

Oskamp, S., Harrington, M. J., Edwards, T. C., Sherwood, D. L., Okuda, S. M., & Swanson, D. C. (1991). Factors influencing household recycling behavior. *Environment and Behavior, 23*(4), 494–519.

Pallak, M. S., Cook, D. A., & Sullivan, J. J. (1980). Commitment and energy conservation. In L. Bickman (Ed.), *Applied social psychology annual* (pp. 235–253). Beverly Hills, CA: Sage.

Rogers, E. M. (1993). *Diffusion of innovations* (6th ed.). New York: Free Press.

Schultz, P. W. (2002). Knowledge, education, and household recycling: Examining the knowledge-deficit model of behavior change. In T. Dietz & P. Stern (Eds.), *New tools for environmental protection* (pp. 67–82). Washington, DC: National Academy of Science.

Stern, P. C., & Aronson, E. (Ed.). (1984). *Energy use: The human dimension.* New York: Freeman.

Stern, P. C., & Oskamp, S. (1987). Managing scarce environmental resources. In D. Stokols, & I. Altman (Eds.), *Handbook of environmental psychology* (pp. 1043–1088). New York: Wiley.

Tedeschi, R. G., Cann, A., & Siegfried, W. D. (1982). Participation in voluntary auto emissions inspection. *Journal of Social Psychology, 117,* 309–310.

Tracy, A. P., & Oskamp, S. (1983/1984). Relationships among ecologically responsible behaviors. *Journal of Environmental Systems, 13*(2), 115–126.

Wang, T. H., & Katzev, R. D. (1990). Group commitment and resource conservation: Two field experiments on promoting recycling. *Journal of Applied Social Psychology, 20,* 265–275.

SECTION II

Influencing Behaviors in the Residential Sector

CHAPTER 2

Reducing Waste

F or the purposes of this chapter's discussion, we will consider waste generated by the residential sector as items that people living in private or multi-unit dwellings dispose of in their garbage, take to the "dump," or just litter, whether deliberate or accidental. In some cases, these items could have been recycled, reused, given "a longer life"—even never produced in the first place.

The Problem

The problem with waste is that the production, distribution, sales, and consumption of products use the earth's natural resources—many of which are nonrenewable. And the disposal of these products, even in landfills, can have negative impacts on the environment, including those from methane gases and leachate, a groundwater pollutant.

To illustrate the market potential for waste reduction, reports from the U.S. Environmental Protection Agency (EPA) provide estimates of the size of the U.S. municipal waste problem, as well as the opportunity. Municipal waste includes residential, commercial, and institutional waste and was estimated to weigh about 500 billion pounds in 2008. (This does not include industrial, hazardous, or construction waste.) As illustrated in Table 2.1, estimates are that as much as 97% of food waste, 87% of plastic containers and packaging, 72% of glass containers, and 62% of aluminum containers that are disposed of could have been recycled or reused. And the potential for this problem is on the rise with—between 1960 and 2008—EPA estimating that the amount of waste each person in the United States created almost doubled from 2.7 to 4.5 pounds per day (U.S. EPA, 2010).

Table 2.1 Generation and Recovery of Products in Municipal Solid Waste (MSW)				
Material	76.6 billion MSW Pounds Generated in 2008	Percentage of Total MSW (500 Billion Pounds)	Percentage Recycled or Reused	Percentage Disposed of (Could Have Been Recycled or Reused)
Containers and Packaging				
Aluminum	3.8 billion	.8%	38%	62%
Glass	20.1 billion	4%	28%	72%
Paper and Paperboard	76.6 billion	15%	66%	34%
Plastics	26 billion	5%	13%	87%
Organic Wastes				
Food	63.6 billion	13%	3%	97%
Yard	65.8 billion	13%	65%	35%

Source: Adapted from U.S. Environmental Protection Agency. (2008). *Municipal solid waste generation, recycling, and disposal in the United States: Facts and figures for 2008.* Retrieved from http://www.epa.gov/epawaste/nonhaz/municipal/index.htm

Potential Behavior Solutions

The top three Rs of the waste management hierarchy are to reduce, reuse, and recycle, providing a rule of thumb guide to relative environmental benefits of waste reduction options. Brief descriptions of each follows, with Table 2.2 then providing a list of related potential behaviors.

Reduce

The best way to reduce our waste stream is to not produce it in the first place. By doing this, we not only decrease the number, size, and environmental impact of landfills but we also decrease use of natural resources, energy, and time that have been used to make and distribute the products. Citizens can be encouraged to reduce consumption most by altering their purchasing behaviors—buying in bulk, buying items with less packaging, paying bills online, giving experiences instead of gifts, and postponing new purchases.

Reuse

Reusing products that have "some life left in them" postpones, even reduces, the use of new resources and the disposal of old ones. As social marketers, we want to develop, promote, incentivize, and/or prompt convenient options to donate or sell unwanted household items such as clothing, furniture, toys, books, magazines, bicycles, cell phones, glasses, garden tools, electronics, and reusable materials from home remodels. We also want to encourage timely maintenance of motor vehicles and appliances to increase their longevity.

Recycle

Recycling is the R that appears to have caught on the best in many countries, making new products out of used ones. Traditional household items that can be recycled include mail, newspaper, glass, aluminum, plastics, and cardboard/corrugated paper. More recently, we are seeing recycling of electronic materials, yard waste, food waste, worn out furniture, clothing, and shoes. Materials for many traditional products are being replaced with ones that have been recycled, including decking from plastic milk jugs and playgrounds from old tennis shoes.

Table 2.2 Residential Behaviors to Help Reduce Waste	
Areas of Focus	**Examples of End-State Behaviors That Might Be Chosen for Adoption**
Reduce	• Purchase remanufactured toner cartridges. • Purchase a reusable coffee filter to replace disposable filters. • Bring a reusable mug to work. • Use a refillable water bottle. • To make a mattress last longer, reverse it end to end twice a year. • Give a battery charger with rechargeable batteries as a gift. • Leave grass clippings on the lawn. • Buy products with the least packaging. • Pay bills online. • Tape a no junk mail sign to mailboxes or mail slots. • Give experiences as gifts.
Reuse	• Donate useful items no longer wanted to charitable groups. • Cut the fronts off of greeting cards and resend them as postcards. • Wrap gifts in materials such as the comics.

(Continued)

(Continued)

	• Use reusable cloth or canvas bags for groceries. • Shop for secondhand items online, at yard sales, and resale stores. • Take unwanted magazines to senior centers. • Use washable table napkins instead of paper napkins. • Hold a neighborhood yard sale. • Follow maintenance schedules on appliances to prolong their use. • Donate unwanted eyeglasses to a charity that will distribute them to those in need. • Return unwanted hangers to cleaners.
Recycle	• Take your Christmas tree to a community "treecycle" event. • Put select food waste and food soiled paper items such as napkins and paper plates in yard waste containers in communities that offer this service. • Give worn out gym shoes to organizations that turn them into basketball courts and playgrounds. • Take worn out clothing or other textiles such as drapes to larger thrift stores that recycle them. • Take unwanted cell phones to an "ecycle" event or electronics collection center. • Sign up for curbside recycling. • Take plastic food bags to recycle locations often found in grocery stores. • Take used tires to a store that sells tires or some other community collection center. • Take used print cartridges to office supply stores for recycling.

Three success stories for this chapter highlight efforts to influence the residential sector to engage in the three Rs: (1) reducing, (2) reusing, and (3) recycling.

CASE #1 No Junk Mail (Bayside, Australia)

Background

Globally it is estimated that 100 million trees are harvested to produce junk mail each year. In Australia alone, 8.2 billion pieces of "occupant/resident" junk mail are sent out annually, along with an additional 650 million promotional letters. Most of this mail is never even read. Even if recycled, junk mail requires further resources to process and remove inks, dyes, and gloss coatings (Latrobe City Council, 2010).

In 2007, two local residents living in Bayside City, a residential suburb to the southeast of Melbourne on the shore of Port Phillip Bay, formed the Bayside Climate Change Action Group (BCCAG) to advocate for firm government action and to persuade other citizens to adopt environment-friendly behaviors (L. Allinson & C. Forcey, personal communication, 2007). Reducing junk mail was one of their first missions, and five volunteer members designed and implemented an impressive, community-based effort to make it happen.

This case story highlights the group's strategic marketing approach, beginning with collection of baseline data to determine the quantity of junk mail being delivered to each household on an annual basis and concluding with an evaluation after 12 months that indicated a third of households (more than 10,000) adopted the desired behavior—placing a No Junk Mail sticker on their mailbox.

Target Audience(s) and Desired Behaviors

The Bayside community is an area of 37 square km and in the last census (2007) had 35,000 households and a population of 92,801. About 43% of residents are 35 to 64 years old. The campaign focused its research and strategies on household heads they described as being well-intended but not active environmentalists. Those in the active environmentalists' segment were tapped for advocacy and volunteer efforts.

The targeted behavior was a single, simple, and doable one—to adhere a No Junk Mail sticker to the household's mailbox. It was anticipated that this highly visible act would have the intended normative effect.

Barriers and Benefits

The project team brainstormed potential barriers to uptake and then interviewed 20 friends and colleagues to deepen their understanding of their audience. They confirmed the following:

- Some people liked receiving junk mail, using it to identify discounts on offers or for food/recipe or product research.
- There was a concern that the No Junk Mail request would also stop delivery of the two free weekly community newspapers.
- Junk mail delivery was a source of income for local teenagers and retirees.
- Some local small businesses regarded the junk mail medium as a key channel to drive customers and might ignore or push back efforts.
- Not all direct mailers respected the request of a No Junk Mail sticker.
- The sticker itself would need to look professional with a nonoffensive design and made of durable and waterproof materials.

For this "well-intended" target audience, benefits included a chance to save trees, as well as declutter the mailbox.

Description of the Program

The product was the No Junk Mail sticker itself, a small (3" x 1") sticker that could be attached to the mailbox, usually located at the gatepost. (See Figure 2.1.) More than 200 distribution boxes were developed and filled with the 10,000 stickers and placed by the volunteer team in outlets around Bayside including coffee shops, bakeries, pharmacies, health clinics, sports clubs, schools, playgroups, youth group halls, local libraries, and council offices (place). Boxes were made from discarded energy bar boxes and covered with the No Junk Mail campaign details. Messages highlighted potential tree savings, emphasized the sticker was free, and included instructions to place it on the household letter box (promotion). The cover of the box also listed online sites for catalogs and support, a contact number for refills and questions, and a link to the BCCAG. Children were also tapped for distribution of stickers, providing them at schools to take home and for Boy Scout troops to distribute (place).

Figure 2.1 A Sticker Signals to the Postal Staff That the Household Declines Junk Mail

Source: Lucy Allinson--co-director of the Bayside Climate Change Action Group (BCCAG).

To accommodate the barrier expressed by several individuals who wanted to read some of the junk mail (e.g., flyers with discount coupons), the BCCAG website carried links to mailings that might have been of interest. In addition, several locations including libraries and coffee shops agreed to make copies of these publications available for customers to read and use.

Though the stickers were free (price), messages on distribution boxes suggested that donations would be appreciated and would be used to help fund the printing of additional stickers. In the end, a total of 350 Australian dollars in donations were collected, fully funding the first as well as the second run of 10,000 stickers each. It was also the intention and belief of the group that citizens would feel a sense of pride for their environmentally responsible action.

Campaign promotions deliberately leveraged the strong community involvement and goodwill toward the BCCAG, which had recently received significant media coverage for a pollution prevention sign on a local beach. The "human sign" was a fun way to get the community to make the call for climate action, featuring people gathered together to form the shape of letters, spelling out the message "Halt Climate Change Now." A picture was then taken from above. Further communications were carried out through a school speakers program and promoted in conjunction with similar BCCAG initiatives. At events related to a solar challenge effort, for example, members were provided stickers and were encouraged to disseminate them to friends and neighbors. At local Al Gore *Inconvenient Truth* events, stickers were handed out as a symbol of a clear and immediate action that an individual could take. Additionally, a press release to local media generated visibility for the effort, and the BCCAG's website (http://www.baysideclimatechange.com/) provided additional information on the impact of junk mail and where and how to get a sticker.

A pilot with 25 houses on two randomly chosen streets in Bayside provided encouraging results:

- Twenty-four houses were approached and offered a sticker.
- Fifteen accepted stickers.
- Seven refused the stickers.
- Two were undecided.

The campaign ran for an initial period of 12 months from October 2007 through September 2008. Campaign effectiveness was evaluated by volunteers auditing eight randomly selected streets within the Bayside City area. Overall, it was estimated that a third of households (10,000) posted one of the 20,000 stickers that had been made available. An audit to estimate impact reported that the average household received over 5,000 pages of junk mail each year (e.g., catalogs, advertising supplements in newspapers). Assuming postal delivery staff observed the No Junk Mail request, as many as 50 million pieces of junk mail were not delivered.

Negative reactions and unintended consequences, especially those of businesses, were addressed in a variety of ways: offering guidance to small businesses on effective alternatives to junk mail including web-based promotions, personally contacting businesses who ignored the stickers, and removing a few of the least productive sticker distribution outlets (i.e., 24-hour fast-food outlets where kids were wasting the stickers at night).

The BCCAG is now (2010) planning to promote this model to other climate groups.

Critical Review

This effort certainly supports what Margaret Mead expressed in her famous quote: "Never doubt that a group of thoughtful committed citizens can change the world. Indeed it's the only thing that ever has." Five volunteers and 350 Australian dollars reduced the amount of junk mail being delivered to a third (10,000) of households in one city in Australia.

What we want to know more about, however, is whether this influenced the behaviors of those upstream . . . organizations developing, funding, and producing the junk mail. Did the post office (midstream) return these mailings to the sender, or did they "simply" recycle them? If it was the latter, we doubt there would be any impact in the reducing the volumes of paper being produced. In an ideal world, this end-state behavior of placing the sticker on a mailbox would have been chosen based on higher potential impact, probability, and penetration scores when compared with alternative behaviors such as influencing citizens to contact organizations to be removed from their mailing list.

CASE #2 Decreasing Use of Plastic Bags and Increasing Use of Reusable Ones (Ireland)

Background

In 1999, it was estimated that around 1.26 billion plastic shopping bags were being handed out free in Ireland each year, with most of the product ending up in the landfill as part of the domestic waste stream (AEA Technology PLC, 2009). Although an unknown smaller proportion of the bags eventually appeared as litter, even the Irish called it their national flag. Some retailers had tried to encourage the reuse of the bags or the use of cloth and canvas bags but had not been successful to date. Most blamed consumer apathy, and although there was robust legislation in place to tackle littering, the ability to enforce violators was understandably difficult.

The Irish government first considered imposing upstream taxes on producers and importers of plastic bags but decided instead to focus on a downstream strategy that would change consumer behavior. In 2002, they introduced a 15 euro cent tax on plastic shopping bags, an amount considered sufficiently high to give consumers pause for thought, and to stimulate bringing their own reusable shopping bags more often (Convery, McDonnell, & Ferreira, 2006). As you will read, the effect has been dramatic, with a reduction in the consumption of plastic shopping bags in excess of 90% and the increase of reusable bags from 36% in 1999 to 90% in 2003 (BBC News, 2007).

Target Audience(s) and Desired Behaviors

The Irish government wanted consumers to bring a reusable bag for their purchases at retail stores, thereby reducing the amount of plastic bag consumption and, ultimately, production and littering.

Barriers and Benefits

Central to their ultimate success were the extensive surveys and consultations the government had with stakeholders that would be affected by the levy, with the following highlights regarding barriers revealed (Convery et al., 2006):

- Consumer "protests" were feared, as many believed increased taxes would benefit the retail stores and/or were primarily a way for the government to increase revenues. Consumers were also concerned they would forget to bring their own bags, having experienced forgetting them frequently in the past.
- Retail industry leaders were concerned that consumers would blame the retailers for "profiteering" and that the levy would encourage shoplifting, making it easier for customers to put items unseen into their shopping bags. Butchers were strongly opposed to any levy that would apply to all plastic bags, warning that various purchases, including meat, need to be wrapped separately for hygiene reasons.
- Revenue commissioners and local authorities were concerned with the amount of additional time, effort, and cost this would require for enforcing, tracking revenue, and allocating funds appropriately.

Perhaps to make this case even more challenging, perceived benefits for each of these groups were difficult to identify.

Description of the Program

A variety of tools were used to address major audience barriers and provide motivators. They are highlighted in Table 2.3.

Program evaluations report the following:

- *Decrease in Bags Distributed:* In the first year after the launch of the levy, there was a 90% reduction in plastic checkout bags distributed, equating to a reduction of 1 billion plastic bags. The number of plastic bags issued per capita fell from 328 to 21. Of interest to some is whether there was then a significant increase in the purchase and use of kitchen "bin liners." Retail data confirmed that there was indeed a 77% increase in the purchase of plastic kitchen bags but that this only equated to 70 million bags. The net effect is still positive, with an overall reduction in plastic bag use of 930 million bags (Evidence, 2005).

Table 2.3 Tools to Address Audience Barriers and Motivators to Using Reusable Bags

Audience	Tools
Consumers	*Incentives and Disincentives (Price)* The 15 euro cent tax was aggressive, but given reluctance among consumers to pay anything for a bag, policy makers were confident it would give pause. A 2000 survey of 1,003 Irish adults aged 18 and over commissioned by the Department of the Environment, Heritage, and Local Government suggested that the proposed tax was more than six times higher than the average amount consumers were willing to pay (around .024 euro cents) and that only 8% of the consumers surveyed felt it was worth paying for a plastic bag at all (Convery et al., 2006). *New or Improved Goods and Services (Product)* Retailers made reusable bags available for purchase and offered the use of recycled cardboard boxes they had a constant supply of for free. *Persuasive Communications (Promotion)* Signage in stores carried messages reminding consumers of the surcharge, as well as encouraging their use of reusable bags.
Retail industry	*New or Improved Goods and Services (Product)* Extensive face-to-face consultations regarding implementation were provided with the main retail industry representative body and the leading retailers. *Incentives and Disincentives (Price)* Exemption was given to plastic bags below a certain size when used for separating food items for hygiene and food safety reasons. *Persuasive Communications (Promotion)* Strong publicity campaigns with the general public were promised and implemented by the Department of the Environment, Heritage, and Local Government. To defray concern that retailers were profiting from the levy, communications stressed the environmental benefit and explained that taxes would explicitly go to funding projects to protect the environment.
Revenue commissioners	*Convenience of Access (Place)* The Irish system appears to have been relatively simple to administer with negligible incremental costs for the retailers as a result of utilizing an existing online levying system. It involved adding another reporting line to the current system of the Inland Revenue's database. *Incentives and Disincentives (Price)* Revenue commissioners were provided with initial setup costs earmarked for new computer systems and increased resources to administer the levy (AEA Technology PLC, 2009).

- *Cost Recovery:* Costs incurred the first year were roughly 1.9 million euros and included the following: 1.2 million for new computer systems and administrative resources needed for launch; 350,000 for annual administering costs; and 358,000 for a promotional campaign to launch the levy. Revenues from the program the first year were 12 million euros, over 6 times the costs of the effort (Convery et al., 2006).

- *Increase in Funds for Environmental Projects:* In the first year, roughly 10 million euros of the revenue were earmarked for environmental projects.
- *Decrease in Litter:* Litter surveys found that prior to the levy launch in the spring of 2002, plastic bags were estimated as comprising 5% of litter in Ireland. By August 2003, they were estimated at .25% of litter and by August 2004, .22%.
- *Consumer Attitudes:* A year after the levy's launch, 100 telephone interviews were completed with a randomly selected sample of householders in Dublin. As indicated in Table 2.4, highlights of findings indicate that the majority of the respondents were either neutral or positive about the expense of the bags and that virtually all felt positive about the environmental impact (Convery et al., 2006).

Table 2.4 Attitudes Toward Bag Tax One Year Later		
	Expense	**Environmental Impact**
Positive	14%	90%
Neutral	60%	10%
Negative	26%	0%

Note: A 43% response rate from the sample was achieved, and there is a + 9.8% margin of error for respondent answers.

- *Retailers Attitudes:* Surveys of retailers were conducted a year after the levy's introduction. Researchers conducted face-to-face interviews with seven leaders in the retail sector, following their completion of a self-administered questionnaire. The cumulative market share of those retailers accounted for 50% of Irish retail sales. Findings indicated that retailers found the effects of the tax neutral or positive, as savings resulting from not having to purchase plastic bags outweighed additional costs of implementation. Findings also indicated that although shoplifting rose initially, it then fell (Convery et al., 2006).

Fast-forward to August 2006 when it was estimated that .52% of litter was from plastic bags, up from .22% in 2003, and the number of plastic bags increased to 30 bags per person, up from 21 in 2003. In July 2007, a press release and statement from the Irish Environment Minister's announced that the tax would increase from 15 euro cents to 22, the first increase since the launch of the levy. "We need to ensure that the success story continues into the future. . . . There has been no increase in the levy since its inception and I am anxious to ensure that its impact is not diminished" (BBC News, 2007).

Critical Review

At first glance, it might seem that the entire strategy for this effort was using a strong "disincentive"—an enforceable tax on the undesirable behavior. In fact, the strength of this effort was in knowing that this was what was needed to achieve the desired behaviors and then developing a program that would be acceptable to the retail industry and convenient and cost efficient for local agencies to implement. Without this upstream and midstream cooperation and support, it is doubtful the program would have been as successful.

As noted, 3 years after the launch of the effort, bag use increased slightly. Although annual use rates (30 bags per capita) were not even close to pre-campaign usage (328 bags per capita), it might be time for new research studies to be conducted to determine the reasons for the near 50% increase. Who brings their own bags and who doesn't? If remembering the reusable bag is a major factor, a few tools that might have helped prevent or deter this decline include a visible prompt to remember the reusable bag either at home, in the car, and/or in the store parking lot. If a perceived norm needs to be reinforced, consider establishing a standard where checkout clerks ask the customer, Did you bring your bag today? And it might be worthwhile to test the power of a pledge where customers commit to using reusable bags.

CASE #3   Increasing Curbside Recycling of Organics (Halifax, Nova Scotia, Canada)

Background

Halifax Regional Municipality (HRM) is a geographically large coastal community comprised of four amalgamated communities: the former cities of Halifax and Dartmouth, the former town of Bedford and the former Halifax County. The population is 375,000 (2006 census) and is spread across an urban area surrounding Halifax Harbour and a larger surrounding rural area. HRM is the capital of the province of Nova Scotia and almost 40% of Nova Scotians live in HRM.

Throughout much of the 1990s, the region sought a new disposal solution for its municipal solid waste. A failed attempt at developing an incinerator (the project failed to receive environmental assessment approval) resulted in a search for a new landfill. In a unique community-led process, a new waste management system was developed for the region.

An important component of the new waste management strategy was separate curbside collection of kitchen and yard waste organics. This was a new system that most people in Nova Scotia had not heard of previously. While communications was an integral component of the introduction of the entire waste management system, more was needed for the successful implementation of this collection program. As you will read, barriers for adoption were significant, and perceived benefits were minimal or, at best, unclear.

When the program was rolled out, each household received a free organic wheeled collection cart, a kitchen container for collecting scraps, and instructional materials that informed them what to put into the container, what not to, and when to set their cart out at the curb for collection.

Target Audience(s) and Desired Behaviors

The target audience for the program was all residents of HRM, in single as well as multifamily dwellings. This included high-rise apartment buildings, condominiums, and townhomes. There were approximately 125,000 households in all. The targeted behavior was to place kitchen and yard organic waste into the new organic collection container.

Barriers and Benefits

Several barriers to adoption were identified and then tested during a pilot. They included the following:

The "Yuck" Factor. For most of their lives, residents were used to placing their household waste into plastic bag-lined containers, sealing them, and taking them to the curb on collection day where they disappeared. Now they were being asked to handle the kitchen organics more than once: First put the scraps into a bucket and then later pour the bucket into the wheeled cart. Further, after it was emptied at the curb, the resident was faced with a dirty cart that had to be taken back up the driveway to the home to be used again. The carts had residual organic material in them that was continuing to decay, and that did not sit well with people who were not used to seeing raw garbage after collection day. Further, the carts had a tendency to smell, although not as much as people predicted they would. And they attracted flies of many types but most often houseflies and fruit flies. The houseflies would lay eggs, and every so often a householder would lift the lid of the cart and be greeted by many maggots crawling around the cart.

Hard to Maneuver. The carts were perceived to be difficult to maneuver. Many seniors and people with physical limitations felt that they would not be able to wield them down their driveways, and many others were concerned that it would be difficult to move the cart around during the winter due to snow and ice.

Room for the Cart. Some people felt that they did not have room for a cart in their yard. This was particularly true of people in multiresidential units where population density was high and yards were small or nonexistent.

Resistance to Change. Many residents saw no need to handle organic material separately from the rest of their waste. In addition to the yuck factor, they did not see any benefit and felt that the new program was inconvenient and did not provide any benefit to them or the community.

Perceived benefits were not formally identified, although program planners stressed several pluses to using the cart, outlined in the following:

Description of the Program

The curbside organic collection program and the kitchen container and cart (products) were positioned as a better alternative to disposing of organic material in the landfill for several reasons:

1. It recovers a valuable resource that will be used to make compost instead of being lost forever.

2. It reduces the amount of methane, a significant greenhouse gas, and leachate, a groundwater pollutant that is produced in landfills.

3. It reduces municipal solid waste disposal and therefore the need for more landfills.

In addition, recognizing that each household was different, municipal staff worked one-on-one with residents who needed an alternate solution. For instance, if people in townhouses and other multiresidential units wished to share a cart in order to save space that was fine. In row houses, where people would have had to pull their cart through their living room in order to bring it from their backyard to the front, alternatives were developed such as accepting bags set at the curb.

There were no increased collection costs for the containers or for pickup (price). In addition, there was an incentive to switch to the new containers. At the same time the cart program was introduced, there was an organics ban instituted at the landfill. Residents were told that if organic material was found in the garbage containers, it would not be collected. They were certainly free, however, to use backyard composters rather than participate in curbside collection if they preferred.

The municipality recognized that in order to be successful the program would need to be as convenient as possible. Each household received their own composting cart and a kitchen container directly from the municipality (place). The kitchen container helped eliminate frequent trips outside to the larger curbside containers. And the containers were dropped off at the end of their driveways. Collection was provided every 2 weeks and was located curbside, just as garbage and recycling collection was.

The program was referred to as the Curbside Organic Collection Program, and significant attention was paid to communications. Residents received materials explaining how to properly use the system. A comprehensive troubleshooting chart was provided to help people with problems that might arise. A telephone hotline allowed people to receive answers to their questions quickly. Key messages included the following, with the first three appearing in major channels:

- The program is *convenient*. In order to dispel the notion that the cart would be difficult to maneuver, a woman in her 90s was shown wheeling it around. Her message was this: If I can do it, anyone can do it.

- The program is *environmentally superior* to landfill disposal.
- The program is *economical.* A financial analysis demonstrated savings from the program—for the municipality and therefore the taxpayers.
- The program is *mandatory.* Organic material will no longer be accepted in the garbage stream.
- Organic material is a *valuable resource,* and sending it to a landfill loses that resource forever.
- Landfills are very difficult to site and cost a lot of money. Diverting organics to beneficial use makes *existing landfills function longer.*

While mass media communications were employed, there was a significant community-based communications effort. This included a network of community volunteers, set up in a database, who were willing to speak at schools, churches, community events, and other places where people were gathered. They were provided with standard materials, presentations, and buttons and business cards that showed they were part of the community network. When a request came in for a speaker on the topic, the database was queried to determine a local contact.

A sticker on the kitchen container provided detailed information on what could go in the container and what could not (prompt).

A pilot test in 1996 of the program was conducted in 2,000 homes in rural and urban areas to see how real the barriers were. There were four areas chosen strategically, one in each of the municipalities, and each test included 500 homes. The areas included urban, suburban, and rural areas, so the program would test different issues, such as use in dense areas, small yards, and long driveways. The pilot began in September and ran through the winter, to test such things as capacity in the fall and freezing and maneuverability in the winter. A hotline fielded questions, concerns, and, in a few cases, "nasty" comments complaining about the unsolicited drop off. Staff encouraged these residents to give it a try. Notably, several of those who had called with complaints actually called back in several months to express their enthusiasm for the program and apologize for their initial reaction.

Initial concerns with the yuck factor and the cart being hard to maneuver did not turn out to be major barriers after all. The kitchen container helped, as it had a handle and was small enough to be rinsed out in the kitchen sink. Concern with room for the cart was handled by encouraging those in row houses and apartment building to share carts. In fact, the pilot acted as a demonstration project. Once people became comfortable with the program, many began to sing its praises. These people were recruited as spokespeople and were referred to the media in order to help build a positive attitude toward the program (diffusion). By the time the citywide rollout began, there was such a positive buzz about the program that people were calling the hotline and asking if they could receive their carts first. Many did not want to wait.

Since the launch of the program in Halifax in 1998, participation in the organics curbside program was at 80%, measured in a curbside sample in 2005 (K. Donnelly, personal communication, 2010).

Critical Review

An uptake of 80% is impressive and most likely a result of two major strategies. First, the ban on the organics (disincentive). Without this, it is unlikely the rates would have been so high. In addition, however, the program should be credited with responding to barriers identified during the pilot, including providing a container for collection in the kitchen (a cart that even 90-year-olds found easy to maneuver), giving an option to share carts to reduce space, and allowing those concerned with the yuck factor to use plastic bags to contain the waste in the cart.

Other Notable Programs

A few additional tools for increasing residential recycling not included in these examples are worthy of brief mention:

Consider Developing a Brand for the Program

A strong brand helps increase awareness, understanding, credibility, and memorability for your program. In 2008, the City of Milwaukee, Wisconsin, launched a campaign to increase the tonnage of recyclables among City of Milwaukee residents by 15% in 2 years. The campaign was branded Recycle for Good. (See Figure 2.2.) Inspiration for the brand came from research with "medium and high" recyclers (target audiences), indicating that a primary motivator for increased recycling was knowing more about the potential positive impacts they could have on the environment.

Figure 2.2   Branded Logo for City of Milwaukee's Program

Source: Department of Public Works, City of Milwaukee, Recycle More Wisconsin.

Communications consistently carried the brand logo, and concrete messages highlighted what "good" recycling would do for the environment as well as the community. A 2010 report indicated recycling had increased by 10.4% (when removing newspaper as an outlier due to significant newsprint generation decline), an indicator the program is well on its way to reaching the 15% goal by the end of 2010.

Consider a "Support Group" Approach

Programs like Weight Watchers have helped millions of people around the world lose weight. They understand the behavior change power of providing programs that offer information, feedback, and support. The EcoTeam concept is similar. In the United Kingdom, EcoTeams were first introduced in 2000, where small groups of households meet once a month for approximately 5 months (product) to map out practical behaviors to reduce environmental impact. They then weigh and measure their waste and report back to the group on their progress. At final meetings, they celebrate their collective achievements and discuss potential next steps and future actions, including commitments they want to make. As of 2008, 3,600 households in the United Kingdom have participated in the EcoTeam project, and results indicate a 19% reduction in household waste and a 5% increase in recycling as a proportion of total waste among these households (National Social Marketing Center Showcase, 2010).

Consider Establishing an Annual Event

Forming and supporting an annual event such as National Cell Phone Recycling Week in the United States has numerous benefits. It provides opportunities for partnerships, with EPA partners including leading consumer electronics manufacturers, retailers and mobile service providers. Consider the benefits of these partner activities: increased convenience, with Best Buy providing a recycling kiosk that has a slot for cell phones; increased communications, with T-Mobile sending text messages during the week to all customers, reminding them they can recycle any brand or model of cell phone at T-Mobile stores; increased product offerings, with Samsung offering educational materials on recycling cell phones as a part of their March to a Million In-School Recycling Program for middle schools and high schools; and increased incentives, with RecycleBank® offering at least 10 points for recycling a cell phone, points that can be redeemed for a variety of popular products and services.

Consider Offering (More) Monetary Incentives

In a growing number of communities around the United States, pay-as-you-throw (PAYT) programs are gaining in popularity. What these programs have discovered is that when the cost of managing trash is hidden in taxes or charged at a flat rate, residents who recycle and prevent waste are not rewarded. In fact, they often pay the same, even more in some cases, than those generating more waste and recycling less. Though PAYT programs vary by community, programs include options such as paying less for a smaller garbage waste container and paying more for garbage waste than recycling waste. Communities typically report reductions in waste amounts of 25% to 35% and an increase in recycling rates (Environmental Protection Agency Pay as You Throw [EPA PAYT], 2010).

Finally, we hope to one day see two additional strategies considered to reduce residential waste—ones we have not seen implemented to date. Our first "wish" is for universal recycling codes (product features). When a citizen experiences different "rules" for recycling at work, home, a friend's home, and while shopping or traveling, not knowing the right thing to do is a major barrier. When different municipalities, states, and countries have a different definition of recyclable food waste, for example, it is not surprising that many concerned citizens then just toss their paper napkin in the garbage, not wanting to "mess up" the recycling container. Second, purchasing decisions that will "reduce use" would be facilitated by providing detailed information on estimated resources used to produce the item and its packaging (benefit), similar to current listings of calories, fat grams, and the like. We recognize this is not a simple or easy request. But it must have been a daunting effort for food manufacturers when this requirement was first imposed on them as well.

Summary

Three chapter case examples highlighted the three Rs of waste management hierarchy: reduce, reuse, and recycle. The reduction of junk mail in Australia demonstrated success using a new product (a sticker) that functioned as a prompt as well as descriptive norm, and community volunteers that made access to the stickers convenient. The effort in Ireland to decrease use of plastic bags and increase use of reusable bags chose a substantial disincentive to move the target audience, with formative research confirming this was what it would take. And the success of the organic recycling program in Nova Scotia reflected the ban on organics in the garbage containers and close attention that planners paid to aligning strategies with perceived barriers (e.g., offering multiunit dwellings an option of sharing a cart).

Questions for Discussion

1. For the No Junk Mail campaign in Australia, how would you determine what was being done with the mail that was not delivered? If it turns out that the post office recycles it, what (more) would you do to decrease the production levels of these mailings?

2. For the Ireland bag, if you were the Environment Minister, would you have increased the bag tax? If so, why? If not, why not?

3. For the Nova Scotia recycling case, take another look at the list of key messages. As noted, the first three were primary messages. Do you agree with that selection? If not, what would you emphasize?

References

AEA Technology PLC. (2009, August). *Welsh Assembly Government, single use bag study.* Issue Number 8. Report to Welsh Assembly Government. Retrieved from http://wales.gov.uk/topics/environmentcountryside/epq/waste_recycling/substance/carrierbags/singleusestudy/?lang=en

BBC News. (2007). *Irish plastic bag tax set to rise.* Retrieved from http://news.bbc.co.uk/2/hi/uk_news/northern_ireland/6383557.stm

Convery, F., McDonnell, S., & Ferreira, S. (2006). The most popular tax in Europe? Lessons from the Irish plastic bag levy. *Environ Resource Econ, 38,* 1–11.

Environmental Protection Agency Pay as You Throw. (2010). *Pay-as-you-throw success stories.* Retrieved from http://www.epa.gov/osw/conserve/tools/payt/tools/success.htm

Evidence to Scottish Parliament, Environment and Rural Development Committee Hearings. (2005).

Latrobe City Council. (2010). No junk mail and spam. Retrieved from http://www.latrobe.vic.gov/au/SustainableLatrobe/Waste/NoJunkMailandSpam/

National Social Marketing Center Showcase. (2010). *Social marketing case studies.* Retrieved from http://www.nsmcentre.org.uk/component/nsmccasestudy/?task=view&id=100&Itemid=42

U.S. Environmental Protection Agency. (2008). *Municipal solid waste generation, recycling, and disposal in the United States: Facts and figures for 2008.* Retrieved from http://www.epa.gov/epawaste/nonhaz/municipal/index.htm.

U.S. Environmental Protection Agency. (2010). *Wastes—resource conservation—reduce, reuse, recycle.* Retrieved from http://www.epa.gov/osw/conserve/rrr/reduce.htm

CHAPTER 3

Protecting Water Quality

The Problem

While World Water Day has been celebrated annually by the United Nations since 1993, it was not until 2010 that the focus shifted from *water availability* to *water quality*. The United Nations cites human activities including population growth, rapid urbanization, chemical discharge, and invasive species as the primary threats to water quality and estimates that over 2.25 billion people live without adequate sanitation. Every day 2 million tons of sewage and other effluents drain into the world's waters, and more than 1.5 million children die each year from waterborne diseases. The situation in developing countries is the worst, where over 90% of raw sewage and 70% of untreated industrial wastes are dumped into surface waters (UN Water, 2010).

The United Nations further proclaims that the top priority should be water pollution prevention. The two other options, treatment and restoration, are viewed as less sustainable, more costly, and more complex. The 2010 World Water Day was intended to raise the profile of water quality by "encouraging governments, organizations, communities, and individuals around the world to actively engage in proactively addressing water quality" (UN Water, 2010).

The U.S. Environmental Protection Agency (EPA) divides water pollution sources into two categories: point and nonpoint. Point sources of water pollution are primarily stationary locations such as sewage treatment plants and factories. The residential sector, the focus of this chapter, is primarily involved in nonpoint source (NPS) pollution, which occurs when rainfall, snowmelt, and water from hoses and sprinklers moves over and through the ground. As the runoff moves, it picks up and carries away natural and human-made pollutants, finally depositing them into lakes, rivers, wetlands, coastal waters, and even our underground sources of drinking water—often killing or damaging plants, fish, and wildlife, while degrading water quality in local watersheds.

And yet, if we were to ask the general public Where do you think the water that goes down your streets' storm drains ends up?, most would likely tell you they believe it goes to a treatment plant where trash, chemicals, and other pollutants are screened out, or neutralized. In other words, they are unaware that pollutants from many of their household activities (e.g., chemicals from fertilizing and pest control, bacteria from pet waste, and detergents and grime from car washing) eventually go directly into our waterways.

Potential Behavior Solutions

Efforts to reduce pollutants from residential properties most often focus on heads of households in single family homes and/or property managers for multifamily apartments, townhouses, and condominiums. Behaviors that are promoted are varied and have been grouped in Table 3.1 by source of pollutant. Notice that the listed behaviors are singular, simple, and doable. They are ones that communicate clearly what you want your target audience to do and ones you will be able to measure as to whether or not they did. Also recognize these are "end-state" behaviors, as described in Chapter 1, and that barriers and benefits for each behavior will vary depending on whether you are targeting heads of households, contractors, or property managers.

Table 3.1 Residential Behaviors to Help Prevent Water Pollution	
Pollution Source	**Examples of End-State Behaviors That Might Be Chosen for Adoption**
Lawn and garden behaviors to reduce chemical runoff	• Apply compost annually to lawns and gardens. • Apply 8 inches of wood mulch over bare soil areas. • Reduce lawn size and replace with trees and shrubs. • Leave grass clippings on the lawn to reduce the need for fertilizer. • Use organic fertilizers. • Use mechanical rather than chemical methods to control weeds.
Paved surfaces	• Reduce the amount of paved surfaces such as patios, sidewalks, and driveways. • Use porous materials such as pavers, bricks, gravel, and/or pervious concrete instead of conventional concrete.
Rainwater runoff from roof	• Disconnect downspouts from municipal drainage systems, allowing water to soak into the ground. • Insert a splash block. • Reroute downspout to a rain garden or rain barrels. • Use mechanical rather than chemical solutions to remove roof moss.
Septic systems and sewage	• Pump septic tanks every 3 years. • Have septic tanks inspected at least once a year. • Don't put grease down sinks. • Never allow trees to grow over or near the drainfield of a septic tank.

(Continued)

(Continued)

Pollution Source	Examples of End-State Behaviors That Might Be Chosen for Adoption
Pets and farm animals	• Keep farm animals out of streams. • Pick up after your pet—even in your own yard. • Dispose of leak-proof, tear-resistant bagged pet waste in garbage bins.
Household chemicals and waste	• Do not dump household trash in streams or rivers. • Use a low or no phosphorus dishwashing detergent. • Pressure wash buildings and pavement with clean water only—use no soap. • Dry unused paint in the bucket before tossing it out with the trash. • Take unused drugs to a pharmacy or other pharmaceutical take-back program. • Take unused paints, finishes, solvents, and other hazardous materials to a household hazardous waste facility.
Motor vehicles	• Fix oil leaks. • Use commercial car washes or wash your car on your lawn so detergents and grime don't contaminate the water. • Take waste oil and fluids to a household hazardous waste facility.
Storm drains	• Let nothing but rain go down the storm drain. • Keep leaves and clippings away from storm drains.

It is important to note that the process for selecting one or more of these behaviors as the focus for a campaign is rigorous. As mentioned in Chapter 1, each should be evaluated and prioritized based on its unique potential impact on water quality, probability of adoption, and current level of penetration in the community under consideration.

In this chapter, we share two related case stories: (1) Influencing Natural Yard Care (King County, Washington) and (2) Scooping the Poop (Austin, Texas).

CASE #1   Influencing Natural Yard Care (King County, Washington)

Background

King County is the largest county in Washington State, with almost a third of the state's population; more than 800,000 households (U.S. Census Bureau, 2008); and numerous lakes, streams, bays, rivers, and marine waterways. Managers at King County's Department of Natural Resources and Parks (DNRP) in Washington State were disappointed when in the spring of 2000 they received the evaluation results of their Natural Lawn Care Program. Over the past 4 years, the county and their municipal partners had spent 1.5 million U.S. dollars on an advertising campaign, and there was little perceptible change in the promoted behaviors, including two to protect water quality: not using pesticides and leaving grass clipping on lawns. Apparently, about all that had been accomplished was to raise awareness of these preferred behaviors. Following the advertising campaign, about 40% of single family homeowners reported they were aware that these were desirable behaviors; however, behaviors had not changed. It was time for a new approach—one that used more than mass communications. As you will read, the new program not only succeeded in changing 24 behaviors but it was accomplished at a fifth of the cost of the annual advertising campaign.

Target Audience(s) and Desired Behaviors

Rather than targeting the more than 500,000 home gardeners in the county, this time they chose a "one neighborhood at a time" approach. They were inspired by studies from the Garden Trends Report indicating that nearly 43% of consumers learn about their garden behaviors from friends and neighbors. A pilot was conducted in two neighborhoods over 2 years, followed by four neighborhoods the next year. Currently, the program targets 10 to 13 carefully chosen neighborhoods per year. Selection is based on partnerships with city governments within the county, and neighborhoods selected tend to have a strong sense of community and older, problematic yards that are maintained by the owners themselves.

Program managers knew from this secondary research who their most likely early adopters of natural yard care best practices would be: those who cared about the environment and understood how their actions could make a difference. Further, they would be most interested if they had recently purchased a home and especially true for first time homeowners. They would be most eager if they were having specific problems with their lawn or garden or found their aging landscape unappealing. And they would be those who had the most time to care for their yard: empty nesters and seniors.

A total of 24 desired behaviors were identified, each fitting in to one of five broad practice components: (1) building healthy soils, (2) practicing natural lawn care, (3) choosing the best/right plants for the site, (4) controlling pests and diseases without pesticides, and (5) watering deeply and less frequently.

Barriers and Benefits

Prior to developing their strategy, the county surveyed 400 households to identify barriers and benefits and to help confirm the selection of target audiences. This research indicated the major barriers to action were not knowing what practices were ideal and in some cases how to "perform" them (e.g., choosing the best and right plants for the site or getting rid of pests without using pesticides). In fact, 66% thought it was difficult to tell which pesticides are dangerous. In addition, many were concerned their lawn would not look as good if not watered frequently and if grass clippings were left on the lawn. Some were concerned that natural pesticides don't work as well. Indeed, 27% of regular pesticide users reported not believing there were any negative consequences from pesticide use. Others believed these natural products would be more expensive and that natural practices would be labor intensive, with 60% of pesticide users believing it would take too much time and effort to maintain a quality lawn without pesticides.

In terms of perceived benefits and motivators, homeowners were most likely to change their behaviors if they could see and hear about their neighbors' success. This was especially persuasive when the neighbor could explain and even demonstrate the how-tos.

Description of the Program

In 2002, the Natural Yard Care Neighborhoods program was launched, offering three, 2-hour neighborhood workshops (product) to help residents learn about and implement the 24 environmentally responsible gardening behaviors. For the first 7 years, the five broad practices listed previously represented major program topics, many presented by well-known local garden experts. Based on participant feedback and suggestions, in 2008 an additional training on garden design was offered at the beginning of the first workshop. The inclusion of this unit resulted in a substantial increase in attendance.

An added value component of the program is a Natural Yard Care hotline, offered through a partnership with an environmental group, Seattle Tilth, which provides expert advice and a quarterly newsletter to workshop attendees as well as to other callers around the county.

Workshops and the hotline are free, and incentives have included door prizes of mulch mowers (with those attending all three sessions having the highest likelihood of winning), garden tools and gloves, books, plants and bags of compost and lime; services such as yard and design consultations; and yard makeovers with new, drought tolerant plants. Each participant receives a free information kit valued at $15, containing informational booklets, fact sheets and DVDs. Advocacy groups such as the Washington Toxics Coalition send representatives to workshops offering free items such as Pesticide Free Zone yard signs, a nonmonetary incentive providing recognition.

The 2-hour workshops are offered on weekday evenings, in the spring and the fall, generally between 7:00 p.m. and 9:00 p.m. They are held in familiar, convenient locations with free parking—such as neighborhood schools, churches, and community centers. Interested participants can register in a variety of ways (place): The majority register by phone or e-mail in response to a direct mail invitation; about a third register when approached by representatives conducting neighborhood canvassing; and a few register at the door.

Key messages to encourage attendance at the workshops stress how easy and rewarding natural yard care can be and that workshops are "fun, informative, and FREE!" Invitations to attend workshops are extended through a few targeted communication channels including a detailed direct mail letter to households in selected neighborhoods, followed by a colorful reminder postcard (see Figure 3.1). In addition, trained natural yard care representatives canvass neighborhoods on weekends for face-to-face interactions with residents, encouraging their attendance at the upcoming workshops. A public relations firm in Seattle, The Frause Group, supports these outreach efforts by securing and managing the canvassers and creating promotional materials (promotion).

Figure 3.1 Postcard to Increase Awareness of Neighborhood Workshop

Source: © 2010 Lida Enche www.lidaenche.com

For ensuring attendance at the workshop, e-mail reminders are sent to those preregistered (prompt). In addition, reminder calls are made to all registrants the day before each workshop. To prompt and reinforce behaviors covered in the workshop, a quarterly newsletter to participants mentions specific preferred seasonal activities. A magnet with the yard care hotline is also distributed to remind gardeners where they can call for help and get answers to questions not addressed during the workshop.

By persuading several residents in one neighborhood (or even better, on one block) to change their gardening practices, it was believed that others would notice these new practices as well—even perceive them to be a new, positive trend (e.g., lawns being replaced with native and drought tolerant plants with surprisingly healthy and beautiful plants). When several homes on one block, for example, let their lawns go "golden" during the summer, those with green lawns suddenly stood out. And when (much to the skeptic's surprise) these brown lawns turned green again in the fall, at least one major concern was visibly addressed.

Part of the rationale for selecting specific neighborhoods (and neighbors) was to capitalize on the motivator that neighbors are key to influencing the adoption of gardening behaviors. To support this diffusion, those attending workshops are encouraged to share their new skills and successes and are provided with materials to give their neighbors to interest them in the techniques as well.

In 2000, a pilot project was implemented in the City of Renton, inviting 35 residents on one two-block street to participate for one summer in Natural Yard Care workshops and techniques. Twenty (57%) of the residents accepted the door-to-door invitation. Personal, on-site interviews with participants 2 years later indicated that all 20 were still "practicing the practices" and that their neighbors had also increased natural yard care techniques.

Based on the success in Renton, four separate neighborhoods were targeted in 2002, all in the City of Shoreline. A promotional strategy utilizing a detailed direct mail letter and door-to-door canvassing was implemented, and door prizes were used as incentives with workshop participants. Ultimately, 57% of those who were approached signed up for the workshop. Within that group, 60% actually attended the trainings, which translates to a third (34%) of those approached.

Based on the success of the Shoreline effort, a total of seven cities signed up in 2003, forming the Natural Yard Care Neighborhoods Consortium. Ten neighborhoods were selected, and each jurisdiction recruited residents from those neighborhoods. A total of 1,058 attended the three trainings that year. In 2005, 2006, and 2007, between 9 and 13 cities offered workshops each year. Average attendance at each workshop was 60, with an estimated 1,200 total workshop participants each year. In 2008, 2009, and 2010, average attendance was about 80, a 20% increase. Though this number may seem small, consider that these are all from one neighborhood in a community, not from households all around the county and is a strategy that supports diffusion and the development of norms for natural yard care ways.

In 2003, the consortium conducted an evaluation using four main survey tools:

1. **Preworkshop Survey:** This survey was used to establish baseline information regarding participant knowledge and behavior. Participants completed this questionnaire at the first workshop.

2. **Workshop Feedback Survey:** This survey was completed at the end of each workshop session and focused on satisfaction with the workshop, increases in awareness and knowledge, and intention to practice behaviors.

3. **Postworkshop Survey:** This survey was used to measure actual changes in knowledge and behaviors. Participants received this questionnaire by mail at three intervals (6 months, 18 months, and 22 months from initial trainings).

4. **Control Group Survey:** This survey assessed how other neighborhood residents were similar or different from participants in the workshop.

Behavior change highlights from one of the 18-month post workshop surveys with 365 participants were encouraging:

- Ninety percent either continued or started setting their mower at 2 inches or higher.
- Ninety percent either continued or started avoiding the use of pesticides.
- Fifty-eight percent began or increased choosing and planting native plants.
- Forty-seven percent began or increased watering deeply but infrequently.
- Forty-three percent began or increased use of organic or slow-release fertilizers.
- Thirty-nine percent planted drought-tolerant plants.
- Thirty-nine percent began or increased applying organic layer of mulch.
- Twenty-six percent had called the garden hotline.

In terms of diffusion, participants shared the workshop and the tips gained with an average of five friends, neighbors and/or family members. Notably, those attending all three workshops shared with seven others, and attendance increased by 35% in 2008 when the garden design component was added.

Of final interest are the per capita costs incurred for exposure to either the workshop itself or the information and skill-building "passed on" by a workshop participant. When including costs for the workshops themselves, as well as the promotion and evaluation expenses, the average cost to reach a gardener, including friends and neighbors of workshop attendees, is $17. This measure and related behavior change outcomes are useful metrics for the county when assessing and comparing potential future alternative strategies (D. Rice, personal communication, 2010).

Critical Review

This case story has several strategies to applaud. First, they recognized that advertising alone was not going to lead to significant behavior change and that the return on investment would be low, even unacceptable to funders interested in behavior change outcomes. Secondly, they funded surveys to monitor results shortly after launch, ones that alerted them to a need for a course correction and then whether the new strategies were working. This then led to increased partnerships with city governments that found the results justifiable—even inspirational. Thirdly, the team chose the target audience wisely, recognizing that those who would attend the workshop would not be "the choir" or the skeptics. Rather, it would be those who saw the need and had the desire and recognized they needed help, inspiring the development and continuous improvement of the workshops.

A few recommendations for enhancement, relative to the tools presented in this book, are worthy of consideration:

- Consider prioritizing the 24 behaviors using the impact/probability/penetration model and then allocate more resources (e.g., workshop time, material space, prompts, incentives) to those behaviors that have the highest impact, highest probability, and lowest current penetration.
- Since data strongly suggest that attending more than one workshop results in greater gains, additional incentive tactics may be warranted.

Consider rewarding completion of all three workshops with some form of recognition such as appointment to a citizen advisory committee in addition to prizes and discount coupons for products and services.

- To expand the market, consider offering "mini" versions of the course for those interested in learning more but not wanting to invest three evenings to training. This might take the form of a one-night or half-day training, concentrating on those behaviors that have the greatest probability of being adopted, as well as the greatest impact on water quality.

- To potentially lower costs "per capita," conduct a controlled experiment that compares results of "door-to-door" visits in a similar neighborhood to the workshop costs of $17/household and related outcomes. Door-to-door representatives could tailor comments and demonstrations to unique yard and homeowner conditions.

- To bring prompts closer in space and time to desired behaviors and to increase their visibility, consider additional and new prompts. An e-mail that encourages a fall mulch application or an adjustment of sprinklers during heavy rainfall might be timelier, as well as more likely to be noticed. A calendar that has monthly recommendations for yard and garden activities might also be more timely and visible.

- To facilitate the development of descriptive norms (i.e., perceptions of how other people are actually behaving), a sign on a golden lawn, or in a front yard native plant garden could help link the new practice to the Natural Yard Care brand and increase interest in these techniques. And to support diffusion, consider conducting tours of select gardens—even a neighborhood.

- To confirm evaluation results and problems associated with "self-reporting" methodologies, consider site visits to a neighborhood where actual behavior change could be confirmed (or not) through observation and face-to-face interviews.

CASE #2   Scooping the Poop (Austin, Texas)

Background

The Humane Society of the United States estimates that 39% of U.S. households own at least one dog (The Humane Society of the United States, 2009). Austinites are no exception, with the current population of canine residents estimated at more than 120,000 and the number of households around 350,000. Further, many consider Austin an especially dog-friendly city, evidenced by off-leash areas in 11 city parks, as well as frequent sightings of dogs with their owners on excursions along neighborhood streets and local trails, lounging on restaurant patios, and attending public events in the parks.

The problem is that pet waste contains dangerous bacteria such as salmonella and E. coli, and harmful parasites such as giardia and roundworms. When not properly disposed of in these public places and as many as 350,000 backyards in the city, it poses a direct contact health hazard for people and pets. And when washed into creeks and lakes, pet waste can make the water unsafe for recreation and can cause aquatic weeds and algae to flourish, eventually reducing levels of oxygen in the water that can result in fish kills. With each dog producing an average of one half pound of waste daily, that adds up to 60,000 pounds deposited each day in Austin (a citywide total of nearly five dump truck loads)—approximately 22 million pounds per year. While bacteria in creeks is not limited to pet waste, the creeks in Austin's more densely populated areas had average bacteria levels that are more than three times higher than those in less-developed areas, with 11 of Austin's creeks listed as impaired because of bacteria.

Since 1992, the city had relied on an ordinance carrying a potential fine of up to $500, requiring that pet owners pick up after their pets. The code is a helpful deterrent but hard to enforce as it requires a law officer to witness the offense and does nothing to increase public concern with the environmental and health impacts associated with pet waste. To increase influence, in 2000 the city's Watershed Protection and Parks and Recreation Departments launched a new effort, one they called Scoop the Poop. As you will read, the program continues to this day (2010), with new strategic components added each year.

Target Audience(s) and Desired Behaviors

Initially, the primary target audience for the effort focused on dog owners taking their pets to public parks. Eventually, in response to citizen complaints regarding neighborhood dogs defecating on private property, the campaign expanded outreach to those walking their dogs in community neighborhoods as well.

Three behaviors for waste disposal were encouraged: (1) scoop the poop, (2) bag it, and (3) place it in the trash (the end-state behavior).

Barriers and Benefits

To identify perceived barriers, program managers interviewed professionals around the country and reviewed existing surveys, including ones from the Center for Watershed Protection. Common barriers to poop scooping and proper disposal included: not having convenient access to disposable bags, not having enough trash cans around in order to be able to quickly dispose of it, finding the task messy and smelly, not believing that "one little pile" is a problem, and some considering it a good/natural fertilizer.

In one survey conducted by the city, potential benefits/motivators were quantified and ranked: 53% expressed that pressure from others would probably make them more likely to pick up after their pet, 46% indicated that more dispensers with plenty of bags would help, 40% said more trash cans were important, 35% wanted more information about why they should pick it up and what to do with it, and 35% "admitted" that enforcement of fines would make a difference.

Description of the Program

In 2000, 25 Mutt Mitt Stations (pet waste dispensers) with disposable bags were installed in city parks (see Figure 3.2). By 2010, there were more than 150 stations in 90 city parks (product). Mutt Mitt plastic bags are degradable and designed to "protect the hand like a glove," easing some of the concerns with mess and smell. Then, in 2002, the program expanded to reach those walking their dogs in neighborhoods and other public places and began giving away reusable pet trash bag holders with a clasp to clip onto a dog leash (see Figure 3.3).

Figure 3.2   Mutt Mitt Dispenser

Source: City of Austin, Watershed Protection Department.

Figure 3.3   Bag Holder Giveaway

Source: City of Austin, Watershed Protection Department.

As noted earlier, there was an existing $500 fine and city code stating, "An owner or handler shall promptly remove and sanitarily dispose of feces left on public or private property by a dog or cat being handled by the person, other than property owned by the owner or handler of the dog or cat" (K. Shay, personal communication, 2008). To make the law more visible and increase the perception of enforcement, citizens are now encouraged to report violators, with the city's nonemergency telephone number (3-1-1) highlighted on signage and promotional materials (disincentive). The city also offers a Green Neighbor program that lists more than 100 action items that citizens can do to improve the environment. Neighborhoods that distribute the Green Neighbor guides to their residents, mark storm drains, adopt a park or perform other earth-wise actions qualify as a Green Neighborhood and can receive a free Mutt Mitt dispenser for their neighborhood (incentive).

To help ensure bags are always available at stations, there is a message on the dispenser with a number to call to let the city know when the dispenser is empty. Yard signs to prompt/remind pet owners to pick up waste on private properties can be ordered online and are then mailed directly to the citizen. Additional trash cans were added in many of the parks to increase the convenience of disposing the waste (place).

Until 2008, primary strategies consisted of the pet waste dispensers with bags (product), signage regarding the city code and how to report violators (price), and increased trash receptacles and a phone number to let the city know if there are no bags in the dispenser (place). And yet, in 2008, water quality monitoring data showed continued problems in multiple locations across Austin. Since much of this bacteria had been tied to pet waste that is not disposed of properly, the city revamped and strengthened outreach efforts.

In 2009, the program was enhanced with more promotional elements to spread the word beyond the city parks and included the following:

- *Broadcast Media:* 30 second animated television spot funded by the Watershed Protection Department
- *Public Events:* Creation of a temporary dirt pile sculpture next to a popular downtown lake; the pile represented one day's worth of poop (60,000 pounds) and was unveiled at a press conference hosted by the mayor and showcasing an original "Scoop the Poop" song performed by local singer/songwriter, Woode Wood
- *Outdoor and Print Media:* Promotional advertisements were placed in newspapers
- *Signage:* Signage based on the Snohomish County, Washington, pet waste campaign was adapted by Austin and placed in many off-leash areas
- *Brochures and Flyers:* Two small Austin Guide brochures were created, one on the Scoop the Poop program and one to describe the particular issues in the off-leash pet areas
- *Enhanced Website:* For downloading program materials and ordering yard signs
- *Program Mascot:* Scoop the Poop's mascot, Eco—Austin's #1 dog for the environment
- *Social Media (e.g., Facebook, Twitter, blogs):* a Facebook page that encourages visitors to interact with Eco, the campaign mascot, with the most popular part of the page the one asking for pet owners to send photos of their dogs who then become "friends" of Eco

- *Articles:* Neighborhood newsletters
- *Face-to-Face Promotions:* Staff talking to dog owners in off-leash areas of park about pet waste and attending environmental-, pet-, and park-themed city events
- *Direct Mail:* Educational postcards mailed to pet-related businesses and organizations to distribute to their clientele
- *Additional Distribution Channels for Program Materials:* Veterinary clinics, animal shelters, libraries, recreation centers

In 2002, Scoop the Poop signs were added to Mutt Mitt stations upon request from citizens who felt the dispensers were being overlooked. Additionally, smaller signs stating the city ordinance and fine were installed below the dispensers (prompt). In 2007, the city produced complimentary Scoop the Poop yard signs. Citizens concerned with pet waste from neighborhood dogs could call or go online and order the 4" x 11" laminated signs. As noted previously, these are then mailed to their home.

Program outcomes, impact, and cost/benefit are tracked and reported every year. As indicated in Table 3.2 outcomes are measured in terms of number of Mutt Mitts distributed, impact is stated in terms of estimated number of pounds of pet waste collected and disposed of properly, and cost per pound disposed of correctly is calculated based on annual program budgets. Number of Mutt Mitts distributed reflects those from the city's dispensers. Impact is based on an assumption of an average of one-half pound per bag. (It should be noted that this number of bags does not include dog owners who carry their own bags, including the 2,000 using the clip-on bag container distributed by the city.) In 2001, approximately $10,000 was spent on the program. In 2008, $72,000 was spent on mutt mitts and dispensers; an additional $20,000 was spent on signs, brochures, giveaways, T-shirts, advertising, and staff time. Yard sign requests have increased from 50 in 2007, to 140 in 2008, to 271 in 2009. Before the campaign, monthly web hits to the Scoop the Poop Austin homepage were under 400. They increased to nearly 4,000 monthly after the campaign.

Table 3.2   Cost Per Pound to Collect and Dispose of Pet Waste Properly

Year	Mutt Mitts Distributed	# Pounds Collected and Disposed of Properly @ .5 lbs. per Bag on Average	Annual Program Budget	Estimated Cost Per Pound to Collect and Dispose of Properly
2001	75,000	37,500 lbs.	$10,000	$.27/lb.
2003	535,000	267,500 lbs.	$53,000	$.20/lb.
2006	967,000	483,500 lbs.	$72,500	$.15/lb.
2008	2,000,000	1,000,000 lbs.	$87,000*	$.09/lb.
2009	2,400,000	1,200,000 lbs.	$92,000	$.08/lb.

*Costs were reduced in 2008 by switching to less expensive bags.

Efforts to Measure Impact on Water Quality

In key waterways, actual impact on water quality has also been evaluated. In 2008, for example, a high level of bacteria was identified in Bull Creek District Park (one of 12 Austin park facilities designated as an off-leash area for dogs), most likely due to use of the park as an off-leash area for dogs. Table 3.3 shows the comparative bacteria levels at various locations along Bull Creek. The levels are also eight times higher on weekends than weekdays when park visitors increase in the off-leash area.

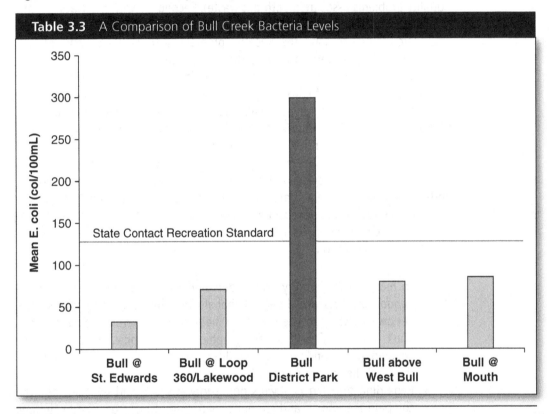

Table 3.3   A Comparison of Bull Creek Bacteria Levels

Note: Sites are presented in upstream to downstream order.

To address that specific problem area, an enhanced campaign effort was initiated March 7, 2008, to persuade these park users to pick up after their pets, with a focus on highlighting health hazards. The campaign included a cleanup event, highly visible signage in the park, installation of additional Scoop the Poop boxes, a press conference with good media coverage, public opinion surveys before and after the campaign, and increased park police and staff presence.

Although the campaign and surveys showed positive results and the bacteria levels in the off-leash area improved, those upstream of the park worsened. It appears that the dog owners either became more conscientious about scooping the poop in the off-leash area or wanted to keep their pets out of the polluted area and moved the problem elsewhere. In May, 2008, a new citizen volunteer group (Bull Creek Dog Off-Leash Group) was formed and has been actively working on park cleanup. There does appear to be improvement. Geometric averages upstream now (2010) meet the health standard and are very close to the actual off-leash area (K. Shay, personal communication, 2010).

Critical Review

This campaign has strong components. First, major strategies appear to be clearly aligned with major barriers (e.g., bag designs that minimize "mess and smell" and face-to-face discussions in off-leash parks to explain the real water quality problems associated with pet waste). Second, as with the Natural Yard Care program, program managers seem committed to a "measure and improve" standard. Efforts to solve the bacteria problem in the off-leash park at Bull Creek, for example, certainly reflect this commitment, as did the decision to take the campaign beyond city parks. The city appears to be *citizen-driven*, responding to desires for yard signs to prompt pet owners to "behave" and providing convenient numbers to call when receptacles are empty of bags. They have stuck with their brand Scoop the Poop for more than a decade and have integrated its use at multiple contact points—from websites to signage to mayoral speeches to having its own popular song. Finally, their cost/benefit tracking and monitoring provides a useful metric, one that can be an inspiration to others as a way to demonstrate constant improvement and to evaluate potential future strategies relative to past outcomes.

A few recommendations relative to the tools presented in this book are worthy of consideration.

- To more clearly identify and understand the target audience, a *doer/ nondoer analysis* would be quite beneficial. What really distinguishes the pet owners who consistently scoop the poop (doers) from the people who don't (nondoers)? Is it a demographic, psychographic, or some related behavior (e.g., nondoers are more likely to walk in nonpublic areas where they feel they are less noticed).
- Regarding *targeted behaviors* going forward, it would be interesting to compare the impact and current penetration of picking up after the pet in their own backyard with picking up their waste in parks and other public areas. In Snohomish County, Washington, for example, research indicated that not only were pet owners less likely to be picking up pet waste in their own backyard (lower penetration) but this is actually where most of the pet waste originates (higher impact). As a side note on this project, one of the major barriers to picking up waste in the backyard is that the owner doesn't see where the pet goes, especially at night. The program then distributed small flashlights with the program logo.
- Since the top motivator identified by 53% of respondents was pressure from others, descriptive norms might help. In Sweden, for example, a bunch of preschoolers in Malmo were inspired to action when one of their teachers nearly fell after stepping in a pile of poop. The young protestors marched on the streets in an attempt to "shame" dog owners into scooping the poop. The kids prepared a batch of very small signs that they put

in each pile of dog poop they came across. According to the local newspaper, cards had personalized messages such as "Pick up after yourself" and "An old woman could slip on a piece of dog poop and break her leg" (WayOdd, n.d.). And in the United Kingdom during National Poop Scoop Week, the Oak Tree Health Nature Reserve in Nottinghamshire unleashed activists with pink spray paint to tint any dog droppings they came across to help draw attention to the mess (Metro UK, 2010).

- As indicated, a variety of promotional tools were utilized. It would be beneficial to evaluate their relative effectiveness by rating each one in terms of estimated reach and frequency achieved. This could then be used, along with expense data, to determine at least a *cost per impression,* if not ideally a *cost per behavior change.* It may turn out that some of the strategies (e.g., television advertising) do not have the payback achieved by others (e.g., news articles and other publicity events).

- Finally, getting people to make commitments should be considered and tested, especially in captive locations such as the dog leash parks.

Other Notable Programs

As evidenced by these two cases, influencing residential behaviors to help prevent water pollution has several unique challenges described in this summary section. In keeping with this book's "what works" theme, we have provided an example of additional notable efforts that appears to be tackling these barriers successfully:

"I Don't Get the Connection"

Water quality program managers conducting barriers research are likely to hear that not only do many citizens not understand how oil leaking from their car in their driveway gets to local waterways but others don't believe that dumping it down a local storm drain could possibly be a problem since they believe it goes to the city's water treatment plants first. Making the connection as concrete as possible will help. Seattle Public Utilities, for example, reports on its website that an estimated 2 million gallons of used motor oil ends up in the Puget Sound waterways each year. And that just 1 pint of oil causes a slick the size of two football fields. To further make the case, a storm drain stenciling program that began in the mid-1990s provides stenciling kits to apply the message "Dump No Waste. Drains to Stream, Lake or Sound" next to storm drains. Volunteers sign up to stencil storm drains in their neighborhoods and communities and include individuals, families, and community organizations like churches, schools, businesses, and youth from Boys and Girls Clubs, and Boy Scouts and Girl Scouts. In 2009 alone, 3,354 storm drains were stenciled with the message, and there are currently (2010) 150 citizens and 48 public schools helping apply the stencils (Seattle Public Utilities, 2010). (It should be noted that many communities prefer drains that have these messages engraved in the drain cover, avoiding any potential problems/pollution from paint when stenciling. On the downside, this reduces citizen involvement.)

"I Don't Know How"

Several of the end-state behaviors identified at the beginning of the chapter require new skills, one such as rerouting a downspout to a rain garden. Even a motivated homeowner wanting to do the right thing to protect the environment will initially wonder, Which downspout? and What's a rain garden? In Melbourne, Australia, these barriers are tackled head-on. Melbourne Water's 10,000 Raingardens Program began in 2008 with an ambitious goal to see 10,000 rain gardens built by 2013. Their website (http://raingardens.melbournewater.com.au/aboutUs.html) breaks the process down into five singular steps, beginning with how to identify a prime location and ending with how to select the best plants. Instruction sheets can also be found at local hardware stores and nurseries and not only give the homeowner a shopping list for materials and plants but also estimated price ranges. And to help build skills, as well as spread the word, the 2010 season of the popular *The Garden Gurus* television show finished the last two episodes of the season featuring the 10,000 Raingarden Program and promoted that rain garden instruction sheets are available on *The Garden Gurus* website. To track progress toward their goal, residents are encouraged to register their raingarden with the local water and sewer utility. Close to 1,000 have been officially "counted" in the first 2 years of the program, and this does not include those the campaign inspired but were not registered on the website.

"I Feel Overwhelmed By All the Requests for Change"

It would not be surprising if attendees at the Natural Yard Care workshops mentioned in Case #1 left with a sense of "so many things to do." After all, 24 singular behaviors are promoted. In Maryland, they took a different approach. Although a few dozen desired behaviors were identified and ranked according to their impact, probability and current participation levels, program leaders decided to initially target just one simple yet important behavior—putting off the use of fertilizer until the fall. They also focused on one major benefit for skipping the spring fertilizing. The program was branded "Save the Crabs, Then Eat 'Em." While people in the Washington, D.C., area may have only limited concern for the bay, many are passionate about their seafood, as is evidenced by the many thriving seafood restaurants throughout the greater Washington, D.C., area. Natural partners emerged. For example, a press event launching the campaign featured local chefs who signed a petition asking Washington, D.C., area residents to wait until fall to fertilize so that they can more reliably serve delicious local Chesapeake seafood. Drink coasters with the campaign slogan and fall fertilizing messages were distributed without charge to local seafood restaurants, to use and hand out to customers to take home. The campaign approach of reframing the issue to appeal to the target audience's stomachs rather than their environmental consciousness was sufficiently newsworthy to gain significant media coverage, enhancing the campaign's reach and legitimacy. In the spring of 2004, before the campaign launched, a telephone survey of 600 area residents indicated that 52% planned to fertilize that spring. One year later, a similar survey found that number had dropped to 39%, a 25% decrease in the number of residents planning to fertilize that spring (Kotler & Lee, 2008). Clearly, residents responded to the benefit that was highlighted, as well as the fewer barriers perceived by one simple behavior.

"This Will Cost Too Much"

Examples of local monetary incentive mechanisms include stormwater fee discounts, expedited permitting, grants, rebates, and installation financing (U.S. EPA, 2009). In 2008, the City of Portland began awarding incentives to property owners interested in installing ecoroofs, a vegetated roof system used in place of a conventional roof. The incentive (up to $5/square ft of installed ecoroof) is intended to increase implementation and defer the increased up-front costs common in a growing market. All building types are eligible for the incentive, which is expected to continue until 2013. The primary target of the program is 43 acres of additional ecoroofs. Multiple outcomes determine the effectiveness of the program:
On the demand side is the following:

- Since 2008, 66 incentive projects were awarded $1,009,515 representing 4.67 acres of ecoroof.
- An additional six acres of ecoroofs are in design or construction (2010).
- On June 1, 2010, 38 applications for two additional acres of ecoroofs were received.
- The program's e-mail distribution list has grown to over 1,000 people since May 2009.

On the supply side is the following:

- The city provides a list of local and regional professionals in the ecoroof industry—a list that has grown 30% since May 2009.
- Vendors participating in the annual vendor fair grew from 35 to 60 in the first year.
- Greenroof Info Think-Tank, a consortium of local and regional industry professionals has grown from 4 to over 130 members in its first year.
- Activity on the City of Portland's ecoroof program website increased from 1,000 in hits per month in 2008 to over 10,000 hits per month by 2010.

The total budget for the city's ecoroof program is $5.9 million, with $5.6 million for incentives and the remaining budget for education, outreach, and technical assistance over the 5-year program. To analyze cost/benefit, the ecoroof incentive is compared to traditional stormwater management systems. Ecoroofs constructed with incentive funding will prevent 17.6 million gallons of stormwater from entering the city's sewer system. If the city had to construct sewer separation projects to manage this amount of annual runoff, the total project costs would exceed $15.8 million. The difference between the incentives and the pipe separation project costs represents avoided costs for future ratepayers of $9.3 million (M. Burlin, personal communication, 2010).

"I Don't Do the Work on My Lawn. My Lawn Care Service Does"

This problem underscores the value and significance of identifying and influencing important "midstream" target audiences. Leaders in Kennebunkport, Maine, recognized this principle (Maine Association of Conservation Commissions, 2009). Linking lawn care to the viability of the lobster catch in the summer resort community of Kennebunkport was a concept that the commission, as well as the town manager, believed citizens would understand and respond to since they wanted the local lobster industry to thrive. He also felt that a compelling story would be more effective than regulation and that persuading lawn care companies would be key to success. The first step in the process was to get the town to formally adopt a set of best management practices (BMPs) for the application of turf fertilizers and pesticides, practices that were then distilled into 10 user-friendly steps. Next, the commission sent a letter on town stationery to all lawn care providers they could identify who worked in Kennebunkport, a community where lawn care companies are responsible for most of the caring for lawns of seasonal residents—residents who want the "perfect lawn" for the few weeks that they are there. They let providers know that if they were willing to follow the BMPs, their business names would be listed on the town website as a "Lawns for Lobsters" partner (incentive). Subsequently, eight of the major lawn care companies signed on, pledging to follow the town's BMPs. Once lawn care companies appeared to be on board, efforts were made to promote the program to the community. One newspaper article included a list of questions they suggested residents ask any lawn care provider that they might employ. And to support diffusion, little flags were given to homeowners who adopted the tenets of the program emblazoned with the Lawns for Lobsters logo and "Fewer Chemicals, Cleaner Water" slogan.

Summary

This chapter focused on strategies to influence the residential sector to engage in behaviors to protect water quality. The first major challenge highlighted was that most citizens are unaware or skeptical, at best, that pollutants from many of their household activities (e.g., chemicals from fertilizing, bacteria from pet waste, and soap from car washing) have any significant negative impact on lakes, rivers, streams, and oceans. Our two featured case stories illustrated the power of developing strategies to overcome perceived barriers. The Natural Yard Care program in King County, Washington, has addressed skill-related barriers by developing and offering neighborhood gardening workshops, a strategy that has achieved remarkable success compared to the mass advertising campaign that had been conducted in prior years that only increased awareness of desired behaviors. The Scoop the Poop campaign in Austin, Texas, has addressed convenience-related barriers by installing more pet waste dispensers throughout the city and ensuring the bags were easy and sanitary to use.

Several additional noteworthy efforts were cited, ones that addressed other common barriers to water protection: drain stenciling in Seattle, Washington, to help make the connection between drains and waterways; promoting the beauty and benefits of rain gardens in Melbourne, Australia; skipping the spring lawn fertilizing in the Chesapeake Bay to save the baby blue crabs; and providing grants for ecoroofs in Portland, Oregon, to reduce pollution from runoff.

Questions for Discussion

1. An additional barrier typical for water quality improvement behaviors is the belief that "my little part doesn't matter." What tools would be most effective in addressing this belief barrier?

2. For the Natural Yard Care case, what do you think of the viability of piloting an alternative strategy to workshops: hiring educators to go door-to-door to work one-on-one with homeowners in a targeted neighborhood? How would you compare the two strategies and decide if a door-to-door strategy would provide a better rate of return on investment?

3. For the Scoop the Poop case, what do you think about the suggestion to influence backyard pet waste collection as well? What unique barriers can you imagine you would discover through research? What tools would be most effective in addressing each one?

References

The Humane Society of the United States. (2009, December 30). *U.S. pet ownership statistics.* Retrieved from http://www.humanesociety.org/issues/pet_overpopulation/facts/pet_ownership_statistics.html

Kotler, P., & Lee, N. (2008). *Social marketing: Influencing behaviors for good* (3rd ed.). Thousand Oaks, CA: Sage.

Maine Association of Conservation Commissions. (2009, Fall). *Lawns for lobsters.* Retrieved from http://meacc.net/achievements/kennebunkport%20Final.pdf

Metro UK. (2010). *Council turns dog poo pink.* Retrieved from http://www.metro.co.uk/weird/187381-council-turns-dog-poo-pink

Seattle Public Utilities. (2010). *Stencil a storm drain.* Retrieved from http://www.cityofseattle.net/util/Services/Drainage_&_Sewer/Keep_Water_Safe_&_Clean/RestoreOurWaters/Volunteer/StencilaStormDrain/index.htm

UN Water. (2010). *World Water Day 2010: Clean water for a healthy world.* Retrieved from http://www.worldwaterday2010.info/

U.S. Census Bureau. (2008). *State & county quickfacts. King County.* Retrieved from http://quickfacts.census.gov/qfd/states/53/53033.html

U.S. Environmental Protection Agency. (2009). Managing Wet Weather with Green Infrastructure Municipal Handbook: Incentive Mechanisms.

WayOdd. (n.d.). *Swedish kids campaign against dog poop.* Retrieved from http://www.wayodd.com/swedish-kids-campaign-against-dog-poop/v/6997/

CHAPTER 4

Reducing Emissions

The Problem

In 2007, there were over 800 million cars and light trucks on the road. The following year saw 68 million added to this total (Renner, 2010). Not only are there even more vehicles on the road but they are also being driven farther. In 1950, the average U.S. automobile was driven roughly 9,000 miles per year; by 2003, that distance had increased to nearly 12,000 miles (Renner, 2005). Collectively, these vehicles consume a staggering 260 billion gallons of fuel (Plunkett Research, 2008) and produce copious amounts of CO_2 emissions. Unfortunately, personal vehicles are associated with numerous other negative impacts, including air pollution, traffic congestion, noise, traffic deaths, loss of agricultural land, obesity, and increased storm water runoff (Newman & Kenworthy, 2007; Zuckerman, 1992). In addition, their usage undermines national security for those countries that rely upon imported oil (Newman & Kenworthy, 2007).

Perhaps the most serious of these issues is the impact that vehicle use has upon greenhouse gas (GHG) emissions. The U.S. Environmental Protection Agency (EPA) estimates that each U.S. light vehicle produces approximately 5.5 metric tons of CO_2 equivalent per year (U.S. Environmental Protection Agency [EPA], 2005). Curbing these emissions will mean altering both *how* and *how often* we use personal vehicles.

Potential Behavior Solutions

Residential behaviors that reduce emissions tend to fall into two broad categories: (1) energy use and (2) transportation. Since residential energy use is dealt with in depth in Chapter 6, here we will focus on reducing emissions related to residential transportation choices. As with residential energy, there are numerous transportation related behaviors that can reduce emissions. As a consequence, Table 4.1 is illustrative rather than comprehensive. Note that seemingly similar behaviors, such as walking or biking to work, must be dealt with as distinct activities as their barriers differ. For example, some of the barriers to biking include owning a bike, sharing the road with cars, and securing a bike while at work—none of which are barriers to walking.

Table 4.1 Residential Behaviors to Reduce Emissions	
Area	**Examples of End-State Behaviors That Might Be Chosen for Adoption**
Vehicle maintenance and purchase	• Maintain correct tire pressure. • Conduct regular engine maintenance. • Purchase fuel-efficient vehicle.
Work-related modal choices	• Ride a bike to work. • Walk to work. • Carpool to work. • Telecommute. • Use mass transit to commute to work.
Driving behavior	• Drive below the speed limit. • Turn engine off when parked. • Do not idle car to warm up engine in winter. • Do not accelerate quickly at stoplights. • Drive the most efficient route to work and errands. • Chain errands together so that they are done at once rather than as several trips.
Child-related modal choices	• Ride a bike to school. • Walk to school. • Ride a bike to recreational activities. • Walk to recreational activities. • Carpool to recreational activities.

This chapter features two case studies. The first addresses a behavior related to how we use our vehicles. The second illustrates how we might impact how often we drive.

CASE #1   Anti-Idling: Turn It Off (Toronto, Canada)

Background

"Idling gets you nowhere" is the slogan for a nationwide campaign in Canada to reduce unnecessary engine idling. For over a decade, the Canadian federal government, working in conjunction with provincial and municipal agencies, has been encouraging motorists to not idle their engines. Engine idling refers to a motorist letting their engine run while they are parked and sitting in the car (e.g., such as waiting for a child to come out of school). Engine idling is not the most impactful residential behavior related to reducing emissions, but it is an activity that Natural Resources Canada (NRCan) believed might be changed easily. Further, NRCan reports that this behavior wastes fuel, produces GHG emissions that contribute to climate change and exacerbates smog in cities with existing air quality problems (Natural Resources Canada [NRCan], 2010). Additionally, if motorists adopted this behavior and engaged in it repeatedly, it was believed that these actions might lead to a heightened likelihood of taking more substantive actions, such as purchasing more fuel-efficient vehicles or carpooling. Canada's nationwide efforts to reduce engine idling began with a community-based social marketing (CBSM) pilot project in Toronto that was instigated by Environment Canada and developed by McKenzie-Mohr & Associates and the Ontario Ministry of the Environment. Multiple agencies funded the pilot project including Canada's Climate Change Action Fund, the City of Toronto, the Ontario Ministry of Environment's Drive Clean Office, and Environment Canada. The Turn it Off Steering Committee included representatives of these agencies, which provided guidance to LURA Consulting and McKenzie-Mohr & Associates, who implemented the pilot project. These consultants worked closely with local agencies including the City of Toronto (Works and Emergency Services; Health Department), Toronto District School Board, Toronto Catholic District School Board, and Toronto Transit Commission [TTC].

Target Audience(s) and Desired Behaviors

Idling is a common behavior that most Canadians engage in frequently. Indeed, NRCan reports that Canadians idle their vehicles for nearly 8 minutes each day (Phase 5 Consulting Group, 1998). This pilot project focused on reducing idling in two locations in which it is particularly common: school parking lots and TTC "Kiss and Ride" sites. Parents frequently idle their vehicles while they are waiting to pick up a child from school. Similarly, idling is common when a motorist is waiting for a partner to return on a train at one of the TTC's aptly named Kiss and Ride sites.

At both school and Kiss and Ride parking lots, the requested behavioral change was simple and straightforward: Turn your vehicle off immediately upon arriving in order to enhance air quality and reduce CO_2 emissions.

Barriers and Benefits

Barrier and benefit research consisted of national focus groups and survey research. These methods suggested the following barriers and benefits:

- Motorists frequently forget to turn their vehicles off.
- They are unaware of the length of time that they should idle their vehicle before turning their vehicle engine off.
- Turning an engine off is not a normative or expected behavior.
- Programs should be delivered during the warmer months, as comfort and safety are important reasons why people idle their vehicles in colder weather.

Description of the Program

Two CBSM strategies were developed to encourage motorists to not idle their engines. In the first strategy, only signs (prompts) were used to encourage motorists to not idle. In the second strategy, signs plus personal contact, commitments, and social norms were applied. Please see Figures 4.1 and 4.2.

Figure 4.1   Anti-Idling Car Window Sticker

Source: "Anti-Idling Commitment Sticker." Natural Resources Canada, 2010. Reproduced with the permission of the Minister of Natural Resources Canada, 2010.

Figure 4.2   Anti-Idling Parking Lot Sign

Source: "Anti-Idling Parking Lot Sign." Natural Resources Canada, 2010. Reproduced with the permission of the Minister of Natural Resources Canada, 2010.

1. *Sign Only Strategy:* A minimum of four temporary signs was utilized per location to encourage motorists to turn off their engines. These signs were mounted on concrete bases and at a lowered height so that motorists could read the signs while parked (the height of many signs makes them difficult to read when a vehicle is not moving).

2. *Signs, Commitment, Personal Contact Strategy:* Public commitments were obtained by asking motorists to place a "No Idling" sticker in the front window of their car. This sticker served as a prompt to remind the motorist to turn their engine off, a public commitment to enhance their motivation to turn their engine off and additionally developed social norms by making the desired behavior visible. Motorists were also provided with an information card that noted that reducing idling would save money, while also reducing air pollution and CO_2 emissions. The following script was used when motorists were approached by trained university students and asked to not idle their vehicles:

"Good afternoon/evening. My name is _____, and I am working with the City of Toronto on a project aimed at reducing vehicle engine idling. We want to decrease the harmful emissions that occur when vehicle engines are left running. These emissions, as you may know, decrease air quality and contribute to climate change. We are asking motorists to make a commitment to turn off their engine when they are parked and are waiting in their vehicle. Would you be willing to join the growing number of people who have made a similar pledge and agree to turn off your vehicle's engine when you are parked and waiting in your vehicle? We are asking people who make such a pledge to turn off their vehicle engine to place this sticker on their window. By doing so, the sticker will both serve as a reminder to you to turn your engine off and as a display of your commitment to reduce engine idling. The sticker has been designed so that it can be easily removed from your window at a later time. Would you be willing to attach this sticker to your window? We are also giving out these information cards, which explain how turning off your engine can save you money, help you breathe easier, and spare the air. Would you like to have one?"

As the script suggests, these conversations were brief in nature and generally lasted less than 1 minute per vehicle. Further, it was found that by sending two people to a school parking lot that most parents and guardians could be reached in the space of two afternoons (afternoon pickup time was used as there was more opportunity to discuss engine idling than in the morning when a parent or guardian is dropping a child off and then quickly leaving).

Unobtrusive baseline measurements were obtained for 10 days in order to determine the frequency and duration of idling at 12 locations (six schools and six TTC Kiss and Ride sites). Random time sampling was utilized to determine when the behavior of motorists would be observed. Random time sampling involves selecting at random small periods of time (e.g., 15 minutes) during which observations will be taken. In this project, however, most of the random time samples were selected from the end of the school day or workday in order to capture the period of time in which idling was most likely to occur. Monitors were carefully trained to collect measurements of idling. The monitors were taught to look for signals that a car was idling (e.g., exhaust, a vibrating tail pipe or antenna, vehicle noise).

Upon completing the baseline measurements, the pilot strategies were tested by randomly assigning the 12 sites into one of three groups: (1) Signs Only Strategy; (2) Signs, Commitment, Personal Contact Strategy; or (3) Control. This process led to there being two schools and two TTC Kiss and Rides sites in each of the three groups, for a total of 12 sites overall.

Upon completing implementing the two strategies, follow-up measurements were obtained for 10 days using the same random time sampling process as in the baseline measurements. In this large-scale project, over 8,000 observations of vehicles in the 12 different locations were made. Importantly, across the 12 sites, fully 53% of motorists were observed idling during the baseline period suggesting that idling is a common behavior for Canadians.

The baseline measurements were obtained during the early spring, and the follow-up measurements were collected during the late spring. As a consequence, it was possible that fewer motorists would be idling their vehicles in the late spring simply because the weather was warming. To control for this possibility, observed reductions in the frequency and duration of idling for the control sites were subtracted from the two strategies.

The sign only strategy did *not* reduce engine idling. However, the combination of signs, personal contact, and commitments reduced idling by 32% and the duration of idling by 73%. This strategy was particularly effective at the schools where idling was reduced by 51% and duration by 72%. In contrast, at the TTC Kiss and Ride sites, this strategy reduced idling by 27% and duration by 78%.

Following the success of the pilot project, NRCan implemented the Turn it Off campaign in two Canadian cities with similar results. Importantly, these broadscale implementations targeted not just schools and public parking lots but municipal fleets as well. Once it was determined that the broadscale implementations had worked well in curbing idling, NRCan, under the leadership of Catherine Ray, developed a "turnkey" toolkit, which provided municipalities across Canada with the necessary resources to implement their own anti-idling campaigns. This toolkit consisted of advice on how to execute an anti-idling campaign along with all the necessary communication materials. Freely available on the Internet (http://oee.nrcan.gc.ca/idling/idling.cfm), this toolkit has led to over 200 Canadian communities implementing their own anti-idling campaigns. Further, over 50 Canadian municipalities have now passed anti-idling bylaws and a number of municipalities in other countries have used the toolkit.

Critical Review

The Turn it Off campaign was tremendously successful. Nonetheless, two alterations would have been useful. First, the measurement of changes in idling was done for 10 days following the implementation of the strategies. This short period of time clearly indicated that idling had been reduced both in frequency and duration. However, it does not indicate whether the changes in behavior were sustained. To assess the longevity of these behavioral changes, follow-up assessments at a later time would be necessary.

Second, idling was selected as the targeted behavior as it was hoped that if motorists altered this behavior they might be more likely to adopt other behavioral changes as well. Motorists are more likely to adopt other behavioral changes if clear links are made between the behavioral change they have already engaged in (in this case reducing idling) and other changes that they might adopt (such as carpooling). Connecting adopted behaviors with other potential changes can be strengthened by the use of a consistent brand across promoted behaviors. Further, the use of a media campaign that meaningfully connects and showcases the behaviors that are being encouraged as part of a national effort to improve air quality and reduce CO_2 emissions will further enhance the public seeing the disparate behaviors as importantly related.

CASE #2   TravelSmart (Adelaide, South Australia)

Background

Australia is a world leader with regard to programs to encourage modal transportation shifts. Across Australia, TravelSmart programs have been implemented with hundreds of thousands of households. The project described here was conducted in Adelaide, South Australia, and is featured as it included some of the most rigorous evaluation methods to date of TravelSmart programs. As stated in the final report, this initiative had the following goals:

- Reduce private car use through behavior change, measured by vehicle kilometers traveled (VKT).
- Achieve ongoing change in travel behavior.
- Engage individuals on a voluntary basis.
- Directly engage people within their own settings and cultural context, capturing interest across all sociodemographics.
- Provide simple, motivating tools and techniques addressing individuals' most significant barriers to behavioral change.
- Build strong partnerships with key stakeholders.
- Integrate continuous improvement into project delivery.
- Independently measure behavior change results using statistically valid methods.

Target Audience(s) and Desired Behaviors

The target area consisted of 65,000 homes and over 140,000 residents with diverse socioeconomic and ethnic backgrounds.

The TravelSmart program targeted a variety of behaviors including trip chaining, journey planning, walking and biking, and alternative practices such as using the Internet for banking.

Barriers and Benefits

Barriers and benefits to the promoted activities were not identified beforehand. Instead, conversations were held with participating households in which they were encouraged to discuss what they found challenging and beneficial with regard to different travel options.

Description of the Program

Each of the 65,000 homes was initially contacted by mail to encourage participation in the project. Follow-up conversations occurred with 22,103 homes via the following methods: telephone (12,342), household visit (8,278), group conversation (1,282), and calls to the TravelSmart office (192). These conversations revolved around four questions that were designed to evoke participants rethinking their transportation choices. These questions were as follows:

1. When were you last in the car and wished that you weren't?

2. What bothers you about getting around in the car?

3. Have you thought about using your car a bit less?

4. Do you use your car the same, more, or less than this time last year?

These questions were designed to identify both the barriers to modal transportation shifts as well as what would motivate residents to change. If residents wished, the TravelSmart officers continued the conversation by coaching them regarding various sustainable travel options and worked with them to develop travel solutions that met their goals (communication). A central tenet of this program was "if behavior changes in travel achieve a personal goal, improve lifestyle or that is compatible with personal values, it is more likely the changes will be maintained in the long term" (Department for Transport, Energy, and Infrastructure, 2009, p. 14). A variety of personalized solutions were discussed with participating households. As noted in the final report, these included

- planning activities ahead, 'trip chaining,' giving someone a lift, etc.;
- walking to nearby shops and using local services;
- participating more in local activities;
- traveling to work by train, bus, or tram;
- walking or cycling; and
- using the Internet or phone for bills and banking.

Based upon participants' interests, the trip advisor provided households with various printed materials to support the behavioral changes that the household expressed interest in. The most frequently utilized of these materials were the local activity and access guides, which were obtained by 28% and 17% of households, respectively. To assist participants in utilizing local alternatives, the local activity guide provided information on local assets, such as shops, services, and activities. The activity guide was primarily for participants who wanted to bike or walk more and provided them with a map showing local routes. The final phase of this project involved creating local capacity to sustain behavioral changes by working with various local community groups.

The overall budget for the project was 1.7 million dollars (AUD), for a cost per household of $77. Adelaide's TravelSmart program was evaluated through two sets of measurements: (1) GPS data and (2) vehicle odometer surveys. Several waves of measurements were conducted prior to and following the household engagement for both forms of measurement, and this was done both with participating and nonparticipating households. Importantly, the nonparticipating households were selected at random and were representative demographically of the pilot project area.

The GPS measurements involved providing each participant in a household that was 14 years or older with a GPS logger for 1 week per year for each of the evaluation years. Interestingly, the GPS device was capable of determining whether someone was walking, biking, taking the bus, or driving, as each transportation mode has its own "fingerprint." Further, it recorded the number of trips made and distance travelled. In total, 218 households were monitored for a 7-day period each year for 3 years.

The odometer survey involved 1,000 households, with each reporting odometer readings from each vehicle that they owned every 4 months for the duration of the project. In addition to recording VKT, data was also collected regarding changes in family size that might impact upon kilometers travelled and whether vehicles were purchased or sold. Unfortunately, the sample size of 1,000 households was too small to be conclusive, and the survey data is not reported here (not all households consistently recorded their odometer readings).

The more reliable GPS data indicated the following:

- Car travel was reduced both on weekdays and weekends, with an average reduction of 10.4 km per day (an 18% reduction in household kilometers traveled).
- Nonparticipants increased their kilometers traveled by 605,030 km over the course of the study, while participants reduced the distance traveled by 229,850 km.
- Participants reduced the number of trips they made by an average of 5%, while nonparticipants increased their trips by 3.8%.
- As measured by time spent traveling, participants traveled more efficiently than nonparticipants.

These results were achieved by participants reducing the number of trips made, decreasing the total distance traveled, using their vehicles more efficiently via trip chaining and journey planning, and by shifting to more sustainable forms of transportation, such as cycling or riding the bus.

Critical Review

This program could have been strengthened in three ways. First, it would have been useful to select the travel related behaviors that were most worthwhile to target using the methodology set out in Chapter 1. Once high impact, high probability and low penetration behaviors had been identified, research regarding their barriers and benefits could have informed the strategies that were used in this project. Third, any time that participants in a pilot are aware that they are being monitored there is the potential of a Hawthorne effect. The Hawthorne effect refers to a General Electric plant in which employees were found to be more productive simply when they were aware that they were being monitored. Why should you be concerned about a Hawthorne effect when you are conducting a pilot? If your pilot participants change their behavior because they know they are being observed, rather than because of the program you delivered to them, there is a real possibility that your program will fail when you transition from the pilot to broad scale implementation. Why? When we deliver pilots, we are often dealing with small numbers of individuals, which makes observing changes in their behavior or resource use doable. However, when we transition to broadscale programs, we are often dealing with thousands of individuals, and personal observation is often impossible. Consequently, whenever possible be careful regarding the use of self-reported behavioral changes and rely instead on either unobtrusive observations (e.g., Are more people walking, biking, or taking the bus?), changes in resource use (e.g., Is water usage decreasing?), or changes in resource quality (e.g., Is watershed or airshed quality improving?). Note that in the last two cases, resource use and resource quality, we are not measuring behavioral changes directly but rather the impact of people changing their behavior. Note also that in the TravelSmart project, GPS loggers were provided to both program participants and nonparticipants. The fact that nonparticipants increased their VKT while participants did the opposite suggests that a Hawthorne effect was not likely operating.

Other Notable Programs

Active and Safe Routes to School

In the United States, the number of children walking and biking to school has fallen dramatically since the 1970s (Kober, 2004). Kober noted that a variety of barriers to active transportation (i.e., walking, biking, skateboarding) have been suggested, including parental concerns regarding abduction, traffic safety, neighborhood crime, distance to school, and weather. In the United States, the percentage of students who walk or bike any distance to school has fallen from 42% in 1969 to 15% in 2001. During this same time period, obesity rates for children 6 to 11 years of age have risen 400% (Hedley et al., 2004). In response to decreasing levels of activity and skyrocketing obesity levels, numerous programs have emerged to encourage children to walk or bike to school. Foremost among these programs is the International Walk to School Month, which occurs each year in October. In 2009, children from 40 countries participated in this initiative (iWalk, 2010). Many of the programs that encourage children to walk to school rely upon a "walking school bus." A walking school bus (product) is a group of children who are led to and from school by older children or parents. Frequently, walking school buses involve children meeting at a certain location and then walking into school together. Walking school buses often also involve picking up children while the *bus* makes it way to school. To learn more about active and safe route to school programs, visit www.iwalktoschool.org and www.saferoutestoschool.ca.

One exemplary school program is Bear Creek Elementary School in Boulder, Colorado (National Center for Safe Routes to School, 2010). Prior to the implementation of their program, only 25% of children were walking or biking to school—despite the fact that two thirds lived within 2 miles of the school. Bear Creek's program focused on encouraging both walking and biking to school through the use of walking school buses and bike safety lessons. Walking school buses are a central part of Bear Creek's success. Parent–volunteers, who wear yellow shirts or vests, carry yellow balloons and wear yellow caps, and use bells and horns to announce each bus stop as they pick children up on their route to school. Each classroom records their walking, biking, and ride sharing and compete in the "Tour de French." Named after a former teacher, the Tour de French rewards students with different colored armbands similar to the leader jerseys of the Tour de France. The principal of the school, Mr. Cruger, also presents a Cruger Cup to encourage students to arrive at school each day without a car. In an evaluation conducted by the City of Boulder, in the first year of Bear Creek's Car Free Commute program, there was a 36% decrease in the number of cars arriving at the school. During the second year of the program, children walked or biked 4,800 miles in the month of September 2008 alone, reducing car use by 6,600 trips during a single month.

Summary

It is common in CBSM strategies to use a variety of behavior change tools to foster a change in behavior. While conducting a pilot allows the program planner to assess whether the strategy worked, it does not normally allow a clear identification of what elements of the strategy were responsible for the behavioral change. This is an important distinction as it is quite likely that most programs include elements that are not actually necessary to foster behavioral changes. These non-essential elements often result in programs that are more expensive to deliver and because of the additional program elements, frequently more logistically challenging. In the case of the Turn it Off anti-idling program, prompts, commitments, and personal contact were all elements of the strategy. While this strategy effectively altered behavior, it is uncertain whether all of the elements are actually necessary. It is possible to tease out which exact program elements are required to foster a change in behavior, but the type of pilot required to individually assess each program element presents a program planner with a conundrum. To assess the individual contributions of program elements it is necessary to utilize an orthogonal design. Orthogonal designs require that each program element be tested to identify its unique contribution to changing behavior. In the case of the Turn it Off campaign, this would have involved a design that looked like the one in Table 4.2.

Table 4.2 Orthogonal Designs		Personal Contact			
		Yes		No	
		Commitment		Commitment	
		Yes	No	Yes	No
Prompts	Yes				
	No				

As is immediately apparent, even with a relatively small number of program elements (three in this case), an orthogonal design quickly becomes unwieldy. When, then, might you use an orthogonal design to pilot test a strategy that you have developed? This type of design is useful in two situations. First, you have three or fewer program elements. Second, when broadly implemented, the program will have significant costs associated with it. Consequently, assessing in a pilot precisely which program elements are necessary to produce behavioral changes is warranted in order to reduce costs for broad scale implementation.

Another design issue affects nearly all programs that rely upon self-reports, but it is often most commented on with regards to transportation behavioral change programs. It is common in modal transportation shift programs to evaluate the program through the use of what are referred to as *travel diaries*. With travel diaries, a subset of pilot project participants (often randomly selected) record their travel choices (e.g., kilometers traveled by car, bus, bike, and walking) prior to altering their travel choices and then again after they alter their travel behavior. These diaries are then used as an assessment of the effectiveness of the program in altering behavior. Two issues are worth noting regarding using self-reports of this type in monitoring the success of a program. First, those individuals who complete the diaries are by the very act of completing a diary not like other program participants. Keeping a diary makes these participants far more aware of both their travel choices and the fact that they are being monitored than other participants. As a consequence, extrapolating from the travel choices made by individuals who are keeping diaries to other participants in the pilot that did not keep diaries is not easily justified.

Questions for Discussion

1. Programs to alter modal transportation behaviors, such as carpooling, frequently involve self-reported behavioral changes. What unobtrusive measurements of travel-related behavioral changes could be collected to authenticate whether these self-reports are accurate?

2. The Turn it Off program assessed short-term changes in idling behavior. How would you assess whether changes in idling were sustained?

3. Increasing concentrations of CO_2 in the atmosphere are undetectable without scientific equipment. What might be done to counteract our perceptual limitations?

References

Department for Transport, Energy, and Infrastructure. (2009). TravelSmart: Households in the West. Retrieved from http://www.transport.sa.gov.au/pdfs/environment/travelsmart_sa/Households_in_the_West_Final_Report.pdf

Hedley, A., Ogden, C., Johnson, C., Carroll, M., Curtin, L., & Flegal, K. (2004). Prevalence of overweight and obesity among US children, adolescents, and adults, 1999–2002. *Journal of the American Medical Association, 291*(23), 2847–2850.

iWalk. (2010). International walk to school. Retrieved from http://www.iwalktoschool.org/index.htm

Kober, C. (2004). *Kids walk: Then and now.* Retrieved from http://www.saferoutestoschool.ca/relatedresearch.asp

National Center for Safe Routes to School. (2010). *Safe routes to school: Case studies from around the country.* Retrieved from http://www.saferoutesinfo.org/case_studies

Natural Resources Canada. (2010). *Toward an idle-free nation: The evolution of Canada's idle-free initiative.* Ottawa, Canada: Author.

Newman, P., & Kenworthy, J. (2007). Greening urban transportation. *State of the world 2007: Our urban future* (pp. 66–89). New York: Norton.

Phase 5 Consulting Group. (1998). *Research related to behavior that impacts fuel consumption.* Ottawa, Canada: Natural Resources Canada.

Plunkett Research. (2008). *Automobile industry introduction.* Retrieved from http://www.plunkettresearch.com/Industries/AutomobilesTrucks/AutomobileTrends/tabid/89/Default.aspx

Renner, M. (2005). Vehicle production sets new record. *Vital signs 2005: The trends that are shaping our future* (pp. 56–57). New York: Norton.

Renner, M. (2010). Global auto industry in crisis. *Vital signs 2010: The trends that are shaping our future* (pp. 15–17). Washington, DC: Worldwatch Institute.

U.S. Environmental Protection Agency. (2005). *Emission facts: Greenhouse gas emissions from a typical passenger vehicle.* Office of Transportation and Air Quality. Report EPA420-F-05-004.

Zuckerman, W. (1992). *End of the road: From world car crisis to sustainable transportation.* Post Mills, VT: Chelsea Green.

CHAPTER 5

Reducing Water Use

The Problem

To view Earth from space, our water supply seems vast, with the majority of the planet's surface covered by water. However, less than 1% of Earth's water is available for human use, the remainder is salt water, polar ice, or freshwater that is inaccessible due to its underground depth (Barlow & Clarke, 2002). This unpleasant fact significantly impacts human welfare, with fully 1.4 billion people living in water scarce regions of the world (Gardner, 2010). Unfortunately, climate change is expected to dramatically increase this number as weather patterns alter, resulting in less available freshwater in several regions of the globe (Flannery, 2005).

The freshwater that is available for human use is under assault. A number of major rivers, including the Indus, Rio Grande, Colorado, Murray-Darling, and Yellow, no longer run to the sea throughout the year as their water is siphoned off for a variety of human uses (Gardner, 2010). Increases in human population will further stress water resources (Barlow & Clarke, 2002). Not only is freshwater a scarce resource but frequently it is polluted and unsafe for human use (see Chapter 10).

Desalinization of salt water is expensive and energy intensive (Barlow & Clarke, 2002). Consequently, we must use water more efficiently. Per capita domestic water usage differs dramatically between developed countries, indicating that there are significant opportunities to enhance domestic water efficiency. For example, the United States and Canada have more than twice the domestic per capita water usage of France (382, 343, and 150 liters, respectively) (World Commission on Water for the 21st Century, 1999). Residential water usage can be reduced in a number of ways. In the summer, 50% of Canada's domestic water consumption is for lawn and garden use (Greenventure, 2010), and 65% of this use is wasted simply due to overwatering and evaporation (Capital Regional District, 2010). It is possible to dramatically reduce domestic water use through alternative irrigation practices, installation of water-efficient devices, such as high-efficiency toilets and showerheads, and alterations in daily tasks such as showering and the washing of clothes and dishes.

Potential Behavior Solutions

A wide array of behaviors exist that affect water use. Below is a list of end-state behaviors that might be targeted to reduce residential water consumption. As explained in Chapter 1, behaviors to be targeted should be selected based upon their relative impact, probability, and penetration. Note also that these behaviors will differ with regard to their perceived barriers and benefits. For example, even closely related behaviors such as installing a toilet dam or placing an item in the tank to displace water differ in their barriers, though both actions reduce water used when a toilet is flushed.

Table 5.1 Residential Behaviors to Reduce Water Use	
Area of House	**Examples of End-State Behaviors That Might Be Chosen for Adoption**
Bathroom	• Install high-efficiency showerheads. • Take shorter showers. • Turn water off while soaping up. • Install high-efficiency toilets. • Install a toilet dam to reduce water use in an existing toilet. • Place item in the tank of an existing toilet to displace water. • Fix leaking toilets. • Install a gray water system that does not rely upon potable water for toilets. • Aerate faucets to reduce water flow. • Fix leaking faucets. • Turn the faucet off while brushing teeth or washing hands.
Kitchen	• Wash full loads of dishes. • When replacing a dishwasher, replace with a high-efficiency model. • Fix leaking faucets. • Wash fruit and vegetables in the sink or a container rather than washing them under running water. • Keep a container of water in the fridge rather than run the tap to obtain cold water. • Reduce meat consumption as meat has a much larger water footprint than grains.
Laundry	• Wash full loads. • Purchase a high-efficiency washing machine.
Yard and general	• Wash vehicles with a pail rather than a hose. • Build homes with cisterns to collect rainwater, and use rainwater for gardening use. • Water lawns in the morning and evening to avoid evaporation. • Fix leaks in hoses and irrigation systems. • Use lawn moisture sensors to control lawn watering systems. • Plant drought tolerant plants in gardens. • Replace lawn or portions of lawn with drought tolerant native plants. • Use pool covers to reduce evaporation.

Two case studies are presented in this chapter that illustrate the gains that can be made in reducing domestic water consumption. The first case focuses specifically on outdoor water use, while the second targets a variety of indoor and outdoor behaviors related to domestic water use.

CASE #1   Reducing Water Use (Durham Region, Canada)

Background

In a study jointly sponsored by the Canada Mortgage and Housing Corporation and the Canadian Water and Wastewater Association, three Ontario, Canada, regions (York, Durham, and Halton) investigated the impact of water-efficiency initiatives in reducing peak day demand (see Bach, 2000).[1] Peak day refers to the day of the year in which residential water usage is at its highest. While the term *peak day* is used to describe one day of the year, in reality most Canadian communities experience roughly 20 days a year in which water usage approaches this peak. These days are important in that municipal and regional governments must have in place sufficient infrastructure throughout the year to meet peak water demands that occur only a few days of the year. For this reason, water used on these days is the most expensive water for local governments to provide to residents. Peak water days fall in the hottest days of the summer when residents are watering their lawns. Interestingly, Bach (2000) noted that while water usage is at the highest on these days, little revenue is actually derived by local governments by peak usage due to the higher costs associated with providing water. Municipalities benefit by reducing peak usage in several ways, including reduced infrastructure costs, ability to service a larger population with the same water resources, and deferral of infrastructure upgrades.

Target Audience(s) and Desired Behaviors

This project targeted residential water usage in the Regions of York, Durham, and Halton. Roughly 500 homes were selected in each community and were similar in age of home, property size, and demographics.

While a variety of outdoor water related behaviors were targeted, the most significant of these was lawn watering. More specifically, residents were encouraged to water their lawns only when necessary and to monitor their watering (often using a rain gauge) to ensure that they were not overwatering their lawn.

Barriers and Benefits

Barrier and benefit research was not reported for the behaviors targeted.

Description of the Program

Each region developed their own water reduction strategy to reduce peak usage. York Region utilized the traditional information-intensive method of dropping off a water-efficiency brochure (communication) and a rain gauge (products) to homes (place) in the pilot area. At a later date, they provided households with a reminder tag (prompt) that could be placed over the outdoor water faucet to remind households to conserve water (Figure 5.1). This program cost approximately $22 Canadian per household and resulted in water savings of 3 liters per household per day or a 1% reduction in water usage.

In contrast to York Region, Durham Region sent college students door-to-door to speak to householders (communication) about the importance of reducing outdoor water use and to request that they reduce their water use. In addition, households were asked to make a public commitment to reduce their use by placing a sticker in the front window of their home that recognized their household as reducing water use (Figure 5.2). They were also asked if a plastic prompt could be placed over their outdoor water faucet that reminded them to think about whether it was necessary to water their lawn. The cost to deliver this program was

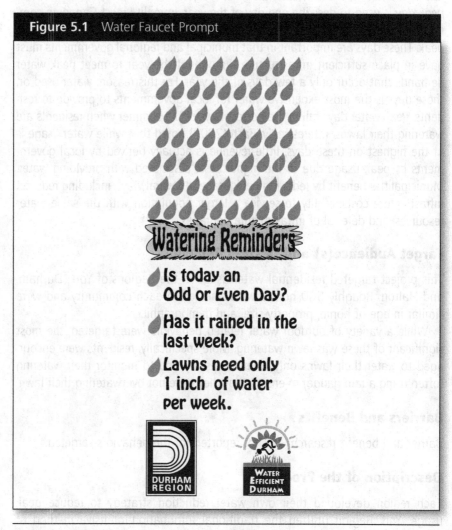

Figure 5.1   Water Faucet Prompt

Source: Graphic provided courtesy of Region of Durham.

Figure 5.2 Commitment Window Sticker

Source: Graphic provided courtesy of Region of Durham.

roughly $44 Canadian per household and resulted in water savings of 215 liters per household per day, a reduction of 32% in outdoor water use.

Halton Region used an approach that was somewhat similar to Durham Region's. In Halton, staff went door-to-door and spoke with householders about the importance of reducing water use (communication). These conversations began by the staff asking homeowners to respond to a survey that begets further conversation regarding water use. They also mailed letters to the households and provided them with rain gauges (prompts) and other educational materials. On a per capita basis, Halton Region spent $18 per household and achieved a 200-liter reduction per household per day, which was a 45% reduction in outdoor water use. Note that Halton Region used staff to deliver this program and the salaries of these staff are not included in the per capita costs.

Not only was water usage monitored in all three regions but the return on investment (ROI) was also calculated. Interestingly, the traditional method of simply providing households with information via the drop off of brochures (e.g., Region of York) was not cost effective. In fact, this approach produced so little in the way of water reductions that it was more cost effective to increase water supply through the building of a new water treatment facility than it was to reduce water usage using these traditional methods. In contrast, in both Durham and Halton Regions the water-efficiency programs were far more cost effective than developing infrastructure to increase supply. Note that water savings in all three regions were monitored via unobtrusive measures that utilized a flow meter that was placed in the water main that serviced these homes. As a result of the use of the flow meters, water usage could be measured in aggregate without the concern that homeowners might alter their water usage because they knew they were being monitored. When participants in a project know they are being monitored they may change their behavior simply because of this knowledge and not because of the program that was delivered to them (see Chapter 4 for a further discussion of the problems that are associated with obtrusive monitoring or what is referred to as the Hawthorne effect).

Critical Review

This project is important for several reasons. First, it demonstrates that it is possible to bring about substantive reductions in outdoor water use through initiatives that carefully target lawn-watering behaviors. Second, it is a careful comparison of the efficacy of traditional information intensive programs versus community-based social marketing (CBSM). Third, not only were changes in water usage unobtrusively monitored but the ROI for each approach was calculated, providing an important benchmark regarding the utility of the region's approach. Too often environmental program planners assess whether a particular approach changes behavior without also addressing the related question of whether the program was cost effective.

As previously noted, Halton Region obtained a 45% reduction in outdoor water use compared to Durham Region's 32% reduction. This discrepancy suggests that regional staff are more persuasive than are students in reducing residential water use. While this might be the case, without having staff go door-to-door in Durham Region and having students go door-to-door in Halton Region, it is impossible to know whether the observed differences in water usage are due to a difference in who was delivering the message, a difference in the receptivity of the communities, or a combination of these factors. To more fully understand the difference between these two communities, students would need to go door-to-door in Halton Region while staff went door-to-door in Durham Region. The relative effectiveness of staff versus students in both communities could then be more fully understood.

Finally, the public commitments obtained in Durham Region likely would have been more effective had they not relied upon householders placing stickers in their front window. These stickers were relatively small in size and would only have been visible to someone who was in close proximity to the sticker. A more effective approach would have been to have a car bumper-sized sticker affixed to the recycling container. A sticker placed on the recycling container would have been visible to anyone who was walking, biking, or driving down the street, dramatically improving the *public* nature of the commitment. Further, public commitments of this sort have the capacity to enhance both social diffusion and social norms (see Chapter 1 for a further discussion of these behavior change tools). It has been the author's experience that householders should not be asked to place these stickers on the recycling containers themselves. In a project in Sonoma County, California, 82% agreed to place stickers on their recycling containers, but only 26% actually did so. In contrast, much higher rates were achieved in Waltham, Massachusetts, by asking householders if they would be willing to place a sticker on their recycling container and then asking if they would simply ensure that their container was placed at the curb on their next recycling day so that staff could place the sticker on the container for them. By simply altering who affixed the sticker, more than twice the number of recycling containers had stickers attached to them in Waltham compared to Sonoma County.

CASE #2   EcoTeams (United States, Netherlands, United Kingdom)

Background

Many environmental behavioral change programs focus on just one change. As a consequence, no matter how successful, their impact will always be constrained by the fact that their program targets one behavioral change. In contrast, the Global Action Plan's EcoTeam approach targets a myriad of behaviors—nearly 100. Founded in the Netherlands in 1990, the EcoTeam (product) program attempts to dramatically alter households' lifestyles such that the amount of water and energy used, waste produced, and transportation choices made along with other sustainable behaviors are all affected. EcoTeam programs have been delivered in 20 countries and to tens of thousands of homes (Staats, Harland, & Wilke, 2004). While the approach varies by country, it normally involves a small group of neighbors and friends meeting once or twice a month for 4 to 8 months. In this case study, programs in the United States, the Netherlands, and the United Kingdom will be featured.

Target Audience(s) and Desired Behaviors

The target audience for the EcoTeam program is usually households; however, it may also involve existing groups such as church groups or civic organizations. The program may also be delivered in workplaces, though the behaviors targeted are usually residential in nature.

The number of behaviors targeted is too lengthy to list. However, it includes a wide variety of actions in the areas of water efficiency, waste reduction, energy efficiency, transportation, and environmentally friendly shopping. In the area of water efficiency, the program targets such behaviors as turning off faucets when not in use, washing full loads of dishes, installing water-efficient showerheads, fixing leaks, and reducing lawn watering.

Barriers and Benefits

Barrier and benefit research was not reported for the targeted behaviors.

Description of the Program

In the United States, EcoTeams (product) comprise 5 to 8 families who meet every 2 weeks for a total of seven times (Gershon, 2008). Each meeting lasts 1.5 to 2 hours, with the first meeting reviewing the themes that will be covered over the course of the program and organizing when and where the meetings will occur. Meetings are facilitated by group members utilizing scripts contained in the EcoTeam handbook (Gershon, 2008). Most meetings involve reporting on actions taken since the last meeting (communication), as well as behaviors that can be adopted to address the theme of the present meeting (e.g., reducing water use). The impact of these actions is recorded by assessing changes in water consumed, waste produced, miles driven, etc. Results vary by community, but organizers report reductions of 25% to 34% in water used, 41% to 51% in garbage sent to landfills, 9% to 17% in energy consumed, 16% to 20% less fuel for transportation, and annual financial savings of $227 to $389 U.S. per household. While a single household can complete the program on its own, the Empowerment Institute recommends participating with other households, a group of friends or coworkers, or a church or civic organization as motivation is enhanced to engage in the behavioral changes if participants are subsequently meeting with others to discuss what they have accomplished. Following completion of the program, participants are encouraged to facilitate the formation of two more EcoTeams. Approximately 40% to 50% of households who are asked to attend a first meeting agree to do so and roughly 85% who attend an introductory meeting join an EcoTeam. The cost per household is a $35 U.S. membership fee (price), which includes the EcoTeam handbook, a volunteer coach, and a subscription to the Global Action Plan's newsletter, *Stewardship*.

In the Netherlands, EcoTeams are normally 6 to 10 individuals in size and are comprised of friends, family, coworkers, etc. (Staats et al., 2004). These groups meet once a month for normally 8 months. As in the United States, these meetings are used to review what was achieved the previous month as well as to plan for activities that will be undertaken as part of the next month's theme. The range of behavioral changes is similar to the United States with waste reduction, energy and water efficiency, transportation, and consumer purchases all being areas of focus. An EcoTeam workbook is also utilized, which provides information on what behaviors to engage in to affect a specific topic, such as water use, and how to monitor changes in that area, such as learning how to read a water meter. Measurements of reductions in water use, energy, waste, transportation, and alterations in purchase behaviors are sent to a central office in the Netherlands, aggregated, and then distributed back to participating households. This aggregated feedback allows participants to know not only what they have achieved but also importantly what is being accomplished collectively. Aggregated feedback is used in a number of countries in which EcoTeams operate.

To assess the effectiveness of the EcoTeam approach in the Netherlands, Staats and colleagues (2004) compared a sample of EcoTeam households with a sample of nonparticipating households who were matched for past environmental practices. Based on self-reports, EcoTeam households altered their environmentally friendly practices from baseline to a follow-up that occurred directly after the meetings completed and sustained these practices in a follow-up that occurred 2 years later. Importantly, in contrast the nonparticipants who were serving as controls marginally increased their environmentally friendly behaviors from baseline to the first follow-up but did not show long-term change in a follow-up survey that occurred 2 years later. Self-report measurements also included data relating to resource use. Participating EcoTeam households reported reducing water use by 7%, solid waste by 32%, natural gas by 17%, and electricity by 8%.

As of 2008, 3,602 U.K. households had participated in EcoTeams (Global Action Plan, 2008). In the United Kingdom, groups meet once a month for usually 5 months and focus on behavioral changes related to water and energy use and waste reduction. Based on self-report data from participating households, U.K. EcoTeams have reduced water use by 15%, waste going to landfill by 20%, their gas/heating energy use by 21%, and their electricity consumption by 7%. CO_2 emission reductions average 17% per household, and average savings per year for water and energy total £148. Post-participation surveys indicated that 94% were "likely" or "very likely" to maintain the changes they had implemented, and 84% would recommend EcoTeams to people they know.

The U.K. EcoTeam program is based upon creating partnerships with local authorities or organizations. Volunteer EcoTeam facilitators are recruited from the community or local organizations and are trained to recruit participants and run their own EcoTeams. In addition to training these facilitators, the national office provides ongoing support in the form of advice and a web-based database for monitoring results.

Critical Review

This research demonstrates perhaps the most important lesson of this book: It is possible to change a wide array of environmental behaviors, in a relatively short amount of time, and sustain these changes. For the innumerable program planners working at the local level, this is very good news. The EcoTeam approach is particularly encouraging as it allows program planners to successfully affect multiple behaviors across multiple domains (e.g., water, waste, energy, transport). This multifaceted approach is both time and cost efficient. Given these positive results, what might be done to further enhance the effectiveness of this approach? Several modifications are worth pursuing. First, it would be worthwhile to compare the behaviors that EcoTeams presently encourage against a careful review of the impact, probability, and penetration of a variety of behaviors within each domain (see Chapter 1 for further information on selecting behaviors). This comparison would allow EcoTeam organizers to ensure that the targeted behaviors have the largest possible impact on water, waste, energy, and transport.

Second, barrier and benefit research for each of the targeted behaviors would allow for further refinement of the strategies that are used to target these behaviors. More specifically, imagine that barrier and benefit research demonstrated that the principal barriers to weather-stripping a house were lack of knowledge regarding how to weather-strip and the inconvenience of traveling to a hardware store to purchase the weather stripping. To address lack of knowledge, EcoTeam leaders could be provided with DVDs that illustrate how to weather-strip as well as a mock window to allow EcoTeam members the opportunity to practice applying weather stripping. To address the inconvenience of traveling to a hardware store, organizers could arrange to have the required materials brought directly to the meetings where they are sold to participants.

Additional scrutiny of which behaviors to target, their barriers, and what strategies might effectively address these barriers could dramatically enhance an already successful program. The third suggestion regards encouraging additional households to participate. At present, EcoTeams frequently rely upon word of mouth as the principal form of recruitment. Each participant is encouraged to recruit new participants in order to expand the reach of the program. Making EcoTeam households more visible in the community could augment these efforts. More specifically, the application of EcoTeam stickers to recycling containers, as discussed in the previous case, would increase significantly the visibility of the program in the community and encourage conversations regarding the program. These conversations can then become an opportunity to recruit additional participants.

Other Notable Programs

Queensland's Home WaterWise Service

In response to one of the worst droughts in Australian history, and associated record lows in water storage, a Home WaterWise campaign was delivered in South East Queensland to substantially reduce residential water use (Local Government and Infrastructure Services, 2010). Funded by the Queensland state government and 21 local councils, and delivered by Local Government Infrastructure Services (LGIS), this ambitious program involved delivering 228,564 home retrofits (22% of homes in South East Queensland) between July 2006 and December 2008. These retrofits (product) involved supplying and installing a water-efficient showerhead as well as aerators on bathroom and kitchen faucets, fixing up to three leaks (two within the home and one outside), installing cistern weights, and providing one-on-one advice via the plumber regarding additional ways in which the household could save water. Homes were also provided with an advice card, fridge magnet, and a washing machine sticker (communication). Householders paid $20 for a subsidized service that was worth $150 per home (price).

While the programs objectives were to achieve a reduction of 21,000 L per household per year, this program far surpassed that objective with actual reductions of 30,600 L per household. Additionally, for those homes that were electrically heated, per household reductions in CO_2 were 932 kg per year. Importantly, follow-up research indicated that high percentages were still using their high-efficiency showerheads (91%), faucet aerators (92%), and cistern weights (85%). Further, nearly half (46%) reported taking shorter showers following the home visit.

Denver Water "Use Only What You Need"

The City of Denver receives 300 days of sunshine a year—more than either San Diego or Miami. As a consequence, managing water resources wisely is a critical issue in Denver (Denver Water, 2010). Denver's water-efficiency program targets both residential and commercial water use. The residential program includes summer water restrictions, incentives for purchasing high-efficiency toilets ($125), washing machines ($150), rain-sensor irrigation controllers (25% of purchase price), and wireless rain sensors ($50) and rain sensors ($25). This program has resulted in annual savings from the residential sector alone of some 2 billion gallons, or approximately 9.9 gallons per person per day.

Summary

A common but mistaken criticism of CBSM is that it narrowly targets one behavior change at a time. It is true that the process of CBSM involves selecting a specific behavior, identifying that behavior's barriers and benefits, and then developing a strategy to address them. The fact that specific behaviors often have unique barriers and benefits associated with them requires that we must identify these barriers and benefits before developing a strategy, but it does not mean that a strategy must target just one behavior at a time. Both of the case studies presented in this chapter demonstrate the importance of being able to target a variety of behaviors simultaneously.

Questions for Discussion

1. Water-efficiency programs target two types of behaviors: (1) repetitive and (2) one-time. Repetitive water-efficiency behaviors include such actions as taking shorter showers and sweeping a driveway off rather than washing it down with a hose. In contrast, one-time behaviors that target water efficiency include such actions as installing high-efficiency showerheads and toilets. How should you decide which of these types of behaviors you should target in your program?

2. Both of the cases discussed in this chapter encouraged the adoption of a variety of behavioral changes simultaneously. What are the strengths and weaknesses of programs that target multiple behaviors at the same time? What selection criteria could you create to assist with determining whether your program should focus on one behavioral change or a group of behavioral changes?

3. Imagine that most households in your community are actively involved in reducing waste through curbside recycling and curbside organic collection. However, little has been done to date to encourage reductions in water use. How might you leverage their involvement with waste reduction to increase the likelihood that they will adopt water-efficiency behaviors as well?

Note

1. This case study is based upon the 2000 report by Cassandra Bach, titled "Outdoor Residential Water Reduction Programs: Do They Really Work?"

References

Bach, C. (2000). *Outdoor residential water reduction programs: Do they really work?* Unpublished report.

Barlow, M., & Clarke, T. (2002). *Blue gold: The battle against corporate theft of the world's water.* Toronto: McClelland and Stewart.

Capital Regional District. (2010). *Water conservation fact sheets.* Retrieved from http://www .crd.bc.ca/water/conservation/education/factsheets/index.htm

Denver Water. (2010). *Use only what you need.* Retrieved from http://useonlywhatyouneed.org/

Flannery, T. (2005). The weather makers: How we are changing the climate and what it means for life on earth. New York: HarperCollins.

Gardner, G. (2010). Water scarcity looms. *Vital signs 2010: The trends that are shaping our future* (pp. 42–44). New York: Norton.

Gershon, D. (2008). *Green living handbook: A 6 step program to create an environmentally sustainable lifestyle.* Woodstock, NY: Empowerment Institute.

Global Action Plan. (2008). *EcoTeams evaluation report: Global action plan.* Retrieved from http://issuu.com/xander/docs/uk_ecoteams/33?mode=embed&documentId=08101 6182632-e70e678d74034a13b2523ec9f01849d8&layout=grey

Greenventure. (2010). *Wise water use.* Retrieved from http://water.greenventure.ca/outdoor-tips

Local Government and Infrastructure Services. (2010). Home WaterWise service end of program report. Queensland, Australia: Department of Infrastructure and Planning, Queensland Government.

Staats, H., Harland, P., & Wilke, H. (2004). Effecting durable change: A team approach to improve environmental behavior in the household. *Environment and Behavior, 36*(2), 341–367.

World Commission on Water for the 21st Century. (1999). The poor pay much more for water . . . use much less—often contaminated. Retrieved from www.worldcouncil.org

CHAPTER 6

Reducing Energy Use

Energy is an essential element of modern life. From automobiles to cell phones to home heating, energy powers our lives. But while energy is the source of our many conveniences and comforts, its use has substantial environmental consequences. In this chapter, we examine programs that aim to change behavior and promote energy efficiency and conservation. Our focus is on residential energy use, particularly electricity. Worldwide, residential uses of electricity account for about 11% of total consumption, although this percentage is much higher in Western Europe, Australia, and North America.

Over the past 50 years, worldwide energy use has increased steadily. Total production has more than doubled since 1971 (International Energy Agency, 2006, 2010). While there are certainly large international differences in the uses of various energy sources, the large majority (83%) comes from fossil fuels like oil, coal, and natural gas. And while recent years have seen a growth in the use of renewable energy sources like hydro, solar, and wind power, almost all of our energy continues to come from nonrenewable sources.

The Problem

The problems resulting from the use of fossil fuels are many and diverse. First, fossil fuels take millions of years to form—they are residues from organic material that accumulated in the ancient past. As a result, they exist in limited supplies and must be harvested from the earth. Yet our energy infrastructure is built around a plentiful supply, and reasonable estimates indicate that worldwide demand for these nonrenewable resources will soon exceed the supply. In addition, the harvesting process itself (i.e., mining and drilling) has large environmental consequences, whether from the disruption of local ecosystems in the arctic (Arctic National Wildlife Refuge, or ANWR) or oil spills like the Exxon Valdez in Alaska or the recent leakage of the offshore British Petroleum (BP) oil well in the Gulf of Mexico.

Second, the use of fossil fuels and other nonrenewable energy sources results in harmful pollutants. Through the combustion process, fossil fuels are burned, releasing their chemical properties into the atmosphere. These pollutants cause many local and global environmental problems, including smog, acid rain, respiratory health problems for humans and animals, elevated cancer risks, atmospheric ozone damage, and ultimately global climate change. The contemporary issue of climate change has attracted considerable attention, and despite the rhetoric, the evidence is clear that releasing carbon and other greenhouse gases (GHGs) can cause major disruptions in the earth's weather patterns, including gradual increases in the global temperature (Intergovernmental Panel on Climate Change [IPCC], 2007; National Academy of Sciences, 2010). In Chapter 4, we discussed social marketing efforts aimed at reducing emissions. In this chapter, we examine the related topic of energy use more generally.

Potential Behavior Solutions

There are two major approaches to addressing the problems associated with energy use. The first is oriented around technology and promoting efficient use of energy. From this perspective, the solution to our energy problems can be found in more efficient technologies—that is, devices that provide the same or enhanced services but with a reduced energy footprint. Consider the case of residential lighting, where a compact fluorescent lightbulb (CFL) produces a similar energy output to traditional incandescent bulbs but uses only about one third of the electricity. And recent developments in light emitting diode (LED) technologies offer even more efficient alternatives.

But technological advances are risky, and there is no guarantee that new discoveries or more efficient devices will solve our energy problems. In addition, focusing on efficiency does not necessarily result in reduced consumption. Efficiency is typically defined as a ratio of input to output (e.g., lumens/watts in the CFL example). But this definition poses problems for comparing across technologies. Consider the case of a flat screen television. A highly efficient 60" television might consume only a fraction of the energy consumed by similarly sized models (making it very efficient), yet the consumption may far exceed that of an inefficient 32" television. As Calwell (2010) stated, "Bigger, more powerful, more functional products get to use proportionally more energy or power and still be labeled as efficient or earn rebates, as long as they use less energy than other equally big, powerful, functional products" (p. 9).

In addition, even when there is a more efficient technology available, there is evidence to suggest that usage patterns can result in zero reduction in energy consumed (see Sorrell, 2007, on rebound effects). For example, a person who realizes that the CFL is using less energy might be less likely to turn it off when leaving a room.

While more efficient technologies can certainly play a role in managing our energy needs, it seems clear that behavioral changes will be essential in addressing energy issues. The behavior change perspective emphasizes conservation and using *less* rather than being more efficient. The role of behavior in efforts to reduce energy consumption has attracted considerable attention in recent years, and many governmental agencies and nongovernmental organizations (NGOs) have embarked on social marketing activities to encourage conservation.

In developing social marketing programs to change behavior, it is important to focus on specific actions. And it is important to connect these actions to the desired outcome (e.g., less energy use or less carbon emissions). A recent analysis of energy consumption in the United States provides a good starting point (Gardner & Stern,

2008). Of all the energy consumed in the United States, 22% is used by households and individuals (excluding transportation), 32% is used by industry, 18% by commercial services, and transportation uses 28%. Table 6.1 shows a breakdown of individual and household energy use.

Table 6.1 Percentage of Total U.S. Individual/Household Energy Consumed by End Use, Ranked in Order of Magnitude	
End Use	**Percent**
Transportation	
Private motor vehicles	38.6
Air travel	3.4
Mass transportation and other	1.4
Subtotal	43.4
In-home uses	
Space heating	18.8
Air conditioning	6.2
Space conditioning subtotal	*25.0*
Water heating*	6.5
Lighting	6.1
Refrigeration and freezing	4.3
Electric (heating elements, small appliances, and small motors)	3.9
Clothes washing/drying*	2.5
Color TVs	2.5
Cooking	1.5
Computers	0.6
Propane and natural gas (swimming pool heaters, grills, and lamps)	0.5
Dishwashers	0.2
Other	3.0
Subtotal	56.6
Total	100.0
Hot water for "Clothes washing" is included under "Water heating."	

Source: Gardner, G., & Stern, P. C. (2008, September/October). The short list: The most effective actions U.S. households can take to curb climate change. *Environment*, 1–10. Retrieved from http://www.environmentmagazine.org/Archives/Back%20Issues/September-October%202008/gardner-stern-full.html

This table provides a useful starting point for developing a social marketing campaign. But the actions are not yet end-state behaviors, so before developing a social marketing campaign, these behavioral domains will need to be focused on specific actions. In addition, it is unclear what is realistically achievable—that is, how changeable are these behaviors?

While social marketers typically conduct surveys and focus groups to better understand their target audience, there are some national-level data from the United States that provide a good starting point. Note that we continue to recommend that program managers utilize local data to understand their target audience, including an assessment of impact, probability, and penetration. But at the national level, data from Dietz, Gardner, Gilligan, Stern, & Vandenbergh (2009) provide a good starting point.

In a report for the National Academy of Sciences, Dietz et al. (2009) estimate the realistically achievable reductions in carbon emissions from U.S. households. Their results identified 17 behavioral areas, and they calculate a *plasticity* estimate using the probability of change utilizing best practices and the percentage of individuals who have not yet adopted the action. Plasticity is calculated as the percentage of the population that has not yet adopted an action (i.e., the inverse of market penetration) multiplied by the effectiveness of the best-practice approach to inducing change over a 10-year period. In Table 6.2, we summarize the key findings from their analysis. To illustrate, household weatherization has a plasticity estimate of 90, because very few households have already adopted this behavior and because best practices identified in prior research has shown that programs can be particularly effective at encouraging residents to engage in weatherization activities such as installing added insulation, caulking and weatherizing windows, and sealing leaks and cracks around exterior doors (Dietz et al., 2009).

Table 6.2 Achievable Carbon Emissions From Household Actions

Behavior Change	Behavioral Plasticity	Percentage Reduction in Total Household Emissions
Weatherization	90	3.39%
HVAC equipment	80	1.72%
Low-flow showerheads	80	.18%
Efficient water heater	80	.86%
Appliances	80	1.87%
Low rolling resistance tires	80	1.05%
Fuel-efficient vehicle	50	5.02%
Change HVAC air filters	30	.59%
Tune up AC	30	.22%
Routine auto maintenance	30	.66%

Behavior Change	Behavioral Plasticity	Percentage Reduction in Total Household Emissions
Laundry temperature	35	.04%
Water heater temperature	35	.17%
Standby electricity	35	.52%
Thermostat setbacks	35	.71%
Line drying	35	.35%
Driving behavior	25	1.23%
Carpooling and trip-chaining	15	1.02%

Source: Dietz, T., Gardner, G., Gilligan, J., Stern, P., & Vandenbergh, M. (2009). Household actions can provide a behavioral wedge to rapidly reduce U.S. carbon emissions. *Proceedings of the National Academy of Sciences, 106*, 18452–18456. Retrieved from http://www.pnas.org/content/106/44/18452

With this general background in mind, we turn now to specific programs that have attempted to change behavior. All of the examples focus on residential target audiences. For social marketing programs targeting business audiences, see Chapter 12.

CASE #1   The One-Tonne Challenge to Reduce Greenhouse Gas Emissions (Canada)

Background

In response to increasing concerns about global climate change, the Canadian government embarked on an ambitious campaign to change behavior. Beginning in 1998, Environment Canada and Natural Resources Canada sponsored a series of public outreach programs with the goal of reducing GHG emissions. The program was supported through a new Climate Change Action Fund and had a stated goal of educating and raising awareness of the threats of climate change. Following ratification of the Kyoto Protocol in 2002, Canada pledged to reduce its GHG emission by 6% from its 1990 levels.

One of the programs funded under this initiative was the One-Tonne Challenge (OTC). The OTC program challenged Canadians to reduce their annual GHG emissions by 20%, or one tonne. Note that because households account for approximately one third of all GHG emissions in North America, a 20% reduction would achieve the targeted goal of a nationwide 6% aggregated reduction. Whereas previous programs had focused on convincing Canadians about the importance of climate change as an issue, the OTC was designed to "encourage and motivate Canadians to take personal action to reduce GHG" (Environment Canada, 2006, p. 5). Funding for the program came from several sources but totaled $37 million over a 3-year period.

The focus was on making modifications to daily activities, purchasing, and lifestyle choices. The campaign was built around the notion that raising awareness and understanding of climate change would lead Canadians to take action and change their behavior.

Target Audience(s) and Desired Behaviors

The overall target audience was "Canadians," and the campaign focused on four key market segments: (1) the general public, (2) business and industry, (3) communities, and (4) youth and educators. For each market segment, unique media and localized activities were developed and implemented.

The program began by recognizing that the average Canadian produced five tonnes of GHG emissions per year. Consistent with the preliminary data noted in the opening section of this chapter, these individual and household behaviors represent approximately one third of the total Canadian emission.

The program targeted direct emissions, like driving automobiles, heating and cooling homes, washing and drying clothes, and using home appliances. The program also targeted indirect emissions, including water consumption (emissions come primarily from transporting water from one location to another) and waste generation (emissions come from processing, manufacturing, transportation, and disposal of materials).

Barriers and Benefits

Because the OTC was an extension of existing GHG programs in Canada, program planners had several large-scale surveys to draw from in designing the program. From the existing data, the program identified two barriers to personal action:

1. Lack of information on how to reduce GHG emissions

2. Perceived inconvenience and difficulties in actually reducing emissions

To address these barriers, the campaign focused primarily on linking specific behaviors to GHG emissions and the environmental importance of emission reductions.

Description of the Program

The program had two key components: (1) a national marketing initiative and (2) a series of partnerships with key organizational entities tied to each of the market segments. The marketing initiative consisted primarily of advertising highlighting the importance and societal benefits of reducing GHG and providing resources to consumers. A media-intensive period was conducted for 3 months in early 2004 with a series of public service announcements, print ads in newspapers, radio spots, and ancillary messages across a variety of media outlets (e.g., MSN, WeatherNetwork) and events (e.g., home and car shows, Earth Day events).

The media portion also contained *Your Guide to the One-Tonne Challenge* and a website that allowed individuals to calculate their personal GHG emission, make a personal pledge, read tips about reducing GHG emissions, and take advantage of existing incentive and rebate programs. The pledge took a variety of forms but typically required the person to use a GHG calculator to identify specific action that would lead to a 20% personal reduction. Then for each action, the person made a pledge by either clicking or writing a check mark. As described in Chapter 1, pledges serve to *commit* an individual to an action, and commitments can serve as an important tool of behavior change.

The partnership portion of the OTC consisted of various organizational and business partners across sectors of Canadian society. These included hubs, community partners, youth organizations, private sector partners, education partners, and "in-reach" to governmental departments and organizations.

Pilot. No specific pilot tests were conducted prior to launching the program.

Implementation. A 2006 report by the Evaluation Division of Environment Canada provides a summary of the project activities and outcomes. Overall, the report notes a high degree of success for OTC messaging and placement. Over the 3-year period, the program distributed 1.2 million *One-Tonne Challenge* guides and received 4.2 million hits to the website. OTC was particularly effective at forming partnerships, and more than 100 organizational partnerships were established to support the campaign.

Evaluation

The effectiveness of the program was assessed through a series of national surveys. In 2003 (prior to the launch of the program), a large national survey was conducted. The results were then compared with results from survey data obtained in 2004 and 2005. Here we highlight three key findings from the survey data.

1. *Exposure.* The survey data showed that the program was very effective at penetrating the target market. In 2004, one year after the launch of the OTC, 6% of survey respondents recognized the program; in 2005, this recognition increased to 51%. When asked where they had heard about the program, a large majority (72%) identified television public service announcements as the primary source. Among Canadians who were familiar with the program, most identified the OTC as a federal program. Survey data also showed that Canadians who were familiar with the program understood what it was trying to accomplish.

2. *Awareness.* The survey data showed that while awareness and concern about climate change was generally high it was not affected by the OTC program. Between 1998 and 2003 (prior to the start of the program), familiarity with climate change as an issue increased substantially (from 54% in 1998 to 77% in 2003). However, between 2003 and

2005 there was no change in the percentage of Canadians who acknowl-
edged that there were steps that they could personally take to reduce
GHG emissions.

3. *Behavior.* Of those Canadians who were familiar with the program, more
than half reported actively participating in it (i.e., to have personally taken
the OTC). And even among those who were not actively involved in the
program, 56% reported a willingness to do so in the future. Yet despite
their willingness, Canadians reported a strong belief that it will be difficult
to achieve a personal target of a 20% reduction. No additional behavioral
outcome data is provided, although our review of the 2003 and 2005
survey reports suggests that there were no changes in reported specific
behaviors (e.g., sealed leaks or drafts in your home, added or replaced
insulation, installed energy-efficient lightbulbs). No assessment was made
of any GHG reductions associated with this program.

The OTC program ended in 2006.

Critical Review

The OTC program is prototypical of many large-scale education programs. It
was well-funded, coordinated through a governmental agency, and systemati-
cally implemented. The program also incorporated a personal commitment
element, linked with specific behaviors for each individual.

However, with regard to implementation, the program was more about
social advertising than social marketing. Like many large-scale education campaigns, the OTC attempted to target a large and diverse audience—in this case,
all Canadians. With such a large and diverse audience there are likely to be a
multitude of barriers and benefits to the targeted behaviors and consequently
creating focused messages that target one or two selected barriers is difficult.
As a result, the campaign resorted to broad-based messages and relied heavily
on mass media like television and radio.

The results reported suggest that the program was effective at reaching the
target audience. A high percentage of Canadians recognized the program and
reported personally taking the challenge. Like many mass media campaigns,
the program was successful at penetrating the market and getting information
into the hands of residents. However, when it comes to changing behavior, the
program came up short. Here we highlight three weaknesses with the OTC, as
implemented.

First, the program overemphasized knowledge and awareness. Prior to the
launch of the campaign, survey data showed that Canadians were already familiar with the issue of climate change. The campaign, therefore, needed to translate
this knowledge into action. Yet campaign messages focused heavily on educating
Canadians about the role of individuals in causing climate change, rather than
on specific actions that individuals could adopt. As discussed in the introductory
chapter of this book, social marketing is about more than education. Research

by behavioral scientists has identified a number of "tools" that can be used to encourage individuals to take action—such as social norms, commitment, financial incentives, or new products or services to increase convenience. Yet these tools were noticeably absent from the OTC. This point was also made in the evaluation report, "...this evaluation concluded that in order to achieve GHG emission reductions, national public education and outreach (PEO) programs like the OTC need to be complemented by additional tools...to assist Canadians in reducing the GHG emissions they produce" (Environment Canada, 2006, p. 3). The use of a personal pledge on the OTC website is a good start, but it needed to be more strongly emphasized in the campaign materials and focused on one or two specific behaviors.

Second, the campaign failed to emphasize specific end-state behaviors. The program attempted to identify individual behaviors for participants, but the program itself did not isolate specific actions. As a result, each participant in the program was left to identify his or her own unique set of behaviors. As discussed throughout this book, behavior change campaigns are more likely to achieve success when they focus on specific end-state behaviors. Because of this personalized approach, the campaign elements provided broad-based messages rather than guidance about specific behaviors. As we have seen elsewhere in this book, general messages that highlight many different behaviors are unlikely to produce change. A campaign that is focused on reducing GHG emissions is nebulous, and while it can be effective at raising awareness, it is unlikely to produce behavior change. It is possible to use a broad-based message as an "umbrella" or overarching brand, but it is important to consider specific focused program elements underneath.

Third, because each participant in the program had a personal set of behaviors, the program was not able to focus on barriers or benefits. No background research was conducted on the barriers and benefits associated with specific behaviors. In essence, the campaign left it up to each individual to overcome the barriers associated with each behavior rather than identifying these barriers and developing a program of messaging to directly address them.

A notable strength of the campaign was its attempt to integrate evaluation. The use of annual surveys provides a good data source for assessing market penetration, awareness, and behavioral responses to the program. However, behavioral evaluations are strengthened by including observational data, like the percentage of individuals observed walking to work, bus ridership, or household energy consumption—that is, evaluations should to go beyond self-reports about behavior and to draw instead on more objective metrics. The evaluation efforts would also have benefited from a control group. In the case of the OTC, the program could have been rolled out to different regions of the country over a period of years, or certain geographic regions could have been selected not to receive the campaign. And finally, the evaluation would have benefited from a pilot test of the messages, prior to placement. In many cases, running a small field experiment or focus group can allow social marketers to test the efficacy of the campaign materials before they are broadly distributed.

CASE #2   ecoENERGY to Promote Home Energy Efficiency (Canada)

In the opening section of this chapter, we presented data for the various household actions associated with energy consumption. These were summarized in Table 6.2. As shown in the table, several of the specific energy-consuming behaviors are related to the characteristics of a dwelling—including such qualities as weatherization, appliances, water heating, and heating/cooling systems. Thus, with regard to impact, encouraging homeowners to upgrade their properties provides an excellent target for a social marketing campaign. Combined, we refer to these behaviors as *home energy retrofits*.

Background

Home energy retrofit programs date back to the early 1970s. The programs typically begin with a home energy audit in which a specialist comes to the home and provides an assessment of the home's efficiency. Such audits are typically offered to residents through their local electric or gas utility, and many are mandated by governmental policy. Yet while such programs are widely available, only a small percentage of residents request them. In areas where home energy audits are available, typically fewer than 5% of residents will have ever requested one (Stern, 1985; Stern & Aronson, 1984). Interestingly, of homeowners who request an audit, a large percentage will adopt at least some of the recommended behaviors—typically more than 50% will implement one or more of the recommendations, but often as many as 70% depending on the program.

While only a small percentage of residents are likely to request an audit, some program elements elicit a better response (Stern, 1985; Stern & Aronson, 1984). In general, programs with more publicity tend to have higher audit rates, as do programs with more convenience (e.g., offering audits on evenings and weekends, rather than just during normal business hours). There is also some evidence that do-it-yourself audit programs are more likely to be utilized, compared with contractor or utility in-home audits. Most residents prefer not to utilize financing options for either the audit or the recommended retrofit actions. And finally, residents prefer to take less expensive actions that will result in direct cost savings, like caulking, weather stripping, installing programmable thermostats, or water heating blankets (Hirst, Berry, & Soderstrom, 1981).

There are also some demographic differences in the types of people who are likely to request an energy audit. While there is some variability, people requesting home energy audits tend to be older and more educated, have higher incomes, and live in larger and more recently constructed homes. Importantly, such dwellings are typically not the ones most in need of repairs, nor the ones most likely to benefit from retrofit activities.

One of the most effective residential retrofit programs was the Hood River Conservation Project (Hirst, 1987, 1988). The program was conducted between 1983 and 1985, with the goal of "testing the upper limits of a utility retrofit program." The campaign focused on electrically heated homes in Hood River, Oregon (about 3,500 eligible homes), and was funded with $20 million that was anticipated in savings from avoiding construction of a new coal-fired energy plant. The program elements included an initial period of intensive media promotion followed by in-person communications from program staff, a free energy audit, and following the audit, free installation of the recommend repairs including new insulation and high-efficiency windows. Note that in testing "the upper limits" the program removed all financial barriers—all program elements were free to residents!

Results from the evaluation showed a remarkable success. Of the eligible homes, 91% received an energy audit, and of these, 92% completed one or more major retrofit activities. Most of the participants heard about the program through word of mouth, although a sizable percentage (28%) cited the newspaper as an important source of information. Careful evaluation of energy savings associated with the program showed an average per home reduction of 2,500 kWh/year. This corresponded to a 15% reduction per home. The program costs averaged $4,400 per house. In summarizing their results, Hirst (1988) concluded that

> The key factors leading to high participation include the offer of free measures, determination on the part of HRCP staff to enlist every eligible household, the use of many community-based marketing approaches, extensive word-of-mouth communication among Hood River residents, ... and the ... personal contacts by staff among the remaining nonparticipants. (p. 317)

We present the Hood River Conservation Project as an example of a highly effective program. However, the program costs far exceed the budgets of most home energy retrofit programs. Yet many of the elements are transferable to other programs, including the intensive period of media coverage, word-of-mouth communication, and efforts to reduce the barriers to energy-efficiency measures, including low-to-no cost, easy-to-understand program elements, and easy access to the home audit. We turn now to an example of a large-scale retrofit program.

The ecoENERGY Retrofit Program

Building on the Hood River Conservation Project, a recent social marketing program in Canada aimed to increase energy efficiency and reduce GHG emissions. The ecoENERGY program was launched in 2007, with $1.5 billion in federal funding (Daily Home Renovation Tips, 2009; MIG, 2010). The program was managed through Natural Resources Canada, a federal agency (see Natural Resources Canada, 2010).

Target Audience(s) and Desired Behaviors

The program targeted single-family and multifamily dwellings across Canada, although funding was also available for commercial and industrial properties. Although the program was available to all properties, there was special interest in reaching older homes, which are most likely to show reductions in energy consumption due to the retrofit measures.

The program specifically targeted home efficiency retrofits, including draft proofing, added attic insulation, window and door improvements, more efficient space heating, and upgraded water heaters.

Barriers and Benefits

No new data was reported as foundation for the program. However, the program did build on a solid foundation of prior studies, including the Hood River Conservation Project previously summarized. The primary barrier addressed through the program was cost.

Description of the Program

To participate in the ecoENERGY program, homeowners must hire a certified energy advisor to perform an on-site audit. From a social marketing perspective, the audit represents a product and the on-site element is the place. Based on the audit, the homeowner receives a checklist of recommended retrofit measures designed to reduce the energy consumption of the home, along with recommendations for reducing water consumption. Following the audit, the homeowner has 18 months to complete the efficiency improvements. After the improvements are made, a second audit is performed to certify the improvements and document the energy savings. The costs for the improvements—up to $5,000—are reimbursed through the program. Additional grant funding offers residents in certain areas another $5000.

In the 2 years following the launch of the ecoENERGY program, 279,363 households received the initial audit, and 94,011 completed the second audit. This corresponds to approximately 1% of eligible households across Canada completing retrofit activities. In addition, the participation rates showed a dramatic increase, from 17,642 completed retrofits in the first year to 94,011 retrofits in the second year. While the funding allowed up to $5,000 per home (plus an additional $5,000 in matching provincial funds in some regions), the average reimbursed retrofit expenses per home was only $1,095. This resulted in a total of $103 million in reimbursed costs.

Evaluation

Based on pre–post on-site audits, the average household reduced their energy consumption by 19% following the retrofit activities.

Critical Review

Overall, the ecoENERGY program provides an excellent model for retrofit programs. Building on the Hood River example, the program was designed to remove the cost barriers associated with retrofit activities. The program shows an increasing participating rate and high energy savings for households that completed the retrofits.

Despite the success, there are several places where the program could be improved. First, the program requires a financial outlay by the homeowner.

While the program rebates these funds to the resident, the initial outlay could pose a barrier for lower-income homeowners. The fact that participants are only spending $1,095 of the available funds suggests that the up-front costs are a barrier. While the program did provide a mechanism for supporting low-income homeowners, it required a separate (and more complicated) process. Second, the program lacks a marketing and outreach plan, and the program is largely unknown to many Canadians. An easy-to-find website, coupled with targeted outreach in defined geographic areas would go a long way toward increasing participation rates. Especially helpful would be in-person invitations from program staff to residents of older homes.

Finally, only 34% of the households that completed the initial audits followed through with the retrofits. This number is relatively small, and while some residents may have implemented the recommendations outside of the program, it suggests that efforts should be made to identify the barriers preventing these interested households from moving forward. In addition, there are a number of tools that could be incorporated into the audit process, including social norms, vivid language, message framing, or commitments on the part of the homeowner (see Stern & Aronson, 1984, pp. 92–96 for specific examples).

Despite the notable success of the program, the Canadian government suspended the program in April 2010. The program is currently under review and may be reinstated pending outcomes of the evaluation.

Other Notable Programs

The cases previously presented provide a good sampling of the types of social marketing programs used to promote residential energy conservation. But there are certainly many other excellent examples, and next in the short section, we briefly mention a few other programs.

The Social Norms Approach: OPOWER

Behavioral science research has shown that social norms can provide a strong motivational basis for residential energy conservation. Social norms refer to a person's beliefs about the prevalence and approval for various behaviors among group members. So, for example, the extent to which a person believes that his or her neighbors are doing things to conserve energy—or that his or her neighbors think conservation is important—are specific types of social norms (Nolan, Schultz, Cialdini, Griskevicius, & Goldstein, 2008; Schultz, Nolan, Cialdini, Goldstein, & Griskevicius, 2007). In a series of studies, Schultz (a coauthor of this book) provided residents with normative messages about specific measures that other households in their neighborhood were taking to reduce energy consumption—for example, "77% of San Marcos residents often use fans instead of air conditioning to keep cool in the summer." Results showed that in the weeks after receiving the normative message, households used 10% less electricity compared to a control group that received tips about ways to conserve (but no normative message).

Drawing on these research findings, OPOWER has developed a program whereby residents receive information about their own level of household energy consumption, coupled with information about the norm for their local community (see www.opower.com). For households that consume more energy than the norm, they receive a "below average" message, whereas households that consume less than the norm receive a "great" message plus a smiley face (see Figure 6.1). Currently, more than 1 million households in the United States receive the OPOWER normative feedback. Results from 23 participating utilities across the country have shown that households that receive the normative message reduce their consumption by an average of 2.4% (Ayres, Raseman, & Shih, 2009; Hunt, 2010).

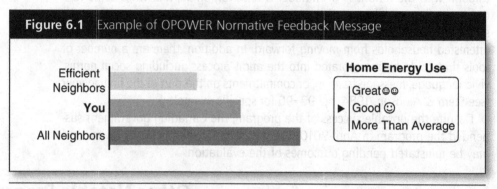

Figure 6.1 Example of OPOWER Normative Feedback Message

Source: Image provided courtesy of OPOWER.com.

The Environmental Protection Agency's ENERGY STAR Program

Launched in 1992 by the U.S. Environmental Protection Agency (EPA), ENERGY STAR has become the most widely recognized symbol of energy efficiency across North America. While the program has grown and changed since its inception, the primary mission remains to provide an objective rating standard for different products (see www.energystar.gov). In 2009, ENERGY STAR was utilized by more than 3,000 manufacturers and differentiated more than 40,000 product models. Similar programs exist in the European Union and in Australia.

For consumers, the ENERGY STAR label is seen as a credible source of information. (See Figure 6.2.) By the end of 2009, 75% of the American public recognized the label, and nearly one third of consumers credited the label as an important factor in their purchasing decisions (ENERGY STAR, 2010). In 2009 alone, more than 300 million ENERGY STAR qualified products were purchased, including appliances, heating and cooling equipment, lighting, and consumer electronics, among others.

While the brand is widely recognized in North America, it is important to look for data about its efficacy at influencing individual purchase decisions. If presented with the two identical models, one with and one without the label, what advantage would the labeled product have? Determining the efficacy of the ENERGY STAR label on purchase decisions turns out to be difficult, given that models with the ENERGY STAR label also tend to have other desirable features. However, in an interesting comparison of washing machine sales, Wallander (2008) reported a 10% price premium due to the label. This price premium shows the added value associated with the ENERGY STAR label, and provides some tentative evidence for its effectiveness at influencing consumer choices.

The success of the ENERGY STAR program is linked with its perceived credibility and its longstanding position in the marketplace (Interbrand, 2007). With the backing of the U.S. EPA and consistent branding, it is easily recognized and utilized. However, its success has also resulted in a proliferation of ENERGY STAR branded programs, which may eventually dilute its credibility in the marketplace. In addition, the success of the program has led manufacturers to seek out ENERGY STAR certification, and very few new appliances or consumer electronics are sold without the label. Given these two trends (brand leveraging and widespread adoption), there is concern that the label may begin to lose relevance for consumer decisions. Yet despite these concerns, ENERGY STAR illustrates the importance of product labels in affecting consumer decisions. In Chapter 12, we examine the ENERGY STAR program's impact on businesses.

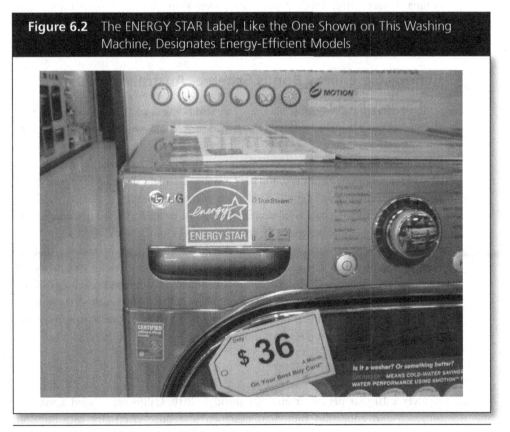

Figure 6.2   The ENERGY STAR Label, Like the One Shown on This Washing Machine, Designates Energy-Efficient Models

Source: The photograph was provided by the authors.

ClimateSmart, Boulder, Colorado

Like many states around the country, Colorado has a long-standing interest in residential energy efficiency. The ClimateSmart program was developed jointly with the City and County of Boulder, using funding from the 2009 American Recovery and Reinvestment Act and a voter-approved carbon tax on electricity (www.beclimatesmart.com). The program focuses on energy efficiency through retrofit activity, encouraging the use of renewable energy sources and community education and training. The program offers home energy audits for a reduced price of $90 and a variety of rebate and loan programs, including Property-Assessed Clean Energy (PACE) financing (for details, see www.pacefinancing.org). PACE financing provides homeowners with funding for retrofit and other energy-efficiency activities by borrowing money to be repaid over subsequent years with a special assessment on their property taxes. To participate in the loan program, homeowners must attend an educational workshop and pay a $75 application fee.

Response to the program has been slow, and even though the program was able to enlist active participation by local utilities and contractors, only 612 residents participated during its first year (the program has funding for up to 2,800 loans). The lackluster results highlight the challenges of overcoming the financial barriers associated with retrofits and illustrates the importance of a simple, convenient, and low-cost program (ClimateSmart, 2010; MIG, 2010). Contrasted with the other retrofit programs described in this chapter, the results from ClimateSmart suggest that financing does not have the same motivational strength as do rebates or direct payment.

Renewable Energy Bonus Scheme, Australia (2010)

In an effort to reduce residential energy consumption, the Australian Department of the Environment launched a program to provide households with a $1,000 direct rebate for replacing an electric water heater with a solar one (see Renewable Energy Bonus Scheme, 2010). The Australian government estimates that water heating accounts for 23% of household electricity use, and a solar system dramatically reduces consumption and carbon emissions. A typical residential solar water heating system costs about $3,500, so the $1,000 rebate is substantial. Within the program, the homeowner selects a licensed contractor to complete the installation, pays for the work, and then submits a rebate form to the government (with signature from the contractor indicating that the work was completed). Payment is made in approximately 8 weeks and deposited directly in the homeowner's bank account. An estimated 1.9 million households will be eligible to receive the rebate. While the program was just recently launched, the simplicity and direct rebate elements of the program are likely to generate a good response. Check www.environment.gov.au for more details.

Flex Your Power

Over a 10-year period, from 2001 through 2010, California funded a massive outreach and education campaign designed to reduce electricity consumption across the state. The campaign included a $200 million advertising campaign focused on changing the behavior of residents, including purchasing energy-efficient appliances and curtailment behaviors like closing blinds on sunny days and planting shade trees to protect southern exposures. Unfortunately, the program was largely information based and did not target specific barriers to home energy conservation. Like the OTC described earlier in this chapter, the Flex Your Power campaign relied on mass media messages to promote broad-based changes. As a result, the campaign failed to produce substantial changes in behavior (Opinion Dynamics Corporation, 2008, 2010). We present it here to illustrate the importance of creating program materials and messages that go beyond raising awareness and instead target specific barriers or benefits associated with conservation behaviors.

Resilient Homes

In a series of exploratory projects, researchers from the University of Manchester have piloted the use of rewards in inducing households in England to adopt energy-efficient measures (Bichard & Kazmierczak, 2009). Unlike prior social marketing programs described in this chapter, the Resilient Homes project focuses on the outcome rather than the specific actions—that is, the program leaves the specific measures up to the homeowner rather than linking the actions to an in-home audit. If the resident achieves certain conservation goals, they receive rewards in the form of products from local businesses (e.g., fruit or produce, meals at local restaurants, or tickets to local entertainment). The Resilient Homes program is similar to other incentives-based programs used to reduce solid waste, like the Nu Spaarpas program in the Netherlands or Recyclebank in the United States (see Seyfang, 2007, for a review of such programs; see also Chapter 2). Results from a national attitudes study of Resilient Homes showed that two thirds of interviewed residents were receptive to the incentive approach and that local businesses saw it as an opportunity for free marketing to potential customers.

Green Power—A Case From the Netherlands

Throughout this chapter, we have presented cases of social marketing programs that focus on reducing residential energy use. However, another important arena for social marketing efforts has been to encourage residents to purchase energy generated from renewable sources. In many countries, electricity consumers can choose to purchase electricity generated from renewable sources, like wind or solar. Typically, these green power options cost more than traditional power, and residents often pay up to a 30% premium. While green power options have been available in many countries since the early 1990s, only about 1% of eligible customers choose this option (National Renewable Energy Laboratory [NREL], 2002).

One notable example of social marketing activities can be found in the Netherlands. Since 1999, all power providers in the Netherlands have offered a green option. In 1999, there were 100,000 customers who had opted for green energy, but in a 4-month period this number jumped by 40%. The change was associated with two activities. The first was a series of tax exemptions that brought the price for green power to parity with conventional electricity, and in some cases it was cheaper (NREL, 2002; van Rooijen & van Wees, 2006). The second was a large-scale media campaign conducted by the World Wildlife Fund (WWF), highlighting these new options and making salient the environmental benefits of switching. In the years following this initial push, Netherlanders have continued to adopt green power, which accounted for 9% of use in 2009. The government has since pledged to continue the tax exemptions and has set a target for 20% of its energy to come from renewable sources by 2020.

Importantly, this case illustrates the strength of combining program elements (i.e., reduced costs) with messaging and awareness. It is unlikely that the WWF campaign would have had near the impact without the tax exemptions; likewise, the tax exemptions needed the media messages to penetrate the market.

Summary

Residential energy use is an important area of work for social marketers. Internationally, the residential sector accounts for a substantial percentage of total electricity use. While renewable sources are slowly increasing in market share, the vast majority of electricity continues to come from nonrenewable sources like coal, oil, and gas. This chapter summarizes some of the many social marketing programs and campaigns aimed at promoting reductions in consumption. We began with a critical look at media-heavy campaigns aimed at raising awareness about energy consumption, and we argued that programs like Canada's OTC tend to produce little in the way of behavior change.

The chapter then focused on a number of very successful social marketing campaigns. Examples include residential retrofit programs, like the Hood River Conservation Project, Canada's ecoENERGY campaign, and the Renewable Bonus Scheme in Australia. We also summarized a range of other strategies, including the OPOWER residential energy reports, and EPA's EnergyStar volunteer labeling program. Taken altogether, these programs illustrate the potential for social marketing programs in the residential energy arena and serve as excellent examples for developing new campaigns.

Questions for Discussion

1. One of the programs discussed in this chapter is Colorado's ClimateSmart residential retrofit program. As mentioned, residents have been slow to respond to the program. What specific strategies might program staff implement to increase response? Discuss at least one program-based change and one marketing or media strategy. Try to utilize the lessons available from other programs discussed in this chapter, but be creative!

2. This chapter began with a summary of the Hood River Conservation Project. What elements of the program do you think were most central to its success?

3. Using the data presented in this chapter about the behaviors associated with energy consumption—and the realistically achievable reductions (see Tables 6.1 and 6.2)—identify three nondivisible, end-state behaviors that could be targeted through a social marketing campaign. For each, discuss potential barriers and benefits that might be addressed with your campaign.

4. Wendy is a program manager for StopWaste.Org, a public agency. Her organization was just awarded a large federal grant to develop and implement a social marketing campaign focused on making homes more energy and resource efficient. Wendy has hired you as a consultant to help in developing the campaign. How might you approach this program? Where would you begin? And what are the key considerations that you would use in developing the campaign?

References

Ayres, I., Raseman, S., & Shih, A. (2009). *Evidence from two large field experiments that peer comparison feedback can reduce residential energy usage.* Paper presented at the 5th Annual Conference on Empirical Legal Studies. New Haven, CT: Yale University. Retrieved from http://ssrn.com/abstract=1434950

Bichard, E., & Kazmierczak, A. (2009). *Resilient homes: Reward-based methods to motivate householders to address dangerous climate change.* Manchester, England: University of Salford. Retrieved from http://admin.cms.salford.ac.uk/__data/assets/pdf_file/0019/9622/report_FINAL_160909.pdf

Calwell, C. (2010). *Is efficient sufficient? The case for shifting our emphasis in energy specifications to progressive efficiency and sufficiency.* Stockholm, Sweden: European Council for an Energy Efficient Economy. Retrieved from http://www.eceee.org/sufficiency

ClimateSmart. (2010). *Home energy 101 workshop.* Board of County Commissioners. Boulder, CO. Retrieved from http://www.bouldercounty.org/bocc/cslp/homeenergy.pdf

Daily Home Renovation Tips. (2009). *ecoENERGY year 2 anniversary results.* Retrieved from http://www.blogcatalog.com/blog/daily-home-renovation-tips-1/26f948f75375eddba5 19eb26ff932153

Dietz, T., Gardner, G., Gilligan, J., Stern, P., & Vandenbergh, M. (2009). Household actions can provide a behavioral wedge to rapidly reduce U.S. carbon emissions. *Proceedings of the National Academy of Sciences, 106,* 18452–18456. Retrieved from http://www.pnas .org/content/106/44/18452

ENERGY STAR. (2010). *ENERGY STAR overview of 2009 achievements.* Retrieved from https://www.energystar.gov/ia/partners/annualreports/2009_achievements.pdf

Environment Canada. (2006). *Evaluation of the one-tonne challenge program.* Retrieved from http://www.ec.gc.ca/ae-ve/F2F5FD59–3DDA-46BC-A62E-C29FDD61E2C5/Evaluation Report-OTC-Eng.doc

Gardner, G., & Stern, P. C. (2008, September/October). The short list: The most effective actions U.S. households can take to curb climate change. *Environment,* 1–10. Retrieved from http://www.environmentmagazine.org/Archives/Back%20Issues/September-October%202008/gardner-stern-full.html

Hirst, E. (1987). *Cooperation and community conservation: The Hood River Conservation Project* (ORNL/CON-235; DOE/BP-11287–16). Oak Ridge, TN: Oak Ridge National Laboratory.

Hirst, E. (1988). The hood river conservation project: An evaluator's dream. *Evaluation Review, 12,* 310–325.

Hirst, E., Berry, L., & Soderstrom, J. (1981). Review of utility home energy audit programs. *Energy, 6,* 621–630.

Hunt, A. (2010). *Social norms and energy conservation.* Cambridge, MA: Massachusetts Institute of Technology, Center for Energy and Environmental Policy Research. Retrieved from http://web.mit.edu/allcott/www/papers.html

Interbrand. (2007). *Building a powerful and enduring brand: The past, present, and future of the ENERGY STAR® brand.* Retrieved from http://www.energystar.gov/ia/partners/downloads/ENERGY_STARBndManf508.pdf

Intergovernmental Panel on Climate Change. (2007). *AR4 synthesis report.* Geneva, Switzerland: Author. Retrieved from http://www.ipcc.ch/publications_and_data/ar4/syr/en/contents.html

International Energy Agency. (2006). *Energy statistics.* Retrieved from http://www.iea.org/textbase/nppdf/free/2006/key2006.pdf

International Energy Agency. (2010). *World energy outlook.* Retrieved from http://www.worldenergyoutlook.org/docs/we02009/WE02009_es_english.pdf

MIG. (2010). *Home energy retrofits: Research report.* Oakland, CA: Association of Bay Area Governments.

National Academy of Sciences. (2010). *Advancing the science of climate change.* Washington DC: National Academies Press. Retrieved from http://books.nap.edu/

National Renewable Energy Laboratory. (2002). *Green power marketing abroad: Recent experience and trends.* Golden, Colorado: Author. Retrieved from http://www.surfingvancouverisland.com/environment/photos2009/greenpower.pdf

Natural Resources Canada. (2010). *ecoENERGY retrofit—home program.* Retrieved from http://oee.nrcan.gc.ca/residential/personal/grants.cfm?attr=0

Nolan, J., Schultz, P. W., Cialdini, R. B., Griskevicius, V., & Goldstein, N. (2008). Normative social influence is underdetected. *Personality and Social Psychology Bulletin, 34,* 913–923.

Opinion Dynamics Corporation. (2008). *2006–2008 statewide marketing and outreach process evaluation: Final report. California Public Utilities Commission.* Oakland, CA: Author. Retrieved from http://www.calmac.org/publications/ODC_Statewide_Marketing_and_Outreach_Process_Evaluation_and_Appendices_Final_CALMAC.pdf

Opinion Dynamics Corporation. (2010). *PY2006–2008 indirect impact evaluation of the statewide marketing and outreach programs. Report for the California Public Utilities Commission.* Oakland, CA: Author. Retrieved from http://www.energydataweb.com/cpuc/home.aspx

Renewable Energy Bonus Scheme. (2010). *Solar hot water rebate.* Department of Climate Change and Energy Efficiency, Australia. Retrieved from http://www.environment.gov.au/energyefficiency/solarhotwater/

Schultz, P. W., Nolan, J., Cialdini, R., Goldstein, N., & Griskevicius, V. (2007). The constructive, destructive, and reconstructive power of social norms. *Psychological Science, 18,* 429–434.

Seyfang, G. (2007). *Personal carbon trading: Lessons from complementary currencies. Centre for Social and Economic Research on the Global Environment.* Norwich, United Kingdom: University of East Anglia. Retrieved from http://infotek.fph.ch/d/f/2277/2277_ENG.pdf?public=ENG&t=.pdf

Sorrell, S. (2007). *The rebound effect: An assessment of the evidence for economy-wide energy savings from improved technology.* London: United Kingdom Energy Research Centre. Retrieved from http://www.ukerc.ac.uk/support/tiki-index.php?page=ReboundEffect&highlight=sorrell

Stern, P. C. (1985). (Ed.). *Energy efficiency in buildings: Behavioral issues.* Washington, DC: National Academies Press. Retrieved from www.nap.edu/catalog/10463.html

Stern, P. C., & Aronson, E. (1984). *Energy use: The human dimension.* New York: Freeman.

Van Rooijen, S., & van Wees, M. (2006). Green electricity policies in the Netherlands: An analysis of policy decisions. *Energy Policy, 34,* 60–71.

Wallander, S. (2008). *Price impacts of the ENERGY STAR label.* New Haven, CT: Yale University, School of Forestry and Environmental Studies. Retrieved from http://cbey.research.yale.edu/uploads/EnergyStar.pdf.

CHAPTER 7

Protecting Fish and Wildlife Habitats

The Problem

This chapter focuses on influencing behaviors that protect fish and wildlife habitats. Although habitats are as varied as the animals that live in them, they are often classified into several major ecosystems including oceans, wetlands, rivers, grasslands, prairies, forests, and backyards. Each has their own problematic situation.

Oceans

Not only do oceans cover more than two thirds of Earth's surface but they are home to thousands of species of fish and invertebrates that are vitally important to people around the world, providing food and supporting jobs. And coastal ecosystems (e.g., shellfish reefs, sea grasses, kelp beds, coral reefs) protect communities from storm damage. Sadly, ocean life today is threatened as never before. People are fundamentally reshaping the marine environment, and no area of the oceans remains unaffected by human activities, ranging from commercial fishing to global climate change (Halpern et al., 2008; Monterey Bay Aquarium, 2009).

Wetlands, Rivers, Lakes, and Streams

Wetlands generally include swamps, marshes, bogs, and similar areas. Some scientists refer to wetlands as nature's kidneys because of the natural cleansing functions they perform (*Importance of wetlands*, 2010). Along with rivers, lakes, and streams, they provide rich habitat for a diverse range of plant and animal species and protect property from flooding and erosion. Unfortunately, according to the U.S. Environmental Protection Agency (EPA), human activities threaten these aquatic environments including runoff from agricultural and urban areas, the invasion of exotic species, and the creation of dams and water diversion. Changes in human behaviors can help restore them (U.S. Environmental Protection Agency [EPA], 2010).

Grasslands and Prairies

In addition to the fact that the world's grasslands are home to nearly 800 million people, many wildlife species also depend on these environments for food, protective cover, and nesting sites. Grasslands help reduce soil erosion caused by wind and water, and they filter chemicals, thus protecting our water supplies. But less than 5% of all grasslands globally have been protected for conservation, and these landscapes face ever increasing threats from the spread of invasive species, the suppression of naturally occurring fire, and the conversion of the landscapes for agriculture and urbanization (NASA, 2010).

Forests and Trees

From the redwood forests of California to the pinewood forests of Scotland to the rainforests of South America, forests blanket more than a fourth of Earth's land mass. Trees renew the air we breathe and provide protection for wildlife. According to The Nature Conservancy, however, nearly half of the planet's original forest cover is gone. And much of what remains is in trouble with diseases and insects slowly wiping out entire species of trees, illegal logging destroying vital wildlife habitat, and woods becoming tinderboxes for destructive fires (The Nature Conservancy, 2010).

Backyards

With thousands of acres of wildlife habitat converted to housing and other development projects each year, many of our native wildlife species will have fewer and fewer places to live and visit. Creating backyard wildlife habitats, sometimes referred to as sanctuaries, are one solution. While many of us may not realize it, a property owner is also a habitat manager. And the things we do, or don't do, in the vicinity of our homes have an effect on the quality of habitat for dozens of wildlife species providing essential elements of shelter, food, water, and nesting sites.

As in other chapters, case examples will demonstrate the successful application of the social marketing model to this environmental area of focus. The two cases featured in this chapter are (1) Seafood Watch: Influencing Sustainable Seafood Choices (Monterey, California) and (2) Reducing Deliberate Grass Fires (Wales, United Kingdom). We conclude with observations regarding the unique challenges that program managers charged with protecting habitats face, illustrating these with a short case example of efforts to influence purchase and planting of native plants in the state of Virginia. We include recommendations that will improve chances for success.

Potential Behavior Solutions

The following list of potential end-state behaviors are only a sampling from the many more that can be chosen for an effort to protect a habitat. As always recommended, actual behaviors selected for a social marketing program should be those that will have the most positive impact on the specific habitat to be protected and, among these, those with the greatest probability of adoption and further market penetration. It should be noted that the behaviors listed in Table 7.1 are ones that would be promoted primarily to individuals (downstream). Certainly efforts might also (or instead) target audiences upstream, including commercial developers and policy makers.

Table 7.1 Potential Behaviors to Protect Wildlife Habitats	
Habitat	**Examples of End-State Behaviors That Might Be Chosen for Adoption**
Oceans	• Buy sustainable fish, ones listed as "Best Choice" on the Seafood Watch Guide. • Leave oyster shells on the beach. • Stay at the offshore side of whales when boating. • Do not stand on, sit on, break, or touch corals. • Do not shine bright lights on the beach at night. • When anchoring a vessel, ensure the anchor is firmly set in sandy areas. • When snorkeling, stay more than 20 feet from sea turtles. • Clean all recreational equipment to ensure not transporting any live organisms.
Wetlands, rivers, lakes, and streams	• When hiking, camping, or picnicking on beaches and coastal areas, dispose of plastic bottles in recyclable containers or take them home. • Plant native plants next to streams, lakes, and rivers. • Use decking on docks that allows sunlight to filter through. • Report sightings of invasive plants in natural waterways to local or state agricultural agent, extension office, or natural resource management agency.
Grasslands and prairies	• Do not throw cigarette butts on the ground. • Stay on trails. • If your property qualifies, apply for a grassland easement through the U.S. Fish and Wildlife Service, which pays you to permanently keep your land in grass.
Forests and trees	• Do not put out a campfire by burying as the fire will continue to smolder and could catch roots on fire that will eventually get to the surface and start a wildfire. • Help plant trees in deforested areas. • Clean boots carefully after hiking in a forest to avoid spreading diseases such as sudden oak death. • Choose wood, furniture, paper, and other products certified by the Forest Stewardship Council (FSC), which promotes responsible stewardship of the world's forests.
Backyards	• Put up a nest box for cavity-nesting birds. • Choose plants that will provide seeds, berries, nectar (flowers), and shelter. • In birdbaths, keep the water shallow—typically 1 to 3 inches at its deepest point. • Scrub small birdbaths a few times each month with a plastic brush to remove algae and bacteria. • To prevent disease and poisoning of birds from bird feeders, every other week remove all seed, fruit, etc.; then clean and dry the feeders.

CASE #1   Seafood Watch: Influencing Sustainable Seafood Choices (Monterey, California)

Background

The Monterey Bay Aquarium envisions a world where our oceans are healthy and people are committed to protecting the integrity of Earth's natural systems. When it opened its doors in 1984, the global catch of wild fish had nearly peaked. That catch is now in decline, and in 2010, it is anticipated that farmed species will for the first time overtake wild-caught fish as the leading source of seafood in the human diet. The concern is that these aquaculture operations have significant negative impacts on aquatic systems, many of which contribute to the decline in ocean health (Monterey Bay Aquarium, 2009).

To help make its vision of healthy oceans a reality, in 1999 the Aquarium created the Seafood Watch program to influence sustainable seafood choices, where sustainable seafood is defined as coming from sources, whether fished or farmed, that maintain or increase production without jeopardizing affected ecosystems. With an estimated two thirds of all U.S. seafood (by dollar value) reaching consumers through restaurants and an additional 24% sold through retail outlets, consumers have an unprecedented opportunity to assist ocean conservation efforts through sustainable seafood choices (Bridgespan Group, 2005). As you will read, its strategy is to use innovative tools that address audience barriers and create incentives that increase marketplace demand for sustainable seafood. Its outcomes, both short term and long term, are inspiring.

Target Audience(s) and Desired Behaviors

The following planned chain of events reflects the program's strategic intent to influence audiences downstream (consumers) to request and make purchases that then influence audiences midstream (purveyors such as restaurants, food service companies, grocery stores and fish markets) to then persuade those upstream (wholesalers and the fishing/aquaculture industry) to change their practices. They began with the end in mind:

1. Consumers decide to buy more (or only) sustainable seafood.

2. Consumers start asking questions and making requests at restaurants, grocery stores, and fish markets, creating salience for the sustainable seafood issue.

3. These purveyors work with their suppliers to increase availability of sustainable seafood.

4. Suppliers shift purchasing.

5. In response to customer demand from major buyers, the fishing/aquaculture industry responds by changing the harvesting practice or shifting to a different operation.

The priority initial consumer audiences were identified as the "green consumer," someone a 2004 survey of 3,690 Americans revealed is likely to be an opinion leader, information seeker, interested in new products, careful in their shopping habits, and, perhaps most importantly, actively engaged in sharing product information related to the environment with others (Wolfe & Lilley, 2004). This audience was also a "natural" for the aquarium as they represent a significant portion of its visitors and those to sister zoos and aquariums as well.

Important additional key audiences included those seen as potential advocates and distribution channels for materials. Outreach partner organizations identified included zoos, aquariums, and science centers; conservation organizations; service organizations; quasi-governmental organizations such as Coastal Commissions; and businesses, especially restaurants and food markets. By formalizing partnerships with these organizations in major metropolitan areas across the country, Seafood Watch "epicenters" could help ensure sustainable seafood messages would reach a far broader, yet still conservation-oriented, audience.

This case example will focus primarily on strategies used to influence consumers and how their actions ultimately influenced audiences further upstream.

Barriers and Benefits

Perceived barriers for consumers to purchase sustainable seafood at the time were significant, even for the "green" consumer:

- Lack of information on sustainable choices at point of purchase, whether in stores or restaurants
- A feeling of being overwhelmed with information to take into consideration when buying
- A concern that sustainable seafood would be more expensive
- Lack of trust for recommendations—concerned with What is their agenda? and wondering How do they know this fish is sustainable and this one isn't?
- Interest in knowing how, if at all, sustainable seafood choices also relate to better personal health

The primary benefit for this environmentally oriented target audience was to contribute to a sustainable supply of seafood.

Description of the Program

The products that Seafood Watch has created over the past decade tackle many of these barriers head-on.

The initiative began with the Seafood Watch Pocket Guides, one for each of six regions in the United States (see Figure 7.1). More than a promotion, this card is designed for point-of-purchase decision making. The most popular seafood options in that region are listed as green (*Best Choices*), yellow (*Good Alternatives*) or red (*Avoid*). Best Choices are defined as abundant, well-managed, and caught or farmed in environmentally friendly ways. Good

Alternatives are an option, but there are concerns with how they're caught or farmed—or with the health of their habitat due to other human impacts. Those to Avoid for now are those items caught or farmed in ways that harm other marine life or the environment. To address health concerns, an asterisk (*) warns whether consumption should be limited due to concerns about mercury or other contaminants for any of the items listed. And to address potential concerns with the credibility of the recommendations, information on the Seafood Watch website explains that categorizations are determined based on reports generated by the aquarium's scientists who review government studies, journal articles, and white papers. They also contact fishery and fish farm experts for input. Their reports are then reviewed by a panel of experts from academia, government, and the seafood industry. From these reports, recommendations are developed and updated every 6 months.

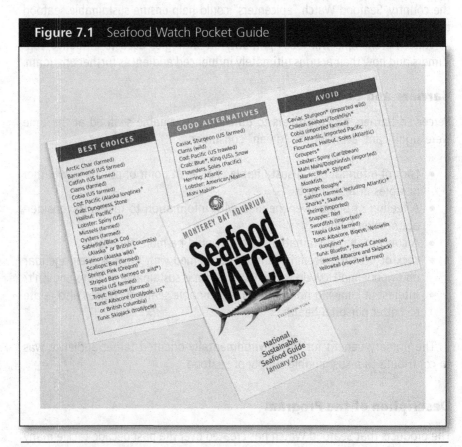

Figure 7.1 Seafood Watch Pocket Guide

Source: Ken Peterson, Communications Director, Monterey Bay Aquarium.

Each month, a Seafood Watch recipe is featured on the website, one created by one of the country's best chefs. In March 2010, for example, the recipe is for Seared Wild Striped Bass with Tomato Sage "Fondue," from Michel Nischan, chef/owner of Dressing Room: A Homegrown Restaurant, in Westport, Connecticut.

And in 2009, a new iPhone application was offered, loading the right guide for the current location using the phone's GPS. The application offers the ability to sort seafood by rank or to search for a rank for a specific fish (see Figure 7.2). A special sushi guide lists fish by Japanese name as well as common market name.

Figure 7.2   Seafood Watch iPhone Application

Source: Ken Peterson, Communications Director, Monterey Bay Aquarium.

Pocket guides are free, including shipping, as is the iPhone application (price). To illustrate a nonmonetary incentive, beginning in 2001, the Seafood Watch program launched an effort to recognize one of its key midstream audiences—chefs. An annual event in May, Cooking for Solutions, honors chefs from across the continent who share their passion for fine food and earth-friendly living at a 2-day, public celebration at the aquarium. Chefs selected are ones demonstrating leadership in promoting cuisine that protects the health of the ocean and the soil. Each year, top awards are presented for the Chef of the Year and Educator of the Year. In 2010, an additional 17 chefs will be honored as Celebrity Chef Ambassadors and 21 as Presenting Chefs.

Pocket guides can be ordered by phone or online and are shipped in small or large quantities. A link to download the iPhone application is provided on the Seafood Watch website. Outreach partners are key to distribution of pocket guides, with aquariums, zoos, and restaurants in major metropolitan areas around the country extending the reach of the guide (place).

Seafood Watch raises consumer awareness primarily through its pocket guides, website, mobile applications, a presence on Facebook and Twitter, and special events (promotion). As the program has gained credibility, it has been featured in a broad array of popular media—from Oprah Winfrey's *O Magazine* to Martha Stewart's television program and, from the *New York Times* and *Time* magazine to websites including TreeHugger.com and Grist.org. Promotional partners for the annual Cooking for Solutions celebration have spread awareness through advertising in magazines including *Coastal Living* and *Sunset.*

An Advocates program launched in 2006 encourages web visitors to take an online pledge to share information about sustainable seafood with friends, family, and businesses in their area. In return, they receive an Action Kit complete with a supply of regional pocket guides, a set of Action Cards, which includes a statistic for each item on the avoid list to leave behind at businesses, and a set of Fish Fact Cards to serve as talking points when discussing items on the avoid list.

Chef partners have their own pledge and spread the word via the Seafood Watch website, featured in Box 7.1.

Box 7.1   Chefs and Culinary Leaders Take the Pledge

Chefs and Culinary Leaders Take the Pledge

As chefs and culinary leaders, we have a special responsibility. Through our menu choices, our purchasing decisions, and the platform we enjoy to reach the public, we are in a unique position to help turn the tide.
We therefore pledge

- to serve no wild-caught or farmed seafood on the Monterey Bay Aquarium's red "avoid" list,
- to communicate our commitment—with peers and the public—so others will join us, and
- to use our talents to introduce new dishes demonstrating that sustainable seafood is also delicious to eat.

The oceans are resilient, and fish populations can rebound—if we give them a chance. Through our actions, we intend to be part of the solution.
Are you a chef or culinary leader who wants to take the Save Our Seafood pledge? Contact us at the Seafood Watch Hotline (877) 229-9990 (toll-free) or e-mail us.

Source: Monterey Bay Aquarium. (2010). Save our seafood: Urgent action by chefs & culinary leaders. Retrieved from http://www.montereybayaquarium.org/cr/cr_seafoodwatch/sfw_pledgechef.aspx

---

One particular pilot with chefs and restaurants is worthy of note. In October 2006, working close to home, Seafood Watch staff approached popular Monterey Bay area restaurants in an effort to persuade them to voluntarily remove all Avoid species from their menus and to provide staff trainings on sustainable seafood choices. Twenty-four establishments signed on, with many distributing the Seafood Watch pocket guides in their guest checks. All participating restaurants were awarded a plaque recognizing their commitment and were highlighted in local ads placed by the aquarium during National Seafood Month. Then, moving north and south of the Monterey Bay area, an additional 17 restaurants joined the program. These pilot programs and their outcomes are now being used as models for regional partner organizations such as aquariums in epicenters to replicate.

Evaluations were conducted for audiences downstream, midstream, and upstream: consumers, partners, retailers, suppliers, and fisheries.

Consumer Outputs and Outcomes

- *Pocket Guides:* By 2010, more than 34 million guides reached the pockets of consumers across the United States. Most were distributed by partners in epicenters, including more than 900,000 to visitors at the Monterey Bay Aquarium alone. Each year, several hundred thousand guides are inserted or reprinted in publications. In 2007, a unique partnership with Warner Brothers Studios inserted 9 million pocket guides in the DVDs of the award-winning film *Happy Feet.*
- *Website:* In 2009 alone, there were 535,559 visitor sessions to Seafoodwatch.org, a 43% increase over 2008. There were more than 1 million page views and more than 200,000 visits the week the State of Seafood Report was released. Currently, Seafoodwatch.org is the #1 search result when a Google search is performed for the word *seafood.*
- *Special Events:* The annual Cooking for Solutions events are attended by close to 6,000 people, and additional presentations at various conferences, trade shows, and special events reach an audience of more than 10,000 each year.
- *Advocates:* To date (2010), more than 1,200 people have agreed to be program advocates and to have their activities tracked via regular e-mail surveys. Surveys completed by a subset of advocates indicted that a majority distributed at least one of the items, 18% distributed everything in the Action Kit, and nearly two thirds (63%) approached at least one restaurant with the materials.
- *Media Impressions (The Estimated Number of People Who May Have Been Seen, Heard or Read Your Messages):* Media coverage for 2006 (including print, online, and broadcast) exceeded 150 placements with a conservative circulation estimate of more than 19 million. Overall, there were an estimated 23,254,000 Seafood Watch media impressions in 2006. As an additional indicator of expanded coverage, a simple survey/content analysis of the frequency with which the phrase *sustainable seafood* has appeared in the media shows more than an eightfold increase between 2002 and 2008.

Partnership Outcomes

By 2010, 161 partnerships had been formed with nonprofit organizations, quasi-government agencies and businesses. This includes 67 *full partners,* those organizations who have formally agreed to distribute at least 10,000 pocket guides per year; develop displays, exhibits, or educational curricula to interpret the pocket guide; and to conduct outreach activities in their area; 45 *associate partners,* who commit to distributing 5,000 pocket guides per year; and 49 *business partners,* primarily restaurants that pledge to remove all items listed in the red Avoid column from their menu.

Retail Outcomes

Several leading supermarket retailers in the United States now have sustainable seafood sourcing policies in place. Most recent commitments were made by Target and Safeway in an announcement in January 2010 (see Box 7.2 and Box 7.3).

Box 7.2   Target Strengthens Seafood Buying Policies

Target Eliminates Farmed Salmon From All Target Stores

Target Owned Food Brands Will Feature
Only Wild-Caught Alaskan Salmon

MINNEAPOLIS (January 26, 2010)—Target® today announces that it has eliminated all farmed salmon from its fresh, frozen, and smoked seafood offerings in Target stores nationwide. This announcement includes Target owned brands—Archer Farms® and Market Pantry®—and national brands. All salmon sold under Target owned brands will now be wild-caught Alaskan salmon. Additionally, sushi featuring farm-raised salmon will complete its transition to wild-caught salmon by the end of 2010. In consultation with the Monterey Bay Aquarium, Target is taking this important step to ensure that its salmon offerings are sourced in a sustainable way that helps to preserve abundance, species health and doesn't harm local habitats. (Target, 2010)

Source: Target. (2010, January 26). Target eliminates farmed salmon from all Target stores. Target owned brands will feature only wild-caught Alaskan salmon. Retrieved from http://pressroom .target.com/pr/news/target-eliminates-farmed-salmon.aspx

---

Box 7.3   Safeway Stores Strengthen Seafood Buying Policies

Target and Safeway Strengthen Seafood-Buying Policies

By Laura Gunderson, The Oregonian

January 27, 2010, 12:38PM

Looking to create a better seafood policy, **Safeway, Inc.** announced it's joining forces with a nonprofit that works to improve the fish industry's sustainability.

As part of the partnership, the Pleasanton, Calif.-based grocer will stop selling grouper, red snapper (Lutjanus campechanus) and monkfish—species it said have been overfished.

Source: Gunderson, L. (2010, January 27). Target and Safeway strengthen seafood-buying policies. The Oregonian. Retrieved from http://blog.oregonlive.com/windowshop/2010/01/target_and_ safeway_strengthen.html

Supplier Outcomes

Two of the largest food service companies in the U.S. Compass Group North America and ARAMARK have made sustainable seafood commitments through agreements with the Monterey Bay Aquarium (see Box 7.4).

Box 7.4   Compass Announces Policy Shift

Compass Group Announces Landmark Policy to Purchase Sustainable Seafood

Seafood Watch Praises Foodservice Provider's Commitment to Protect Threatened Fish Supply

CHARLOTTE, N.C. (Feb. 13, 2006)—Compass Group USA announced today a major policy to shift the company's purchases away from threatened fish species and toward sustainably sourced supplies. The new policy will impact approximately one million pounds of fish purchased annually by Compass Group.

Under the policy, scheduled to begin implementation on March 1, 2006, Compass Group will replace Atlantic cod, a species which leading conservationists have recommended consumers to avoid, with the more environmentally-sound Pacific cod, Pollock, and other alternatives. Compass Group also plans to seek ways to decrease its use of shrimp and salmon that are farmed in an unsustainable manner. These two species are extremely popular with consumers but are of concern to environmentalists. The company will eliminate all other 'Avoid' species from the Monterey Bay Aquarium's Seafood Watch list, and increase its use of 'Best Choices.'

Source: Compass Group. (2006). Seafood choices evaluation prepared for the David & Lucile Packard Foundation. Boston: Bridgespan Group.

Fisheries Outcomes

Fishery eco-certification is on the rise. Seafood Watch staff work with the MSC, the world's leading certification and ecolabelling program for sustainable seafood, having developed standards for sustainably managed and traceable wild-caught seafood. As of 2009, 51 fisheries worldwide are MSC-certified, representing more than 3.8 million tons of seafood with an estimated retail value of nearly $1 billion. Additionally 112 fisheries are engaged in the assessment process to become MSC-certified (K. Peterson, personal communication, 2010).

Critical Review

Several strong components of this program are contributing to its apparent success. First, there is an impressive "work plan" for audiences downstream, midstream, and upstream. It is unlikely that the Seafood Watch program would have been as successful had their efforts been directed only at consumers, or only at restaurants and fish markets, or only at suppliers. The magic is in their integrated approach which covers all influential bases. Another strength of the program is the targeted response to consumer barriers—the pocket guide and now the mobile applications that support consumers at the actual point of decision making. And the diffusion through partners at epicenters is a model that can inspire others wanting to extend reach in an efficient manner.

We think it would be interesting for Seafood Watch's program managers to consider the following:

- Label fresh fish signs at grocery stores and fish markets with a "green label" of sorts, certifying that it is a Best Choice. Eventually, this could work similarly to the organic label and would be one that consumers would learn to look for—even ask about. A variety of symbols could be considered (e.g., a green smiley fish or the MSC logo), but the point is to make it even easier to identify the right choices. Its visibility would prompt purchases of green fish, especially for those who had heard of the program but did not have a card.
- To increase the number of participating restaurants, conduct barriers research with targeted restaurants to identify concerns/reasons for not participating as partners. As with most barriers research, this should be conducted using a methodology that would support ranking barriers, perhaps an online survey to solicit as high a response rate as possible.
- To report on impact, as well as return on investment, work to quantify the amount of "red" fish not purchased as a result of this program, and, using budget information regarding expenses, calculate a cost per pound "avoided." When presenting these findings, these statistics would likely be motivating to current and potential funders as well as volunteer partners and advocates.

CASE #2   Reducing Deliberate Grass Fires (Wales, United Kingdom)

Background

Mountain fires and grass arson are significant problems in parts of Wales, with over 7,000 of these fires each year. It is known that almost all (95%) are deliberate, with the remaining 5% due to controlled burning practices or camp fires that get out of control. These fires endanger the lives of firefighters and the public as well as putting property at risk. And they are extremely detrimental to the countryside where wildlife and their habitats are destroyed.

To date (2010), no one has been convicted of grass fire arson. Not only is it difficult to catch and prove that an individual has started a grass fire but a prosecution is not possible if no one owns the land or the land owner is not willing to pursue a case.

In 2008, South Wales Fire and Rescue Services (SWFRS), one of three Welsh Fire and Rescue Service areas, commissioned the development of a social marketing project to influence behaviors to reduce deliberate grass fire arson (S. Peattie, personal communication, 2010). The hope was that outcomes from this pilot would not only inspire the other two fire and rescue service areas but that the model could also be used to tackle other behavior-related issues within SWFRS. A concrete goal was set to reduce the incidence of deliberate grass fires in the Tonypandy target area by 15% during the 2-week school Easter period (March 26–April 12, 2010) in comparison to the control area of Aberdare (allowing for any variance in weather or other external factors).

Target Audience(s) and Desired Behaviors

All fire incidents, whether accidental or deliberate, are recorded in detail by SWFRS. An initial analysis of 5 years of incident data indicated that one area, Rhondda Cynon Taf, consistently had the most grass fire incidents. Two stations within this area, Tonypandy and Aberdare, displayed similar results, with both having significantly higher grass fire calls than neighboring stations. Tonypandy was then chosen as the pilot area for the social marketing intervention, with Aberdare the control area.

Incident data also revealed the peak "grass fire season" takes place between February and May, particularly March and April, which covers the Easter period. Closer scrutiny of quantitative findings revealed the following:

- Incidents are significantly worse during the 2-week school Easter holiday.
- Incidents peak between 5:00 p.m. and 8:00 p.m. on all days of the week.
- Friday is the quietest time of the week, especially between 7:00 p.m. and 9:00 p.m.
- Sunday is the busiest day.

Although the recorded data was able to provide extremely useful and precise information on when and where deliberate fire incidents were taking place, there was very limited information on who the perpetrators were and why they were setting these fires. A series of focus groups and in-depth interviews were conducted to begin to build a profile of the perpetrators, an understanding of their barriers, and what would motivate them to stop engaging in this behavior. The first rounds of interviews were conducted with key members of SWFRS as well as partner organizations such as police service representatives. Phase 2 interviews included ones with youth and their parents. The consensus from all interviews was that

- perpetrators were predominantly male;
- they worked in groups;
- ages ranged from 7 to 17, sharing an interest in lighting fires;
- younger age groups set fires closer to home while older ones went further up the mountain;

- the least number of incidents occurred on Friday evenings when parents of the younger children were out socializing, making it more likely the children would hang out in their homes, while older children were gathering and drinking in the village center;
- perpetrators are not necessarily just the "naughty" ones, as evidenced by the comment of one young perpetrator: Why does it have to be naughty kids? I'm not from a deprived family, have A grades, and I've done it;
- the behavior is often associated with underage drinking and drugs; and
- the lighting of fires was primarily due to boredom, thrill seeking, attention seeking, peer pressure, natural curiosity, and experimentation.

The primary target audience was then defined as 13- to 16-year-olds (grades 9–11) who live and attend school in the Tonypandy area. This group was chosen because this age group tends to be socially independent from their parents and still influenced by peer pressure. In addition, they can also act as role models to younger children.

Although significant emphasis was also placed on encouraging support and coordination of key community groups (e.g., firefighters, schoolteachers, police officers), this case example will focus on strategies targeting the youth and to some extent, their parents.

The desired behavior was clear for the planning group. They wanted to influence prior and "would-be" fire setters to refrain from doing this.

Barriers and Benefits

Insights from focus groups and interviews conducted by the group revealed deeply engrained attitudes:

- This is harmless fun.
- It's only grass; it will grow back.
- My parents did it, and my grandparents did it. In fact, it has been a social norm since the 1970s when it began as an act of rebellion against the Forestry Commission Wales who began planting trees on the mountains.
- There is lack of value or ownership of the land as a community resource.

Straight talk with parents confirmed these challenges:

- Most did not know whether their children were lighting fires.
- Some did not care what they were doing as long as they were out of the way and not causing trouble in the street.
- Many did not feel it was an issue, remembering how they used to light grass fires themselves.
- A few attributed the behavior to lack of parenting skills and positive role models.

A few potential motivators were tested but did not get a promising response. For example, one that was tested in focus groups included persuading citizens observing suspicious activities to contact Crime Stoppers, an independent organization that allows a person to phone in anonymously to report crimes. It was seen as ineffective by respondents, with the major concern that those reporting might be retaliated against. Another, publicizing the cost of the fires, was also not considered a deterrent unless the money would come back to the community.

At this point, program planners knew they needed to focus their attention on developing something "cool, fun, free, and popular" that could take the place of these activities and to make real the harm this current "norm" was causing wildlife and their habitats.

Description of the Program

Strategic planning began with forming a youth panel to help brainstorm and prioritize key strategies—ones that would resonate with and gain support of young people in Tonypandy. This Youth Advisory Panel was comprised of 8 young people (5 boys and 3 girls), ages 13 to 16, who attended school in Tonypandy and were seen as popular with their peers.

The panel had their first meeting in February 2010. Their agenda was to assist in judging a "brand competition" for the program that had been organized in December 2009 and had produced 63 entries from young people ages 12 to 17. In the end, they chose a sheep named Bernie as the mascot and the slogan "Grass is green. Fire is mean." Bernie is now the face and identity for the project, with protocols for using the brand in order to maintain its integrity (see Figure 7.3).

Figure 7.3   A Bernie Poster

As noted earlier, the challenge facing program planners and the Youth Advisory Panel was to develop what is often called by marketers a great substitute product. Effective substitute products offer target audiences similar benefits they seek and enjoy from existing competing products. In this case, the assignment was to create alternative activities that would also be seen as cool, fun, free, and popular—ones that could be done in groups during the prime Easter weeks. Several activities were developed and described on Bernie's website as follows:

- *Graffiti Art:* "Learn how to design and produce a piece of graffiti art with the help of a qualified graffiti artist. Round up a group of friends (maximum of 10) to try your hand at this arts based workshop lasting approximately an hour and a half, and take the completed piece of art work away with you."
- *Survival Skills:* "Bushcraft courses are an introduction to fundamental outdoor survival skills with plenty of hands-on experience to back it up. Conducted in a woodland environment our syllabus will equip you with a wide range of useful knowledge and techniques including safe use of cutting tools, fire lighting, collection and purification of water, shelter building, game preparation and cooking; wild food walk."
- *Ceramics:* "Learn how to throw a pot on a potter's wheel. Take part in a one hour workshop and take your finished piece away with you."
- *Arson Rap:* "Make and record your own CD. Take part in a one and a half hour workshop and experience writing, performing, and recording. Don't be shy, no musical ability necessary just the urge to have a go at something new."
- *Firefighter for a Day:* "During Firefighter for a Day you will have the opportunity to spend a day at a Fire Station and take part in Firefighting activities such as ladder climbing, spraying a hose, working in a team, and carrying out a search and rescue exercise in a simulated incident. There will also be an opportunity to learn about the hazards encountered by fire and rescue service personnel during their daily activities and understand the impact of incidents such as grass fires on your community." (Southwales-Fire, 2010)

All activities are free, and a packed lunch and/or refreshments are provided at each event (price). As a deterrent (nonmonetary disincentive), it was also decided there needed to be increased visibility of fire crime enforcement, with special patrols during peak periods and locations based on data regarding of incidents. In addition, it was important that citizens witnessing burning events be (more) assured their call to the tip line would be anonymous.

More than 35 workshops/classes were held 1 week before and 1 week after Easter. Times offered varied throughout the day, with some available in the evenings. Youth could register for the events online or by phone, with messages inspiring action by stressing that space is limited—in some cases to only 10 participants. All activities were either held or started at Tonypandy Fire Station, which is located in the center of Tonypandy and therefore within walking distance and easily accessible to all young people (place).

In terms of promotion, program planners stressed the importance of agreeing (and sticking with) one term to refer to these fires. In the past, a variety of terms had been used including grass fires, mountain fires, and wildfires. For grass and mountain fires, there was no recognition it was illegal and wildfires could be perceived as natural and/or glamorous and depicted so by the media. It was agreed that the term deliberate fires would be consistently used. A variety of media channels were used to get the word out about the Easter weeks' activities:

- PR events for local press, media, and the general public launched the event with banners, fliers, balloons, key rings, car stickers, activity brochures, all incorporating the Bernie logo.
- A Bernie hoodie (sweatshirt) became very popular with boys and girls, with a 16-year-old girl from Tonypandy even wearing one on a BBC TV program *Over the Rainbow*.
- A special Bernie website was developed.
- Bernie has a Facebook page.
- The Year 10 drama students in Tonypandy produced a 10-minute drama as part of their course work. Inspired by the Bernie Project, the students decided to base their drama on the problem of deliberate grass fires. In preparation, the students were provided with information on the fires and a visit to the Tonypandy Fire Station was arranged. This enabled the young people to meet and ask questions of the operational crews to gain a better understanding of the fire service role and problems faced when dealing with deliberate grass fires.
- Similarly, the Year 10 media students in Tonypandy who are required to produce a film chose the Bernie Project, deciding to film the drama students performing the grass fire production.
- For 3 weeks prior to the intervention period, fire service personnel were in daily attendance at the school during lunchtime to book students into activities. In addition, there was full support from the school staff to assist in encouraging the young people to attend activities.
- Students in classes on personal, social, and health education were introduced to the Bernie Project.
- An information booth was set up outside ASDA (Walmart) in the Tonypandy town center to discuss the project with the public and to promote enrollment in the activities.

To improve knowledge and change attitudes associated with deliberate grass fires, including dispelling long held myths, additional campaigns include ones using the following media channels:

- Press advertising
- Street stencils
- Leaflets
- Signage with key messages
- Website
- Facebook
- Press release

Youth engaged at the Easter activities were provided a certificate for participating in an activity that included the following pledge: "I am helping and supporting Bernie in reducing deliberate grass fires across Wales." In addition, a paper petition was distributed in the school and the town for people to sign.

Campaign evaluation was based on the number of incidents of deliberate grass fires in Tonypandy compared with the number of fires in Aberdare. Results displayed in Figure 7.4 indicate that Tonypandy had 53% fewer deliberate grass fires (64 versus 135 in Aberdare) during the 2-week Easter period, and 78% fewer in the month of May (17 versus 76 in Aberdare) following the Easter break.

Additional output and outcome data reported that more than 600 Bernie hoodies were distributed; a total of 1,022 people became friends of Bernie; and 312 youth attended workshops, with an even 50/50 split of female and male.

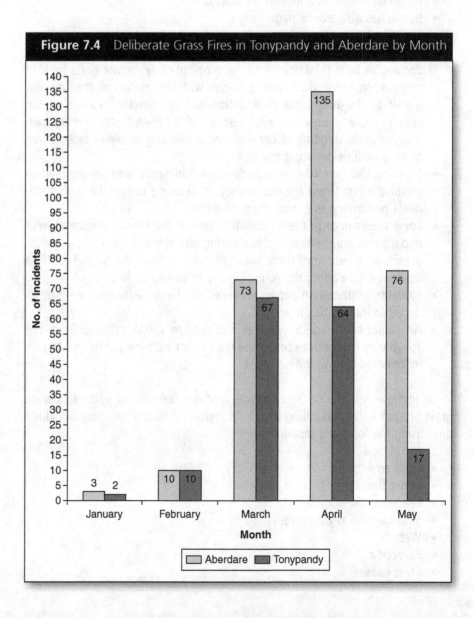

Figure 7.4   Deliberate Grass Fires in Tonypandy and Aberdare by Month

Critical Review

One of the clear strengths of this program was the extensive secondary research that was used to understand more about where and when the fires were being set and then the qualitative research to identify who was setting them and why. Deciding to develop a competing/substitute product versus just influencing the youth to "abstain" is a strong approach. Additionally, multiple partners and stakeholders appeared to be working together in an efficient and integrated way. Finally, making the effort to conduct a pilot, and selecting a "control" city provided strong strategic guidance for future programs. A few ideas to consider include the following:

- Is there a more sustainable "substitute product" idea, one that would be available throughout the year, and perhaps more accessible (e.g., not needing to sign up and get a parent permission)?
- Some of the activities that were offered addressed their motivations for thrill-seeking, natural curiosity, and experimentation (e.g., the Survival Skills and Firefighter for a Day) and others appealed to boredom (e.g., Arson Rap and Graffiti Art), but this still leaves 50 weeks during the year that might result in a return to old ways. It would be interesting to query students for their ideas of what's missing for them in the community (e.g., a youth activity center) that would provide some of these same benefits on an ongoing basis.
- Consider the use of (more) prompts at locations where and when fires are most likely (e.g., reminders to anonymously report suspicious activities or actual deliberate fire settings).
- Evaluation results certainly point to an intervention success. It would be interesting, however, to understand more about which components of the campaign contributed the most to the changes in behavior. Was it the workshops, the school-based activities, the increased visibility of enforcement, media coverage, or a combination of these?

Other Notable Programs

Influencing behaviors to protect wildlife habitats have many of the challenges common to any environmental behavior change effort. There are also a few that are unique. To illustrate several typical barriers to change, we will use a third case example from a social marketing project of the Virginia Coastal Zone Management Program initiated in 2009 to increase the use of native plants on Virginia's Eastern Shore. (Information for this case provided by Virginia Witmer, Outreach Coordinator, Virginia Coastal Zone Management Program.) One of the long-term objectives of the Plant Eastern Shore Natives campaign is to increase habitats for the millions of migratory birds that rely on Virginia's Eastern Shore for a "stopover."

"I Don't See the Problem"

This barrier is particularly common for habitat protection efforts, as most of us can't tell when there are fewer Chinook salmon, see the dolphin that got tangled in a gill net, or notice the butterflies having a problem finding the right plants for their eggs. Making the problem visible and concrete is paramount. Consider key messages in Virginia's Plant Eastern Shore Natives campaign that helped make the problem real:

> Native plants are critical to the millions of migratory songbirds that visit the Eastern Shore of Virginia each spring and fall. The Eastern Shore is one of only a few rest stops along the Atlantic coast for songbirds traveling thousands of miles to their winter homes in Central and South America. That's quite a long trip for birds that can weigh as little as half an ounce! Native trees and shrubs provide the berries and insects that songbirds eat to fuel their long journeys. . . . Even the smallest yard can provide a "stopover habitat" for hungry migrants.

It might be even more persuasive if the actual number of birds was cited (versus "the millions"), how "few" rest stops there actually are, how many "don't make it" to their destination because they didn't have a chance to rest, and how this has changed over time.

"I Can't Find These Products They Recommend I Buy"

Sometimes the reason well-intended target audiences can't find a product being promoted is because the retailer or supplier doesn't have them in their inventory (e.g., liquid detergents without phosphates). Just as often, interested customers don't know how or where to find them, as the labels don't clearly identify the preferred option (e.g., sustainable seafood choices). For Virginia's campaign, focus groups and a written survey identified one of the greatest barriers as the lack of availability of natives at local garden centers. Garden center managers explained this was due to limited demand. In addition, consumers also commented they didn't know how to recognize native plants, even if the nursery carried them. In response, planning team members visited local garden centers and nurseries prior to the launch of the campaign to encourage their partnership in the effort and to share with them what marketing materials would be provided through the campaign: tags they could put in the pots of native plants, a banner with the campaign slogan and message EASTERN SHORE NATIVE PLANTS SOLD HERE, and recognition on the campaign website including a downloadable inventory of native plants available at the center, and campaign radio ads encouraging gardeners to buy from their local garden centers (see Figures 7.5a and 7.5b). In return, garden centers were asked to hang the banner in a prominent location, tag all native plants, provide reference to a new guide to Virginia Eastern Shore native plants, and track the numbers of native plants sold.

"I Am Not Convinced My Property Will Look as Good"

Unfortunately, many gardeners are skeptical about the priority that environmentalists and the government place on "function over form." In other words, the sense is that how the yard and garden will look is not as important to campaign sponsors as is minimizing its impact on the environment. The barriers and benefits research for

Figure 7.5a and 7.5b   Banners and Plant Tags and Partner Nurseries

(a)

(b)

Source: Coastal Zone Management Program at Virginia Department of Environmental Quality.

Virginia's effort revealed that many felt that native plants were scraggly and weedy and that what would motivate them would be if they discovered that natives were actually quite colorful and attractive plants. Based on this research, the campaign focuses on the beauty of natives, with the slogan "They're Shore

Beautiful." Messages included ones such as "Native plants not only offer many practical, low cost, environmental benefits over non-native plants, many also offer an appealing display of foliage and flowers that surpass non-native ornamentals. By planting natives, you will join an increasing number of gardeners who have discovered that wildflowers, trees, shrubs, grasses and annuals native to their region are not only important to protecting local water supply and wildlife, but are simply gorgeous." A handsome free guide contains close-up color photos of at least 100 plants native to Virginia's Eastern Shore, most with beautiful flowers and many with lovely berries. This is the first guide produced specific to the region's natives. In addition, to illustrate the appeal and beauty of the native plants, five demonstration sites have been installed to date, including a "shady garden," a "maritime forest," a "pollinator garden," and a "shoreline garden." A "healing" garden is being installed at a local health center and "habitat" garden is being planted adjacent to a songbird habitat restoration forest at a state park. The demonstration sites are listed on the campaign's Web site and include a list of all the native plants to be seen at each site.

"These Changes Cost Money"

When monetary costs are a major barrier, or even moderate concern, we have several tactics to consider. We can reduce monetary costs by working with others to provide discount coupons, bulk discounts, rebates, or grants. Although sometimes these costs may need to be absorbed by the campaign budget, often they can be picked up by suppliers or retailers for the products being promoted. On the other side of the equation, we can emphasize how the behavior will result in cost savings, both monetary and nonmonetary. If, for example, the cost of an Eastern Shore native plant is greater than that of a nonnative species being considered, it may be a barrier for some in our audience. To address this, the native plant guide being distributed widely to gardeners and also available at the point of sale at garden centers and nurseries argues that native plants are a value in comparison to nonnative plants, as they last longer since they are more resistant to insects and disease and require less water, fertilizing, and time to maintain.

Results from a mid-campaign evaluation of this native plant campaign were encouraging, with one of the largest Eastern Shore garden centers reporting that native plant sales were up almost 10% in 2009. Another garden center/nursery has decided to grow their own stock of over 40 species of native plants in anticipation of greater demand, and a new garden center opened that will not only provide an Eastern Shore native plant section and adopt maintenance of a nearby demonstration garden but will also provide environmental and best management practice lectures and classes as well.

It is important to note that in this Eastern Shore example, as in other watershed quality efforts, program managers need to rely on measuring changes in behavior (outcomes) versus change in water quality, wildlife saved, or habitats preserved (impact). This would require more controlled experiments, a larger scale implementation, and a longer time frame in order to show significant improvement in watershed quality.

Summary

This chapter focused on strategies to influence behaviors that protect fish and wildlife habitats, in both the residential and commercial markets. Our two featured case stories, as well as one additional brief example, all demonstrated the use of a variety of tools to address barriers, especially the product tool.

The Monterey Bay Aquarium's Seafood Watch program was designed with a strategic intent to influence audiences downstream to purchase more sustainable fish. They developed a new product, a consumer's pocket guide, and iPhone application to address audience barriers related to knowing what fish are sustainable when shopping or eating out. Outcomes were inspiring, with increased consumer interests and preferences eventually reshaping the marketplace. The second case, one to reduce deliberate Wildfires in Wales, demonstrated the power of a substitute product, one that offers similar benefits to existing, competing products. Outcomes suggest that activities developed and offered to youth in the community were apparently as cool, fun, free, and popular as wildfires. An additional noteworthy effort to increase purchasing and planting of native plants in Virginia addressed common barriers to habitat protection including the following: I don't see the problem; I can't find these products they recommend I buy; I am not convinced my property will look as good; and These changes will cost money.

Questions for Discussion

1. For the Seafood Watch case, would you put the time and effort into getting an icon for sustainable fish to prompt purchasing in grocery stores and fish markets? Why or why not?

2. Also relative to the Seafood Watch case, what should program managers do if some state decides to take issue with the classification of a fish as red, when they believe it should be green?

3. For the Wildfires in the Wales case, what other substitute product might appeal more to target audiences?

4. For Virginia's Native Plants case, how would you propose to make "the problem" more concrete?

References

Bridgespan Group. (2005).

Compass Group. (2006). *Seafood choices evaluation prepared for the David & Lucile Packard Foundation.* Boston: Bridgespan Group.

Gunderson, L. (2010, January 27). Target and Safeway strengthen seafood-buying policies. *The Oregonian.* Retrieved from http://blog.oregonlive.com/windowshop/2010/01/target_and_safeway_strengthen.html

Halpern, B. S., Walbridge, S., Selkoe, K. A., Kappel, C. V., Micheli, F., D'Argosa, C., et al. (2008). A global map of human impact on marine ecosystems. *Science, 319*(5865), 948–952.

Importance of wetlands. (2010). Retrieved from http://legacy.ncsu.edu/classes/nr400001/ gradpage/Wetland_Mitigation_Home/wetland_importance.html

Monterey Bay Aquarium. (2009). Turning the tide. *The State of Seafood,* 11.

Monterey Bay Aquarium. (2010). *Save our seafood: Urgent action by chefs & culinary leaders.* Retrieved from http://www.montereybayaquarium.org/cr/cr_seafoodwatch/sfw_pledgechef.aspx

NASA. (2010). *Earth observatory: Grasslands.* Retrieved from http://earthobservatory.nasa .gov/Features/Grassland/

The Nature Conservancy. (2010). *Forest conservation.* Retrieved from http://www.nature.org/ initiatives/forests/about/

Southwales-Fire. (2010). *Arson rap.* Retrieved from http://www.southwalesfire.gov.uk/ English/bernie/Pages/ArsonRap.aspx

Target. (2010, January 26). *Target eliminates farmed salmon from all Target stores. Target owned brands will feature only wild-caught Alaskan salmon.* Retrieved from http://press room.target.com/pr/news/target-eliminates-farmed-salmon.aspx

U.S. Environmental Protection Agency. (2010). *Threats to aquatic biodiversity.* Retrieved from http://www.epa.gov/bioiweb1/aquatic/threats.html

Wolfe, L., & Lilley, L. (2004). *Seafood Watch Literature Review.* Section 5.2.3. Quadra Planning Consultants Ltd. Galiano Institute for Environmental Social Research.

SECTION III

Influencing Behaviors in the Commercial Sector

CHAPTER 8

Reducing Waste

This chapter will focus on reducing solid waste generated by organizations in the commercial sector. For our purposes, we will consider the commercial sector as traditional commercial establishments including hotels, motels, restaurants, wholesale businesses, retail stores, laundries, and other service enterprises; religious and nonprofit organizations; health, social, and educational institutions; federal/national, state, and local governments; and establishments engaged in manufacturing and agriculture.

The Problem

Waste in this more broadly defined commercial sector consists of some items similar to those in the residential sector (e.g., food waste, paper, yard waste, plastic containers, aluminum cans, glass) but is unique in its inclusion of items used in the manufacturing, packaging, planting, harvesting, and transporting process as well. The United Nations estimates that, worldwide, in the 67 countries where municipal waste is collected, 1.8 trillion pounds of waste are generated each year, and more than two thirds of this (69%) ends up in the landfill (United Nations, 2010).

Potential Behavior Solutions

One solution to the waste problem in the commercial sector is to count on these organizations to change their waste management practices, without any "nudging" from outsiders. A better and more effective strategy is for a change agent to work with these organizations to help them identify promising new practices and then demonstrate potential benefits and address real and perceived barriers.

Although change agents are most likely to come from governmental agencies and nongovernmental organizations (NGOs) with environmental protection missions, it is also possible that a for profit business might be influential in changing the waste management behaviors of their employees or even other companies. Traditional governmental organizations working with the private/commercial sector include federal/national agencies such as the U.S. Environmental Protection Agency (EPA), state agencies such as a Department of Ecology, county agencies such as Departments of Natural Resources, and municipal agencies such as a utility's Solid Waste Division. NGOs involved in waste management practices in the commercial sector range from those interested in protecting wildlife habitats to those working to reduce greenhouse gases (GHGs) to ones focused on alternative energy sources.

Benefits change agents may highlight include monetary ones such as cost savings and nonmonetary ones such as increased brand loyalty. Barriers that will need to be addressed include lack of skills and knowledge, requirements and related incremental costs for new systems and infrastructures that a change in practices would require, and a lack of data and tracking systems related to waste generation and recovery.

As in the residential sector, waste reduction in the commercial sector has the same reduce, reuse, recycle behavior hierarchy. A sampling of potential behaviors for each appears in Table 8.1.

Table 8.1 Commercial Behaviors to Help Reduce Waste	
Areas of Focus	**Examples of End-State Behaviors That Might Be Chosen for Adoption**
Reduce	• Make computer files, not paper files when possible. • Set photocopiers and printers to print on both sides by default. • Remove business names from unsolicited mailing lists. • When buying cleaning agents by the case, buy those that do not have cardboard dividers between the bottles. • Remove former employees from your mailing lists. • Use lighter weight packaging. • Save documents on floppy disks instead of printing hard copies. • For health care organizations, require vendors to reduce packaging or use durable packing that can be repeatedly reused. As much as 80% to 85% of a health care facility's waste is nonhazardous solid waste (Practice Greenhealth, 2010). • Provide condiments in bulk dispensers. • Use cloth roll towels in restrooms. • Use refilled or rebuilt fax and printer cartridges. • Reuse envelopes and send them through the mail again whenever possible. • Reduce beverage container weight.
Reuse	• Make scratch pads from paper that was used only on one side. • Buy refurbished toner cartridges. • Encourage staff to use reusable coffee mugs. • Invest in rechargeable batteries and battery chargers. • Reuse packing material whenever possible. • Set up a system for returning cardboard boxes and foam peanuts to distributors for reuse. • Sell or give old furniture and equipment to employees or donate to a local charity. • Install reusable heating, ventilation, and air-conditioning filters.

Recycle	<ul><li>Purchase a worm bin for your office to convert food waste into high quality potting soil.</li><li>Contact a community recycling coordinator for technical assistance, listed in the government section of the phone directory.</li><li>Recycle paper cuttings and excess paper from job overruns.</li><li>If in a large office building and there is no recycling program, encourage management of the property to implement one for the entire building.</li><li>Label bins clearly to indicate what goes in the container and what doesn't.</li></ul>

Case stories highlight these 3Rs and include Green Dot®: Europe's Packaging Waste Reduction Efforts (European Union), Fork It Over! Reusing Leftover Food (Portland, Oregon), and Anheuser-Busch: A U.S. Environmental Protection Agency WasteWise Hall of Fame Member (United States).

CASE #1   Green Dot®: Europe's Packaging Waste Reduction Efforts (European Union)

Background

In the early 1990s, Germany's landfill capacity was shrinking, and at the same time, packaging waste generated by the commercial sector continued to grow. Product packaging already accounted for an estimated 25% to 30% of the waste in European landfills, and apparently, there was little being done by the industry to reduce it (Green Dot® Compliance, 2010). After Germany passed legislation aimed at reducing the amount of packaging waste ending up in the landfill, other countries in the European Union followed suit. By 1994, five (Germany, Belgium, Austria, Sweden, and France) countries had national packaging compliance organizations that managed their country's packaging recovery programs.

Europe recognized next that corporations, especially those with operations in several countries, would have a tough time complying with several versions of a packaging directive. In late 1994, the EU passed the "Packaging and Packaging Waste Directive," an attempt to integrate and strengthen national efforts. The EU also recognized the need for an umbrella organization to assist corporations in complying with this directive and developed PRO EUROPE (Packaging Recovery Organization Europe) in 1995. Its mission is to assist national recovery organizations by providing a knowledge and best practice exchange forum for members and support for the establishment of markets for secondary raw materials that would minimize costs associated with recycling and recovery efforts. One of its strengths is that it involves all actors in the packaging chain, including packaging manufacturers, fillers, distributors, as well as local authorities and citizens. The system also collects data on packaging waste generation and waste management, which is helpful to the member states to fulfill reporting requirements. This also assists policy makers when evaluating the effectiveness of current directives (PRO EUROPE, 2010).

One of the major responsibilities of PRO EUROPE is to help administer the use of the Green Dot® logo, a symbol of producer responsibility and efficient packaging waste—the focus of this case.

Target Audience(s) and Desired Behaviors

Companies targeted by PRO EUROPE for the Green Dot® are those using any material to contain and protect their goods or to aid in their handling, delivery, or presentation. This includes plastic and paper wrappings, fillers, and other shipping materials such as cardboard, metal, and wood.

Green Dot® is a registered trademark of Duales System Deutschland (Dual System of Germany), and the logo signals consumers that a company has voluntarily joined a packaging reduction and recovery scheme in that country. Members pay a fee that then funds a company in their country to recover, sort, and recycle the manufacturers' used consumer packaging. By doing so, the company is in compliance with the EU's Packaging and Packaging Waste Directive. Importantly, the PRO EUROPE organization that manages the Green Dot® program also works directly with manufacturers to reduce the amount of packaging for their products.

Barriers and Benefits

Not all manufacturers were eager to jump on board, having one or more of several concerns including

- paying annual membership fees, as well as prorated fees based on weights and types of packing;
- following guidelines for reducing, packaging, and reporting on progress;
- knowing what types of packaging are covered; and
- understanding how the Green Dot® program guidelines differed from the existing directive.

What would appeal to targeted companies were benefits that would reduce their costs and increase their sales. They were motivated by evidence demonstrating that consumers would associate products displaying the Green Dot® logo with companies that had good environmental stewardship. They would be interested to know if retailers would give Green Dot® products shelf space preference, even reject those without the logo. It would be reassuring to them if they knew there would actually be fewer problems following the Green Dot® guidelines than those in the official directive.

Description of the Program

PRO EUROPE offers a variety of value-added services to members (products).

The organization provides opportunities for members to join working groups for a variety of topics including international marketing strategies, information exchange networks, and packaging systems development. Through these working groups, PRO EUROPE's members have become important discussion partners for the European Commission and the European Parliament. Working groups also participate in clarifying definition-based questions, for instance what falls under packaging and products.

Trainings provide evidence that best practices related to reducing packaging can mean increased efficiencies and profits. An example cited was one for Procter & Gamble. By doing away with the high density polyethylene thermoplastic handle, and the steel fastening rivets on their traditional box, the weight of the cardboard packaging dropped from 180.4g to 109g. Vacuum filling also reduced both the volume and the weight of the plastic bag from 17g to 13g. These changes in packaging allowed 50% more primary packaging to be placed on a pallet and transportation volume to be reduced by more than 30%. Approximately 55 truck journeys were saved with detergent packages made of cardboard, while 257 fewer journeys were needed for refill bags (PRO EUROPE, 2006/2007).

Green Dot® fees paid by members are used to influence reduction in packaging, as well as provide services for consumers to dispose of packaging from Green Dot® products. There are two types of fees that might be charged—an annual license fee and/or a variable fee based on the type and quantity of packaging generated by the company. Some countries charge both the membership as well as material fee; others charge only one or the other.

Members have a financial incentive to reduce packaging placed on the market, as in most countries, license fees are calculated on the basis of the material and weight of the packaging. The system encourages waste reduction since manufacturers that cut down on packaging waste ultimately pay less in fees. In addition, by joining the Green Dot® program, companies are exempt from creating their own program to take back used sales packaging, a process many companies find impractical as well as costly. If not exempt, regulatory authorities in the individual countries impose fines for noncompliance. Fines can be significant and are enforced. Finally, communications to potential members also provide evidence that they may encounter resistance from distributors and retailers to stock their products.

Manufacturers can register to join the Green Dot® program online with a system in their respective country (place).

The Green Dot® logo signals to consumers that the manufacturer pays a fee to support the recovery, recycling, and/or reuse of its packaged materials. Importantly, the logo communicates a "connection" with the recycling brand logo, even though it does not assure the packaging has been made with recycled materials (see Figure 8.1).

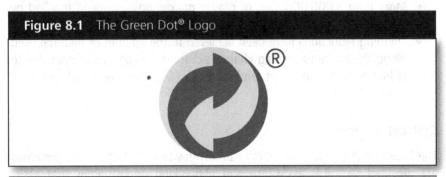

Figure 8.1 The Green Dot® Logo

Source: Pro Europe, Packaging Recovery Organisation Europe.

PRO EUROPE's publications, reports, and websites stress the environmental as well as economic advantages for producers to minimize packaging (promotion). Examples are tangible and include evidence from well-known producers including Laughing Cow cheese, which removed a false bottom in the carton, and Nescafé coffee, which reduced the thickness of their glass jars.

European consumers are reached through intensive communication campaigns and media activities designed to increase awareness regarding the impact of packaging and provide instructions on how to separate waste. Many activities are conducted as partnership programs in conjunction with producers, local authorities, recoverers, recyclers, and the trade. Green Dot® compliance schemes hold open days each year at waste disposal and recovery plants and invite people to road shows on the subject of waste avoidance, recycling, and recovery. In France, Eco-Emballages has set up programs and seminars for public relations officers or "recycling ambassadors" who have direct contact with the public and inform them in a professional manner about waste separation and recycling (PRO EUROPE, 2006/2007).

Communications create perceived norms by highlighting the participation of 22 European countries: Austria, Belgium, Bulgaria, Cyprus, Czech Republic, Estonia, France, Germany, Greece, Hungary, Ireland, Latvia, Lithuania, Luxembourg, Malta, Poland, Portugal, Romania, Slovakia, Slovenia, Spain, and Sweden. In addition, PRO EUROPE has developed cooperative agreements with similar systems in the United Kingdom, Iceland, Finland, and the Ukraine.

Members agree to report all quantities of packaging they put into circulation and to pay the corresponding license fees (commitment). Collection service providers agree to educate consumers and companies on ways to reduce, reuse, and recycle packaging.

A variety of metrics provide evaluative measures:

- As of 2010, about 170,000 companies in 26 countries are registered with the Green Dot® system.
- More than 360 million citizens have access to separate collection financed by PRO EUROPE member systems.
- About 31,000,000 tons (62 billion pounds) of packaging have been recovered by PRO EUROPE member systems in 2008 alone.
- More than 24 million tons of CO_2 equivalent has been saved by the work of PRO EUROPE member systems in 2008 alone.
- More than 3,000,000 tons of plastic packaging have been recycled by PRO EUROPE member systems in 2008.
- Ongoing reductions have been achieved in the amount of material used along the entire packaging chain. Packaging has become lighter due to reductions made in weight and materials (J. Quoden, personal communication, 2010).

Critical Review

The Green Dot® program appears to be a win-win-win situation. Corporations are provided technical assistance and networking opportunities that assist them in reducing packaging and ultimately saving production costs and avoiding fines for not complying with the existing government packaging directive. Governments in the near 30 European countries are reducing their need for expanding landfills. And consumers are provided a convenient opportunity to reward "green companies" with their purchase decisions.

It would be interesting to know more about the companies that haven't become members. How do they differ from those who have? Does membership prevalence vary by business sector, size, geographic location, waste management practices, or some other factor? Assuming PRO EUROPE wants to increase its membership, this "doer vs. nondoer" analysis would provide insights for future target audiences and barriers/benefits research. It might also be worthwhile to consider what additional, even alternative, environmental practices the Green Dot® could signify, including recycling and reuse of materials used in production. This might also defray concerns that some might express that the Green Dot® is simply a way to avoid meeting the requirements of the packaging directive.

CASE #2   Fork It Over! Reusing Leftover Food (Portland, Oregon)

Background

Some might have called the situation in 2000 in the Portland Metropolitan area "the perfect storm." It was estimated that 180,000 tons (360 million pounds) of food were being disposed of annually in the region's solid waste system. Metro, the directly elected regional government servicing the 1.5 million people in the three-county metropolitan area, was looking for ways to reduce this waste. Although the Metro region boasted an overall solid waste recovery level of 57%, the rate was lower in three key areas: (1) business recycling, (2) construction and demolition debris, and (3) organic food waste. At the same time, the Oregon Food Bank was struggling to provide new sources of fresh, nutritious food to Oregonians, as the state of Oregon had one of the highest rates in the nation for the incidence of hunger and food insecurity. Most of those who were hungry were employed full time but not making enough money to have a secure source of food from month to month. The pairing of a food bank and a solid waste agency was not necessarily intuitive, but it proved to be very fruitful. The sharing of resources and contacts led to the growth of coordinated programs that remain in operation today (J. Erickson, personal communication, 2010).

Fork It Over! serves as a model program that has been adapted throughout the state and the country. The concept is fairly simple: Provide food businesses a safe and convenient way to donate their perishable and surplus prepared foods to agencies that serve the hungry, ones this initiative refers to as "Food Rescue Programs." Community partners include the Oregon Restaurant Association, Chef's Collaborative, Oregon Food Bank, Sysco Portland, Tri-County Lodging Association, the region's three counties and 25 cities, the Food Alliance, and more (see Figure 8.2).

Figure 8.2   Handing Over the Surplus Food

Source: Photo courtesy of Metro and/or C Metro, Portland, Ore. 2010.

Target Audience(s) and Desired Behaviors

For food donations, target audiences are primarily restaurants, cafeterias, grocery stores, and schools. Rescue agencies include food banks, churches, Boys & Girls Clubs, group homes, child care centers, YMCAs, senior centers, the Salvation Army, shelters for the homeless, and more. The role of Fork It Over!, an initiative staffed by Metro, is to create lasting partnerships and relationships between donors and food rescue agencies, ones that make it safe and convenient for food businesses to donate and supported agencies to be responsive and reliable.

Barriers and Benefits

In 2003, Metro conducted a comprehensive study to identify barriers and benefits that food industry managers perceived relative to donating surplus food. Seventy-two businesses were interviewed, and a comprehensive literature search was conducted. This study gave Metro a relatively solid picture of the target audience needs and concerns, how the industry communicates internally, what sources of information they trusted, and how food moved through their businesses. Major concerns included the following:

- Will the food be considered safe?
- Could we be liable in the case of any problems?
- How much additional time and labor will this require?
- How hard is it to find a food rescue agency?

- How reliable, professional, and responsive will these agencies be? Will they be here at a regular time and day?
- Where and how will I store food items until they get picked up?

Surprisingly, to program planners, the biggest perceived benefit to food donation was not tax write-offs, savings on garbage fees, or other financial benefits, as assumed by both Metro and food banks. It was simply that reducing waste and fighting hunger at the same time was "the right thing to do"— that what had once been surplus was now a precious resource.

Description of the Program

Services were developed to provide potential donors with several convenient avenues to participate in the program from a simple online (place) self-help system to having a local government Recycle at Work specialist visit their business and set up the program for them (product). The online program instructions at www.forkitover .org are simple. Donors enter their location and the food they wish to donate, and the system displays a list of the closest food rescue agencies that match their needs. The information displayed includes the contact information for the agencies along with who they serve and whether they provide pickup service. This allows potential donors to choose the agency that is geographically closest to them as well as one that suits their needs. Businesses can also call (place) Metro's recycling information line for personal assistance with finding a food rescue agency (product). Once in touch with an agency, businesses take responsibility for working out pickup details and maintaining the longer-term relationship.

As noted earlier, the biggest perceived benefits of donation were not monetary in nature. Although potential tax write-offs and savings on garbage fees were "nice," it was the opportunity to do the right thing (nonmonetary incentive) that was most appealing.

Participating businesses are also likely to see an increase in employee morale and pride in working for a business that cared enough about the community to ensure that food went to those in need and not to waste. (One hotel currently in the program even offers the surplus first to staff and then to food rescue agencies.)

To assist the food rescue agencies with their capacity limits, grants were given by Metro to purchase refrigerated trucks, coolers, freezers, and/or other equipment needed to recover, transport, store, and distribute perishable foods safely.

In November 2003, armed with results of the comprehensive Food Donation Barrier and Benefit Identification Study, a promotional strategy team was formed that included a marketing firm, the former marketing director from Oregon Food Bank, a public relations firm specializing in the food industry, a media outlet willing to provide public service TV spots, and well-known food industry personalities willing to provide feedback and guidance.

Research of other food rescue program logos and taglines found that most programs used the same tried-and-true (and tired) motifs such as cornucopias, sheaves of wheat, hearts, and hands. Metro wanted something different and catchy that would stand out and be forceful. Fork It Over! was chosen as the program name, and a logo was designed (see Figure 8.3).

Figure 8.3 Program Logo

Source: Photo courtesy of Metro and/or C Metro, Portland, Ore. 2010.

To promote the program, advertisements were placed in the food section of the daily paper, articles and ads were placed in industry publications, press events were held, and mailings were sent to targeted food industry businesses. An editorial article in the local newspaper, as well as a feature story, lent an additional level of legitimacy to the program. County Health Department restaurant inspectors distributed Fork It Over! brochures during their regular annual inspections. And as noted in Figure 8.4, a flyer highlighted key benefits, ones that addressed major barriers.

Magnets were distributed to prompt businesses to call Metro to sign up for the program and to receive ongoing assistance. To engage customers of food businesses, listings were placed in telephone directories under restaurants and caterers to remind patrons to ask businesses to Fork It Over!

A new campaign was launched in June 2004 with a focus on targeted food businesses to make written, public commitments to donate food regularly. These commitments were then reinforced and publicized using print advertising, web postings, and earned media. Brochures and posters provided detailed program information. Pioneer donors were recruited as spokespeople, demonstrating that donation was safe, simple, and the right thing to do (see Figure 8.5). These pioneers were also asked to sign letters to their peers encouraging participation (norm appeal). Early adopters of the program were also asked to sign a commitment form and received posters and window clings touting their participation in the program. The names of businesses that have asked for assistance and committed to the program were also included in advertisements and posted on the website (incentive).

- Between 1999 and 2005, an estimated 9,000 tons (18 million pounds) of food was "forked over" to food rescue agencies and a total of $700,000 in grant funds were allocated to assist agencies in transporting and storing the food.
- In a 2002 study, the avoided disposal cost of this food recovered to date (5,181 tons was estimated at $647,650) and the dollar value to food banks of the additional recovered food was $17,305,208; on average, for every dollar of grant funds disbursed, there was a $31 benefit.

Figure 8.4   A Program Flyer

Source: Photo courtesy of Metro and/or C Metro, Portland, Ore. 2010.

- Visits to the program website increased from 34 in 2004, a month before the campaign began, to 948 for the month of July 2004.

Critical Review

Fork It Over! can certainly inspire others to see threats as opportunities and fulfill needs with untapped existing resources. Program managers also understood the power of audience research. Not only did they take the time and make the effort to listen to the wants and needs of both target audiences (food businesses and rescue agencies) but they acted on what they heard. Without this effort, they might not have known how important it would be to the food businesses to know of their limited liability and to easily find an agency, one that would be convenient and reliable. They might not have "raised many eyebrows" if they had only

Figure 8.5   Early Adopters of the Program Touted That "Prepared and Perishable Foods Are Easy and Safe to Donate and Are in High Demand by Food Rescue Agencies"

Source: Photo courtesy of Metro and/or C Metro, Portland, Ore. 2010.

touted the potential cost savings for the businesses and did not highlight how many hungry people their waste would feed. And they might not have realized how "stuck" their partners, the food banks, would be without access to grants to help fund additional equipment and storage devices.

Although it appears some effort was made to signal customers that a business was participating in Fork It Over!, the program might benefit from even more visibility with customers (diffusion). If customers at a restaurant regularly saw the program's logo on menus, much like we do a heart symbol for healthy food, they might not only become more loyal customers of those establishments participating, they might even ask those not participating to Fork It Over!

CASE #3   Anheuser-Busch: A U.S. Environmental Protection Agency WasteWise Recycling Hall of Fame Member (United States)

Background

In 2005, the U.S. EPA "cheered" Anheuser-Busch for "Brewing a Better Environment" and inducted them into the WasteWise Hall of Fame, the highest honor awarded to WasteWise partners. WasteWise, a free, voluntary EPA program that supports members in their efforts to eliminate solid waste, pointed to several impressive accomplishments for Anheuser-Busch in just the past year. Since joining WasteWise as a charter member in 1994, they had achieved a company-wide goal of recycling 97% of solid waste generated in the brewing and packaging of their beers. Recycled materials included beechwood chips, aluminum, glass, brewers' grain, scrap metal, and cardboard. In 2004 alone, they recycled 100% of the number of cans that the company's breweries use to package their products; ensured that shrink wrap used for transporting beer would be recycled; transitioned to smaller lids for cans, expected to save 20 million pounds of aluminum; reduced the thickness of their paper packages, saving 2.8 million pounds of paperboard; converted from hardwood to 100% polypropylene pallets, reducing energy and transportation costs; and increased use of web-based electronic forms (WasteWise/U.S. EPA, 2010).

In response, Anheuser-Busch's group vice president of Brewing Operations and Technology saluted "each of our employees," for the company believes that it has been the ideas and actions of employees that helped to reduce, reuse, and recycle nearly all of the materials generated in the production processes.

This case story will focus first on what the company has done to influence these employee actions and then highlight strategies employed by WasteWise.

Description of the Program

Employee Target Audience

Anheuser-Busch employs around 42,000 people, operates 12 breweries in the United States, and is a wholly owned subsidiary of Anheuser-Busch InBev, the leading global brewer. Based in St. Louis, Anheuser-Busch is the leading American brewer, holding a 48.9% share of U.S. beer sales to retailers. The company brews the world's largest-selling beers, Budweiser and Bud Light (Anheuser-Busch, 2010). The 3 Rs are a familiar focus of the corporation's environmental efforts, emphasizing with employees that reducing waste at the source provides the greatest environmental benefit and that some of the greatest ideas for doing this have come from employees themselves.

Partners in Quality and Excellence Thru Ideas are the main vehicles for Anheuser-Busch employees to suggest new ideas to save the company money, improve operations, and enhance customer satisfaction (product). It is through this channel that employees suggest specific environmental improvements including reducing waste. Local environmental teams look for ways to lessen their facility's impact on the environment. Simple, easy to overlook ideas are explored for their waste reduction potential. For example, one brewery team focused on altering the practice that employees' work gloves were thrown out when they became soiled. The team located a laundry service that would sort and clean the gloves and return them for reuse. Housekeeping staff placed bins throughout the facility to collect the soiled gloves (place) and encouraged fellow employees to participate in the program (diffusion). Employees are encouraged to communicate their environmental ideas and concerns via electronic bulletin boards and e-mail (place). A variety of communication channels support employee involvement. In the past 2 years, for example, every issue except one of the company's newsletter, the *Eagle*, has contained articles on environmental actions such as the glove project, within the company. An annual event called Green Week is held the week of Earth Day and features activities designed to inspire employee participation in idea sharing (WasteWise Update, 2010).

Beginning in 1995, employees were recognized for their environmental efforts by creating the Pledge and Promise Environmental Stewardship and Leadership Awards. More than 60 employee teams entered the award competition in the first year alone (incentive).

Anheuser-Busch as a Target Audience

WasteWise, launched in 1994, provides technical assistance (product) on reducing purchasing and minimizing waste to more than 2,400 partners spanning more than 50 industries. A variety of practices are promoted to reduce solid waste and industrial waste associated with procurement, production, packaging, and transportation. Assistance is available through a toll-free helpline (place), as well as online resources and links, publications, case studies, and educational materials. The *WasteWise Update* is the WasteWise program's principal technical assistance periodical. Each publication details a single waste reduction strategy and provides case studies of organizations that have successfully implemented that strategy. Regional forums provide networking and info-sharing opportunities.

Each year, the EPA recognizes outstanding achievements of partners with awards in categories including business, government, and educational sectors (incentives). To qualify, partners must submit complete annual reporting forms that detail tonnage of waste reduced, associated cost savings, and promotion of the WasteWise program to employees, customers, and suppliers. Awards presented include the following:

- **Hall of Fame** is the highest honor awarded to WasteWise partners and indicates a continued commitment to progressive waste reduction activities.
- **Partners of the Year** recognizes overall waste reduction achievements, efforts to purchase or manufacture recycled-content products, and activities to promote WasteWise.
- **Endorser of the Year** award recognizes an organization for outstanding efforts to promote the WasteWise program and include members from state and local government agencies, trade associations, and nonprofit organizations and businesses that support other members in their waste reduction efforts (diffusion).
- **Gold Achievement Awards** recognizes partners' achievements in focus areas such as climate change, green buildings, product stewardship, and beneficial use of secondary materials.
- **Honorable Mentions** are awarded to partners who made noteworthy accomplishments in waste prevention, recycling collection, and buying or manufacturing recycled-content products.

In terms of the environment, perhaps one of the greatest services the program offers is a data management and reporting system that partners use to collect, organize, analyze, and report their municipal solid waste information. Regardless of the number of facilities, WasteWise Re-TRAC enables members to track and standardize waste management data for their entire operation. With this system, the EPA is able to report (and praise) organizations like Anheuser-Busch with public statements such as the following:

> Anheuser-Busch's aluminum recycling and source reduction efforts in 2004 yielded significant environmental and energy savings benefits. Using EPA's Waste Reduction Model (WARM), we calculated that their 2004 efforts reduced greenhouse gas emissions by 1.76 million Metric Tons of Carbon Equivalent, which is equal to the annual emission from 1.3 million cars. (EPA Newsroom, 2006)

Critical Review

Anheuser-Busch and the many other companies participating as members of WasteWise are clearly making a difference for the environment. Employees evidently have increased pride, and customers aware of the brewery's efforts are most likely impressed. It might also be beneficial for the EPA/WasteWise to consider assisting members in tracking and reporting monetary benefits of their behaviors as well. Perhaps this could be accomplished by augmenting the current tracking system (WasteWise Re-TRAC).

Most recent reports indicate that to date (2010) there are around 2,400 member partners across the United States. Given the apparent waste reduction success among members, it would be interesting—perhaps even important—to understand more about businesses who are high producers of waste and are not members. What are their barriers to joining, and what strategies would address their concerns? Are they aware of and value member benefits? If not, what would motivate them? Similarly, relative to employees, what would motivate more employees and teams to submit their ideas?

Other Notable Programs

In this section, we mention a few additional successful examples of waste reduction in the commercial sector. We use each as a chance to illustrate one of seven recommendations on how change agents can persuade those in the commercial sector to change their businesses practices. We encourage you to stress the potential for one or more of the following corporate benefits often realized (Kotler & Lee, 2008):

Supporting Brand Positioning

Kotler and Armstrong described a brand's position as "the complex set of perceptions, impressions, and feelings that consumers have for the product compared with competing products" (Kotler & Armstrong, 2001, p. 269). Subaru has a desired positioning as "an automobile that offers a high-level blend of ride, environment and safety." Their recycle rates help secure this positioning, reporting on their website that 97% of excess/leftover steel, plastic, wood, paper, glass, and other materials goes to recycling outlets, and that the remaining 3% is shipped to an incinerator to help generate steam (Subaru, 2005).

Creating Brand Preference

In a 2004 Citizenship Survey conducted by Cone, Inc., 86% of U.S. citizens said "yes" to "I am likely to switch from one brand to another that is about the same in price and quality, if the other brand is associated with a cause" (Cone, Inc., 2004). This helps explain some of the success of ENERGY STAR, the joint program of the U.S. EPA and the U.S. Department of Energy mentioned in Chapter 6 that helps consumers save money and at the same time protect the environment. The ENERGY STAR label helps create brand preference for the manufacturers of products deemed energy efficient (ENERGY STAR, 2010).

Building Traffic

Best Buy makes it free and convenient to recycle unwanted electronics including cell phones, print cartridges, DVDs, CDs, computers, and more. Every U.S. Best Buy store has free kiosks, just inside the door . . . perhaps one you'll then go through to purchase replacements for items you are recycling. In 2009, Best Buy recycled 60 million pounds of old electronics (Best Buy, 2010).

Increasing Sales

Better World Books is a for-profit social enterprise that collects used books and sells them online to raise money for literacy initiatives worldwide. Founders consider their job to be finding new homes for unwanted books and refer to the company as the "Online Bookstore with a Soul." The company has successfully diverted more than 32 million books from landfills and in the process has raised over $7.6 million for its nonprofit literacy, library, and college partners (Better World Books, 2010).

Improving Profitability Through Reducing Costs

In the first case featuring the Green Dot® program in Europe, the potential for increased profitability for program members was highlighted, mentioning Laughing Cow cheese reducing packing by 13% after removing a false bottom. Green Dot® publications also mentioned others including Coca-Cola, which reduced the quantity of materials in their can by 23%, and Philips, which made one of their cell phones smaller, resulting in 34% reduction in packaging weight (PRO EUROPE, 2010).

Attracting Enthusiastic and Credible Partners

Consider how important all sectors (private, public, and nonprofit) were to the success of Fork It Over! It took food businesses to donate surplus food; food banks to be responsive and reliable for pickup; and a public agency, Metro, to create a program that would overcome barriers, ensure benefits, and facilitate the relationship.

Having a Real Impact on Social Change

Verizon Wireless shareholders and employees can feel proud of the impact that the company has made from collecting, refurbishing, and reselling a total of 660,000 used cell phones in 2006 alone. They made a real contribution. Selling the refurbished phones enabled their HopeLine® program to donate $1.3 million to nearly 300 domestic violence prevention and awareness organizations that year (Verizon, 2010).

Summary

The three cases presented in this chapter highlight the 3Rs of waste management in the commercial sector. It is interesting to recognize that in all three of these success stories, we witnessed a win-win-win situation: a win for the change agent, the corporation, and the environment. PRO EUROPE's Green Dot® program helped fulfill the organization's environmental mission, saved businesses money, and even gave consumers a chance to reward "green" companies. Metro's Fork It Over! initiative reduced organics in the region's waste stream and gave food businesses a convenient and reliable way to "do the right thing" and food banks more resources for their clients. And EPA's WasteWise program delivered on its mission to provide technical assistance and network support that contributed to Anheuser-Busch's award-winning recycling rates and induction into their Hall of Fame. In a final section, we mentioned a few additional successful examples of waste reduction in the commercial sector, ones that illustrate seven recommendations on how change agents can persuade those in the commercial sector to change their businesses practices. Additional corporate examples included ones for Subaru, ENERGY STAR, Best Buy, Better World Books, and Verizon Wireless.

Questions for Discussion

1. Table 8.1 (Commercial Behaviors to Help Reduce Waste) mentions several examples of end-state behaviors. What is at least one more for each of the 3Rs?

2. For the Green Dot® program, what do you think of the recommendation in the Critical Review section to expand the businesses practices associated with the program to include recycling and reuse practices as well?

3. For the Fork It Over! case, what tools would you use to increase consumer advocacy with food businesses?

4. For the Anheuser-Busch case, what additional tools would you consider to increase employee involvement, either in suggesting new ideas or implementing recommended practices at their work location?

References

Anheuser-Busch. (2010). *Welcome to Anheuser-Busch, where making friends is our business.* Retrieved from http://www.anheuser-busch.com/company.html

Best Buy. (2010). *e-cycle. Frequently asked questions for electronics recycling program.* Retrieved from http://www.bestbuy.com/site/null/null/pcmcat174700050009.c?id=pcmcat174700050009

Better World Books. (2010, March 22). *Better World Books awarded 2009 WasteWise Gold Award.* Retrieved from http://www.betterworldbooks.com/custom.aspx?f=wastewise-award

Cone, Inc. (2004). *2004 Cone Corporate Citizenship study: Building brand trust executive summary citizenship study.* Retrieved from http://www.coneinc.com/stuff/contentmgr/files/0/84d3119 bfe09009ccba4134a2c9fd5ae/files/2004_cone_corporate_citizenship_exec_summary.pdf

ENERGY STAR. (2010). *Overview of 2009 achievements.* Retrieved from http://www.energystar.gov/ia/partners/annualreports/2009_achievements.pdf

EPA Newsroom. (2006). *Anheuser-Busch: Brewing a better environment.* Retrieved from http://www.epa.gov/osw/inforesources/news/2006news/04-busch.htm

Fork It Over poster C Metro, Portland, Ore. 2010.

Fork It Over program logo C Metro, Portland, Ore. 2010.

Green Dot® Compliance. (2010). *About Green Dot and Europe's packaging waste recovery efforts.* Packaging Waste Compliance Europe Green Dot Consultants. Retrieved from http://www.greendotcompliance.eu/en/about-green-dot.php

Kotler, P., & Armstrong, G. (2001). *Principles of marketing.* Upper Saddle River, NJ: Prentice-Hall.

Kotler, P., & Lee, N. (2008). *Corporate social responsibility: Doing the most good for your company and your cause.* New York: Wiley.

Practice Greenhealth. (2010). *Waste reduction. Why focus on waste?* Retrieved from http://cms.h2e-online.org/ee/waste-reduction/

PRO EUROPE. (2006/2007). *Effective packaging—Effective prevention.* Retrieved from www.pro-europe.info

PRO EUROPE. (2010). *About PRO EUROPE: Mission statement.* Retrieved from http://www.pro-e.org/About.html

Subaru. (2005). Reusing and Recycling: Manufacturing without waste at SIA. *Drive magazine.* Retrieved from http://www.subarudrive.com/Sum05_SubaruDifference.htm

United Nations. (2010). *United Nations Statistics Division—Environmental statistics. Municipal waste treatment.* Retrieved from http://unstats.un.org/unsd/environment/wastetreatment.htm

Verizon. (2010). *HopeLine® from Verizon Wireless.* Retrieved from http://aboutus.vzw.com/communityservice/hopeLine.html

WasteWise Update. (2010). *Employee education.* Retrieved from http://www.epa.gov/wastes/partnerships/wastewise/pubs/wwupda4.pdf

WasteWise/U.S. Environmental Protection Agency. (2010). *Anheuser-Busch: Brewing a better environment.* Retrieved from http://www.epa.gov/wastes/inforesources/news/2006news/04-busch.htm

CHAPTER 9

Protecting Water Quality

Water is the most precious natural resource on the planet. It is the source of all life, and clean water is essential to a sustainable planet. Yet across the planet, we see the harmful consequences of human activity on water quality. From contamination of freshwater reserves to pollution of the oceans, water quality stands as a critical environmental issue.

Water pollution worldwide varies dramatically by region and by body of water. For example, in developing countries, access to clean, potable water is a critical issue. The United Nations estimates that 1.1 billion people live in regions without access to an improved water supply, and an additional 2.4 billion people do not have access to any type of improved sanitation facility (United Nations, 2008). As a result, fecal pollution of surface water is an important international issue, and about 2 million people die each year from waterborne diseases.

In addition to the direct consequences of freshwater pollution, pollution of the world's oceans and coastal areas is producing serious environmental problems. The large majority of marine pollution worldwide originates from land-based activities, with chemicals, litter, and waste washing into streams and rivers, and ultimately reaching coastal waterways. The by-products from human activities upstream drain into lower regions through water runoff, and as a result, pollution ultimately reaches estuaries, wetlands, bays, and oceans. Every region of land contributes to one or more watersheds, and human behavior in these watersheds is the primary cause of water contamination worldwide.

The Problem

While every area faces its own unique set of water quality issues, here we highlight several general types of water pollution (U.S. Environmental Protection Agency [EPA], 2009).

- *Dissolved Oxygen.* Dissolved oxygen is necessary for most aquatic organisms—especially fish and invertebrates. Plant matter such as leaves and grass, along with food and other organic waste, reduce the amount of oxygen in the water, ultimately harming fish and other biological organisms.
- *Pathogens.* Bacteria and other microorganisms (e.g., salmonella, viruses, giardia) can cause illness and death when consumed or contacted by other organisms. While such pathogens are more typical in areas with inadequate sewage treatment, they are also found in water contaminated by leaky sewage systems and in areas with high concentrations of livestock.
- *Chemical Pollutants (Organic).* There are a number of organic chemicals that are frequently discharged into waterways, including detergents, food wastes such as grease and fats, petroleum and oil, and hygiene and cosmetic products.
- *Chemical Pollutants (Inorganic).* Nonorganic discharge comes primarily from silt and sediment dislodged during construction or logging activities, but it also includes nitrates and phosphates from fertilizers; metals such as mercury, lead, copper, and arsenic; and chemical waste from industrial processes (e.g., dioxins, polychlorinated biphenyls [PCBs]).

Sources of water pollution can be classified as either a point source or a nonpoint source. Point sources include discrete, identifiable sites, such as a factory, sewage treatment plant, or a city storm drain. Nonpoint sources include cumulative effects from many small contributors, such as nitrogen from fertilizers used in agricultural regions or runoff from city streets and neighborhoods. While historically water pollution has originated from point sources, today it is widely recognized that nonpoint source pollution is the leading cause of water contamination (U.S. EPA, 2010). In essence, it is the aggregated effects of human activity and not the single indiscretion of a company or business that causes most pollution. As a result, social marketing provides an important tool for protecting and improving water quality.

Potential Behavior Solutions

Water pollution worldwide is caused by human behavior. While industrial processes have historically been the major culprit for water pollution, today it is the cumulative impact of nonpoint sources. In many instances, the contaminants found in the water can be traced back to a specific behavior or to use of a specific product. For example, construction activities often result in dirt and sediment draining into local waterways, clearing ice and snow from roadways in the winter can result in salt discharges, and restaurants hosing down mats and equipment can discharge grease and fats.

Because each area faces its own unique water pollution issues, it is important to follow the contaminant upstream to its source. From a social marketing perspective, this is a central first step in developing a campaign. Water monitoring and testing will show the levels of specific contaminants, and each of these can be compared to a local or regional limit—that is, the Total Maximum Daily Load (TMDL). For an example and discussion of TMDLs, see the U.S. EPA's website at www.epa.gov/owow/tmdl.

At a global level, the United Nations has summarized the primary causes of oceanic water pollution worldwide. These are shown in Figure 9.1 and reflect the myriad of human activities that result in discharge. The figure shows the impact of various types of human behavior on estuaries— intertidal and wetlands—and the open ocean. Of course, each of these categories of activity needs to be reduced to more specific end-state behaviors, but it's helpful to consider the types of behaviors that are having the largest impact. Of particular note is the role of commercial entities as a primary cause of water degradation—from construction, agriculture, logging, and mining, commercial entities play a central role in water quality.

This chapter focuses on commercial entities and social marketing activities that involve businesses. Such activities can take a number of forms. Our focus in this chapter is on social marketing activities with commercial entities as the target audience—that

Figure 9.1   Causes of Water Pollution Worldwide

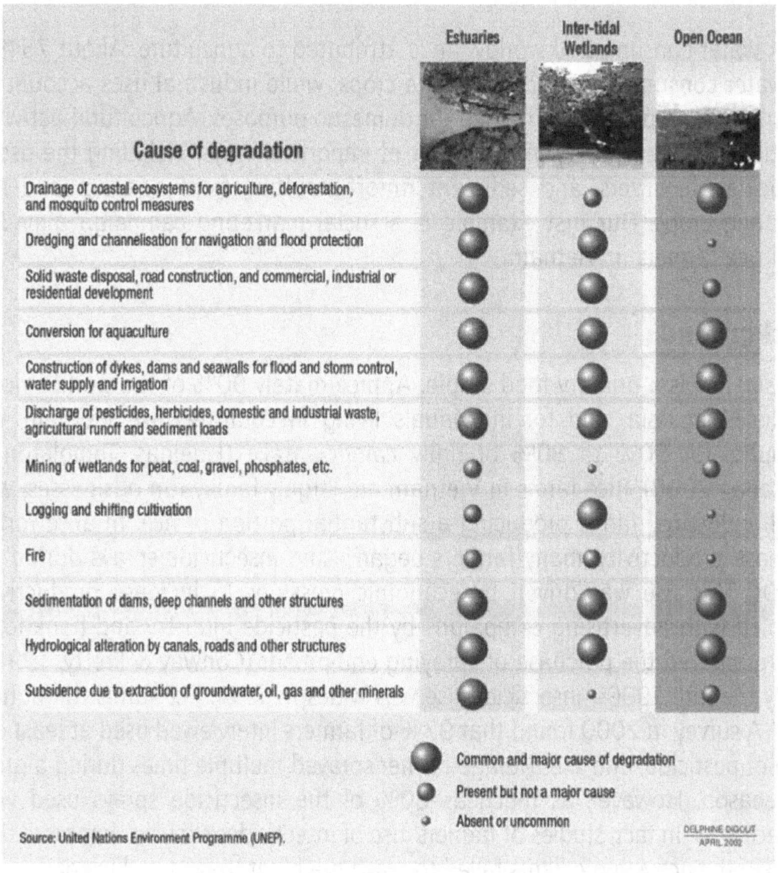

Source: United Nations Environmental Programme, http://www.unep.org/dewa/vitalwater/jpg/0321-human-actions-EN.jpg. Reprinted with permission.

is, social marketing programs that attempt to promote changes in business practices. However, it is important to point out that social marketing activities can also target employees and aim to change the behavior of individuals in their workplace—for example, encouraging workers on charter fishing boats to use the onboard storage tank for human waste rather than dumping it into the ocean. And finally, social marketing activities can occur through commercial channels but target customers. For example, a social marketing program aimed at reducing pesticide runoff might work with local businesses to establish an exchange program to collect products with specific chemicals. As an example, the pesticide Diazinon was recently banned in the United States, and many communities are now developing programs to collect unused product.

We turn now to examples of social marketing programs aimed at inducing change in the commercial sector.

CASE #1   Chuyen Que Minh (My Homeland Story): Reducing Insecticide Use Among Rice Farmers (Vietnam)

Most water consumption worldwide is attributed to agriculture. About 75% of all water consumed is used to irrigate crops, while industrial uses account for about 20%, and only 5% is used for domestic purposes. Agricultural activities are tied to water quality in a number of important ways, including the use of pesticides, fertilizers, and sediment runoff resulting from clearing land and irrigating crops. Our first example is a social marketing campaign aimed at rural rice farmers in Vietnam.

Background

In Asia, rice is a primary food staple. Approximately 90% of the world's rice is produced in Asia, and for individuals living in countries like Vietnam, rice accounts for 50% to 80% of daily caloric intake (Huelgas, Templeton, & Castanar, 2008). Rice farms in Vietnam are largely family-run businesses, with small individual farms producing a substantial portion of rice. In an effort to increase productivity, many farmers began using insecticide sprays during the 1980s. This rise was driven by economic pressures to increase productivity, coupled with advertising campaigns by the pesticide industry and bank loans that promoted the purchase of spraying equipment (Conway & Pretty, 1991).

By the late 1990s, insecticide use was widespread on rice farms throughout Asia. A survey in 2000 found that 97% of farmers interviewed used at least one type of pesticide, and the average farmer sprayed multiple times during a growing season. However, as much as 80% of the insecticide sprays used were unnecessary. In fact, studies of farmers' use of insecticides showed that more than 75% of the active ingredients failed to reach the plant targets and instead ended up in the water and soil. While agricultural studies showed that leaf-feeding insects had little impact on rice yields, farmers generally perceived leaf-feeding insects as the most important pest (Escalada, Heong, Huan, & Chien, 2009).

While the proper use of pesticides can help to increase crop yield, the effects are generally short-lived, and they can have serious harmful consequences. First, the chemicals result in human health problems, including asthma, eye irritation, and pulmonary disorders. Second, the chemicals contaminate the soil and in the long term can reduce crop yield. And third, the chemicals have harmful effects on other plants and animals in the region (cf. Heong & Escalada, 1997). For example, in rice farms that are pesticide free, it is possible to farm certain types of shrimp along with rice. However, cofarming of shrimp or other types of fish cannot happen in areas with pesticide use because of the resulting water contamination.

Target Audience(s) and Desired Behaviors

The target audience for the campaign was Vietnamese rice farmers living in Vinh Long province, an area south of Ho Chi Minh City. The province has a total population of more than 1 million, of which 883,000 live in a rural setting. The main economic activity in the region is agriculture, and the area produces nearly 1 million tons of rice per year.

The target behavior was the indiscriminant spraying of insecticides. Rather than attempting to eliminate insecticide use, the campaign aimed to promote a more efficient use of insecticides and to encourage Integrated Pest Management. The targeted behavior was to avoid spraying during the first 40 days after planting, during which time insecticide use has little benefits. In addition to the 40-day period, the campaign promoted more efficient use of fertilizers and seeds and nonchemical solutions to pest management.

Barriers and Benefits

Survey data from Vietnamese farmers had been conducted for more than 15 years prior to the program. The existing data showed the widespread use of insecticides, and the general belief among farmers that leaf damage would reduce crop yield. There was also a finding that some farmers viewed insecticides as "medicinal" and believed that they would generally result in healthier farmland.

Description of the Program

The campaign consisted of a radio soap opera, Chuyen Que Minh (translated as My Homeland Story). The radio show was broadcast on several major Vietnamese stations twice per week for 1 year. Each of the 20-minute episodes told the story of a farming family, as family members faced their daily challenges. Embedded throughout the stories were the principles of Integrated Pest Management and the desirable farming behaviors. The characters in the story were based on a real-life farming family, identified through demographic analyses to represent the typical family in the region. In developing the scripts, the production team visited the family regularly to learn about the activities, behaviors, and common expressions that could be integrated into the episodes.

The materials were developed through a series of workshops with members of the farming community, including input on the radio scripts, posters, and leaflets (pilot). In addition, all materials were pilot tested through regional "radio clubs" before being finalized and distributed. (See Figure 9.2.)

A total of 104 episodes were broadcast over a 1-year period, from 2004 to 2005 (implementation).

Evaluation

Survey data was used to assess the impact of the program on Vietnamese farmers. An initial survey was conducted with 605 farmers in the target region to

Figure 9.2 Chuyen Que Minh: A Vietnamese Radio Soap Opera to Reduce Pesticide Use Among Rice Farmers

Source: Photograph provided courtesy of Kong Luen Heong, International Rice Research Institute.

identify beliefs and practices and to inform the campaign materials and development. Then, prior to the launch of the program, a pretest survey was conducted with 600 farmers. And finally, at the conclusion of the program, another survey with 609 farmers was conducted.

During the 1-year period, 41% of farmers reported listening to the soap opera. In comparing the pretest and posttest surveys, a number of significant effects were noted. First, the percentage of farmers who believed that spraying insecticide was necessary during the first 40 days of planting dropped from 80% to 48%, and the percentage of farmers who believed that leaf damage would mean reduction in crop yield dropped from 59% to 38%. In addition, farmers were more likely to believe that spraying insecticides on their farmland could negatively affect their health (from 62% at pretest to 86% posttest).

With regard to behavior, the program reported a significant reduction in insecticide spray rates. During the pretest, the average farmer reported spraying 1.9 times per season, and at posttest, the average farmer reported spraying 1.3 times—a reduction of 31%. The effect was particularly strong for farmers who reported listening to the soap opera, among whom the posttest surveys showed a 60% reduction in the number of sprays. In addition, farmers who reported listening to the soap opera were substantially more likely not to use any insecticide (54%) compared to farmers who did not listen (15%). See Heong and colleagues (2008) for additional details.

Critical Review

The Chuyen Que Minh radio soap opera provides a creative example of a social marketing program designed to promote changes in a diffuse commercial context. The authors refer to the approach as "entertainment-education" but it is really much more than simple education. Through the radio stories, the episodes convey a social norm for the proper behavior. That is, the episodes provide role models for adopting the targeted behavior and convey a message that such actions are common and accepted. Bandura (2002) has argued that such "serial dramas" serve to empower viewers and to install a sense of self-efficacy. See Dagron (2001) for other examples of serial dramas.

The results from the Chuyen Que Minh campaign show clear effects. Particularly noteworthy is the program's focus on community involvement and the efforts throughout the campaign to involve members of the Vietnamese farming community in developing and pilot testing the materials. Another program strength was the focus on a single behavior: avoiding insecticide use during the first 40 days after planting. And the survey data collected before, during, and after the program provide a good method for evaluating the overall impact.

The Chuyen Que Minh campaign provides a clear example of "what works." However, there are several elements that could have strengthened the program. First, the evaluation relied exclusively on survey data, and while the pattern of results is clear, behavioral observations would have strengthened the findings. Examples of behavioral data might have included water testing at randomly selected farms throughout the region, observations, and sampling of seedlings during the first 40 days of planting, or pesticide sales receipts from local vendors and retail locations.

Second, the program relied heavily on passive radio messages. As described elsewhere in this book, mass media messages are particularly effective for increasing awareness or promoting favorable attitudes, but they often struggle to induce lasting behavior change. To strengthen the message, the campaign could have added program elements to directly reach farmers—for example, recommendations by retail staff at the point of purchase for pesticides, community workshops designed to promote and reinforce positive pest management behaviors, or personal contact with farmers through an agricultural extension network.

Third, the evaluation would have benefited from a control group. That is, comparable survey or behavioral data obtained from farmers in similar regions of the country where the soap opera was not aired. The results previously reported were based on pre-post comparisons, and while the results show clear effects, it is unclear what would have happened without the program. Perhaps regional trends were already moving toward less pesticide use or there was a dramatic increase in the cost of insecticides. These external events could have been responsible for the reported results, and while they may seem unlikely, using a control group can help to eliminate these alternative explanations and to isolate the causal impact of the campaign.

The success of the program led to the development of related programs in Vietnam and other areas of Asia. One example is Que Minh Xanh Mai (translated as Forever Green My Homeland), which was launched in 2006 to educate rice farmers about environmental issues and conservation and to reduce harmful farming practices. For another example, see the 3R3G program described at the end of this chapter.

CASE #2   Dirty Dairying (New Zealand)

Background

Our second example of social marketing to protect water quality comes from New Zealand. Water quality in New Zealand is generally good, and the country boasts thriving tourism and recreational industries. However, despite an overall record for clean water, contamination of nitrogen and phosphorus levels have increased steadily since 1990 (New Zealand Ministry for the Environment, 2007). Water contamination from point sources has been notably improved, but pollution from nonpoint sources has increased.

One identified source of water pollution in New Zealand is dairy farming. While livestock have been a central economic activity in New Zealand for the past 100 years, recent trends have shown an increase in cattle and dairy farms. This increase in the number of cattle in New Zealand has been directly linked to deteriorations in water quality, particularly from animal effluent in rainwater runoff, rivers, and catchments (Hamill & McBride, 2003). Current practice in New Zealand dairies allows cows to graze freely in open land. However, this practice means that the cows regularly cross streams and that dung and urine are washed into catchments and waterways. In addition to animal waste, economic pressures toward increased productivity of dairy farms has resulted in increased use of fertilizers on grazing land, which also contributes to the phosphorous and nitrogen.

While a number of structural and policy solutions have been proposed, there remains an important role for social marketing and encouraging dairy farmers to adopt practices that limit water contamination. One specific behavioral practice is for farmers to fence off streams in order to keep cattle from defecating directly in the water (Environment Waikato, 2004). Fencing also serves to protect other aquatic habitat and prevent bank erosion. However, dairy farmers have been slow to implement fencing solutions (Bewsell, Monaghan, & Kaine, 2007).

In an effort to raise awareness among the New Zealand public about the role of dairy farms in water contamination, Fish and Game New Zealand launched a campaign in early 2000.

Target Audience(s) and Desired Behaviors

There were several target audiences for the Dirty Dairying campaign. First (and foremost) were dairy farmers themselves, and the ultimate goal of the campaign was to promote changes in dairy farming practices that contribute to water contamination. However, secondary audiences were New Zealand residents, and by raising awareness about the issue, the campaign hoped to apply pressure to local politicians and decision makers.

The primary behavioral target was fencing and encouraging dairy farmers to fence off streams and waterways in the grazing areas. A related behavior was the installation of bridges at central water cross points to keep the cattle out of the water.

Barriers and Benefits

While no barriers and benefits data were collected prior to the launch of the campaign, the increased interest in the topic led to several subsequent studies of dairy farmers. Bewsell and colleagues (2007) report the results from interviews with 30 dairy farmers in four catchment regions in New Zealand. The interviews focused on the farmers' decision to engage in best practices and the perceived benefits of these behaviors. Target behaviors included fencing streams, managing effluent by installing a pond system, reducing fertilizer use, installing bridged water crossing points, and performing several other specific behaviors. Our focus here is on the results for fencing. The qualitative results were used to segment farmers into different groups.

The results suggest that farmers were more likely to engage in fencing activities when there was a perceived benefit to the farm or to comply with local laws and regulations (not necessarily out of environmental concern). The interviews showed that farmers' decisions were based largely on contextual factors of the farm, including plans for expanding or redesigning the farm operations, streams that serve as boundaries to the farm, needs for fencing to manage stock movement (to improve dairy operations), and the existence of wetlands or boggy areas (where cattle can get stuck). Note that each of these contextual factors is linked to the efficiency or convenience of operating the dairy and not necessarily to broader considerations of downstream pollution. The authors concluded that, "adoption may be slow in the absence of on-farm benefits" and that "promotion of stream fencing needs to be strongly linked to on-farm benefits" (Bewsell et al., 2007, p. 201). In the absence of these direct farm benefits, regulation was seen as a central reason for compliance and the threat of fines or reduced sales.

Description of the Program

The Dirty Dairying campaign consisted of a series of media messages distributed to areas throughout New Zealand. The campaign materials highlighted the role of dairy farming in polluting lakes, rivers, and streams and the negative consequences for the people of New Zealand. The messaging platform was one of shame and general disapproval for current dairy practices.

Evaluation

While few details are available on public perception or recognition of the issue, the campaign is widely recognized as the impetus for the New Zealand Dairying and Clean Streams Accord in 2003. This was a voluntary agreement between Fonterra (a large farming cooperative group with more than 10,000 New Zealand farmers as members), the New Zealand Ministry for the Environment, the Ministry for Agriculture and Forestry, and regional councils. The accord aimed to promote changes in dairying practices, and to reduce water pollution. The accord also set specific targets, such as preventing cattle from entering streams (50% of all cattle by 2007 and 90% by 2012) and building bridged crossing points for cattle on dairies (50% by 2007 and 90% by 2012). In an effort to achieve these targets, a monitoring and enforcement plan was adopted that allowed for fines on farms not in compliance.

A 2008 report noted an 83% compliance rate for excluding cattle from waterways and a 93% compliance rate for bridging waterway crossings (New Zealand Ministry for the Environment, 2008).

Critical Review

The Dirty Dairying campaign illustrates the power of social marketing. However, unlike many of the examples discussed in this book, the campaign was successful because it influenced public policy and key decision makers (most notably, Fonterra). The campaign's use of shame to raise awareness and leverage social pressure on dairy farmers prompted a quick response by policy makers and industry leaders.

The policies voluntarily adopted by Fonterra resulted in a monitoring and enforcement program. Rather than encouraging or incentivizing farmers to adopt the desirable farming practices, the policies imposed sanctions and fines for noncompliance. While this approach has been effective in New Zealand, it is important to consider several aspects of fines and sanctions that impact their efficacy as a behavior change tool. In general, inspection and enforcement programs are most effective when they are the following:

1. *Visible.* Enforcement programs need to be clearly communicated to the target audience, with visible indicators of their presence. Examples can include posted signage or print messages in local trade magazines or at retail locations. In addition, a few highly visible busts can go a long way toward maintaining the salience of the program.

2. *Enforceable.* The targeted behaviors need to be clearly defined, the penalties need to be explicit and strong, and there needs to be a mechanism for enforcement. In addition, the entity responsible for imposing the sanctions needs to be legitimate and ideally associated with a governmental organization.

3. *Equitable.* The monitoring and enforcement needs to be applied fairly across the target audience, with systematic inspections and uniform penalties.

4. *Sustainable.* Once imposed, the policies and fines need to remain in effect for a long period of time. Because the motivation to engage in the behavior is external to the individual (i.e., individuals are doing the behavior in order to avoid the penalty), compliance will only persist as long as the threat of punishment is in place. If the program stops, or its salience and enforcement decline substantially, individuals are likely to "take their chances" and compliance rates will drop.

With these considerations in mind, monitoring and enforcement can play a role in social marketing activities. As illustrated by the Dirty Dairying campaign, fines and sanctions can quickly change the behavior of a target audience. However, such programs also come with some severe limitations. These include program costs associated with the staffing and infrastructure required to monitor and process the cases. Enforcement programs are also generally disliked by members of the target audience, and there is likely to be some political resistance on the part of the individuals to comply. And third, the changes induced by such programs will be specific to those behaviors that are enforced, and typically, individuals will do the least amount necessary to comply. It is rarely the case that monitoring and enforcement programs will spill over into related behaviors. For instance, in the case of the New Zealand dairy farmers, if the program is specific to stock management practices such as fencing, it's highly unlikely that a farmer will also voluntarily work to reduce fertilizer use in order to bring down nitrogen rates in the water (unless, of course, the discharge is monitored and enforced rather than the specific behaviors).

Other Notable Programs

The cases presented in this chapter provide good examples of social marketing programs used to reach commercial entities and protect water quality. But there are certainly many other excellent examples, and in the next short section, we briefly mention a few notable programs.

3R3G: Three Reductions, Three Gains

Building on the success of social marketing programs targeting rural farmers in Asia, the 3R3G campaign was designed to promote three behaviors: reduce seed use, reduce the use of nitrogen fertilizer, and reduce the use of pesticides (the "three reductions"). The benefits associated with these changes in farming practices were to reduce production costs, improve the health of rice farmers, and protect the environment (the "three gains"). The campaign targeted farmers in the Mekong Delta region of Vietnam, an area consisting of 13 provinces and accounting for 52% of national rice output (about 36 million tons per year). The 3R3G campaign utilized the Chuyen Que Minh soap opera, coupled with a number of on-the-ground outreach activities with farmers. These included expanded media placements (i.e., billboards, TV, print, pamphlets) and community events including demonstrations and "farmer field days." As a result of the media and community events, the authors noted that, "it became nearly impossible for a farmer not to hear about 3R3G" (Huelgas et al., 2008).

Data evaluating the program came from a series of surveys conducted with random samples of farmers from each province. The surveys were supplemented with focus groups, price data from retail shops in the provinces, and through interviews with local government officials, extension workers, and seed growers. Results showed that after the yearlong campaign, 80% of farmers were aware of the program's message. The authors attribute this to the widespread media placement, but also note that " . . . it takes more than awareness to affect practices." In this regard, the community events and community-based activities of the extension workers helped to promote behavior changes. "The media campaign . . . made it easier for the technicians to motivate farmers in taking small risks by reducing inputs gradually from one season to the next. This eventually led to adoption" (Huelgas et al., 2008).

Think Blue San Diego

Like many coastal areas around the world, the City of San Diego faces pollution from storm water runoff. Runoff from rain, along with irrigation and other water-use activities (e.g., washing cars, hosing off walkways), collects contaminants from the urban region and deposits them in the bays, estuaries, and along beaches. Many of these contaminants are the direct result of specific behaviors by residents and businesses in the surrounding community, so reducing pollution will require changing behavior. Preventing storm water pollution generally occurs by managing specific pollutants like pet waste, fertilizers, and automotive fluids, but it also involves preventing water runoff. Examples of reducing runoff include properly adjusted landscape irrigation, using brooms to sweep off walkways rather than hosing them down, or planting groundcover to prevent erosion and water runoff. To help foster these changes, the City of San Diego developed its Think Blue campaign. Think Blue was launched in 2001 to "educate residents, business and industry leaders about the effects of storm water pollution and about ways to prevent that pollution from harming our environment" (Think Blue, n.d.).

Think Blue has adopted community-based social marketing (CBSM) as a guiding framework for developing, implementing, and evaluating its programs. Each program activity targets one or more specific contaminants and emphasizes positive behavior change among a specific target audience. Thus, while the Think Blue brand provides an umbrella message, the program also conducts specific outreach activities in response to regulatory requirements (e.g., TMDLs) and behavioral priority areas. One such program was a business outreach program conducted in La Jolla Shores (Tabanico & Nichols Kearns, 2009).

In conducting its regular water quality monitoring studies, the city identified bacteria levels in the La Jolla Shores Cove as a priority. The La Jolla Shores region has been designated by the California State Water Resources Control Board as an Area of Special Biological Significance (ASBS), and it serves as a regional hub for tourism and recreation. Bacterial contamination leads to beach closures, affects water quality, and ultimately has harmful consequences for the marine life in the cove. The targeted program began with community observations, in an effort to identify sources of bacterial contamination. The observations revealed a number of potential target behaviors, including litter (trash and cigarette butts), pet waste, and standing water on the streets, gutters, and alleyways. Separate interventions were developed for each of these, including a pet waste program for residents and added trash and ash receptacles in the public areas. For businesses, the program specifically targeted water discharge. Observations suggested four business practices that were linked with water runoff, including

- hosing off beach equipment (surfboards, kayaks) by rental shops,
- hosing down storefronts and sitting areas by local merchants,
- overwatering of potted plants and landscaping in the areas outside the stores,
- overflowing Dumpsters, and
- hosing down mats and equipment by restaurants (particularly in the alleyways at closing time).

Following the observations, the team conducted interviews with local businesses in the La Jolla Shores area, with questions about various practices related to water runoff, and also barriers and benefits to several best management practices (BMPs). From these interviews, the team developed a series of training materials and conducted one-on-one sessions with business owners and employees. The trainings were conducted jointly by staff from the City of San Diego and a local coastal protection nongovernmental organization (NGO) (Coastkeeper). Each training session was tailored to the type of business, and they included a site inspection, educational materials and literature, customized BMPs, utilized vivid language focusing on positive behaviors (rather than listing what not to do), and concluded by providing the business with a Think Blue window decal to be placed in the entryway.

Evaluation data were collected using behavioral observations conducted in the La Jolla Shores business area and in a similar business area in San Diego that did not receive the CBSM business outreach program (Windansea). The social marketing program lasted 18 months, and the same observation protocol was used at pretest and posttest. Relative to the control community, several outcomes were identified that were unique to the La Jolla region:

- Observed water in the gutter decreased by 67% over the 1-year period. For the control region, water in the gutter also decreased slightly but not as much as for the treatment community.
- Water flowing from weepholes along the street decreased by 67%; for the control region, weephole drainage increased slightly during the same period.
- Debris in the gutter decreased by 77% in the La Jolla region; it increased slightly in the control region.
- Standing water attributed to washing beach equipment decreased by 85% in the La Jolla region.

In addition to these changes, several of the observed behaviors did not differ between the treatment and control areas. Overwatering of plants, puddles, and standing water in alleyways and amount of wet pavement did not change during the treatment period. In addition, no differences were noted between the treatment and control sites in the amount of litter or in the amount of pet waste.

Smart About Salt, Region of Waterloo, Canada

In cold weather regions around the world, salt and sand are used to remove snow and ice from roadways and walkways. Salt is cheap, and when mixed with other products like sand or calcium chloride, it provides an effective mechanism for melting ice and improving traction. But the widespread use of salt for deicing also has many negative side effects. First, salt is corrosive to metal and causes damage to vehicles and metal structures like bridges and posts. Salt also has environmental consequences: It contaminates drinking water, is harmful to freshwater fish and other biological organisms, and can attract animals to roadways increasing deaths and accidents (e.g., moose and deer often lick the salty surfaces).

In an effort to reduce the harmful effects of salt from deicing, the Waterloo Region in Canada developed a Smart About Salt program. The program was launched in 2008 to reduce salt application rates while maintaining pedestrian and motorist safety and targeted private snow contractors and facility owners who used salt on their parking lots and sidewalks. The program involved training, accreditation, and ongoing monitoring by businesses. The training focused on best management practices and implementation of specific strategies for the storage, management, and application of salt. In the first year following its launch, the Waterloo program accredited 12 contractors and registered an additional 40 for the program. In addition, the program received support from several trade associations and a commitment from an insurance company that specializes in the snow and ice industry to provide a 5% discount to accredited contractors. As a result of the program's success in attracting contractors and business, it is currently being expanded to cover the entire province of Ontario (see www.smartaboutsalt.com).

Summary

In this chapter, we have examined social marketing programs that aim to change business practices and protect water quality. Nowhere is the effect of human activity more evident than in water quality. Water is fundamental to life on our planet, yet lakes, oceans, and aquatic areas worldwide are being polluted. While historically much of the water pollution came from single point sources, such as a factory or manufacturing facility, today nonpoint sources account for the majority of water pollution. And many of these nonpoint sources are small commercial entities, like stores, farms, or contractors.

The chapter presented two detailed cases illustrating the role of social marketing in changing business practices. In the first case, we examined the Chuyen Que Minh radio soap opera targeting Vietnamese rice farmers. The "entertainment-education" approach provided information about effective farming practices, but it was embedded within a larger serial drama about the daily challenges of a rural farming family. Over the 1-year program, farmers in the targeted region reported spraying insecticide on their crops 31% fewer times, and the effect was especially strong among farmers who reported listening to the show.

In the second case, we examined the Dirty Dairying campaign in New Zealand. One of the largest commercial activities in New Zealand is dairy farming, but herd management activities can have a direct impact on water pollution. The campaign led to the adoption of a regional accord requiring dairy farmers to adopt specific practices. By 2008, 83% of farmers had adopted fencing strategies to keep cattle out of the streams, and 93% had installed bridging for water crossings.

Questions for Discussion

1. Leanne is helping to develop the Smart About Salt program in Canada. The core element of the program involves training and certification for contractors who run small snow-removal businesses. From a social marketing perspective, what other elements could be added to attract contractors to the program? Be specific.

2. Tim is a program officer for the Think Blue program in San Diego. In an effort to address coastal bacteria pollution, Tim is developing a social marketing campaign to prevent litter from entering the storm drains in the Chollas Creek business area. He began by conducting observations in a retail location to identify the sources of litter. From these observations, Tim noted a high percentage of intentional littering behavior by shoppers in the retail areas. Nearly half of the individuals who disposed of items in these areas littered. The most frequently littered items were cigarette butts, food remnants, plastic wrappers from

purchased items, and food wrappers. Tim wants to conduct a social marketing campaign to reduce litter. Using the findings from his observations and your knowledge of social marketing, how would you proceed? What next steps would you recommend?

3. The Chuyen Que Minh radio soap opera described in this chapter reported a number of positive results and changes in the practices of rice farmers in Vietnam. Do you think that a radio soap opera would be an effective channel of communication for addressing water quality issues in your region? In thinking about this marketing approach, consider different target behaviors, their barriers and benefits, and various target audiences.

4. Liz works in the Newport Bay region. A recent water quality report showed a high level of dissolved copper in the marine water. The reading was 29 ppb, and the state standard allows for only 3.1 ppb. Studies have shown that much of this copper is coming from anti-algae paint applied to the bottom of boats (which contains copper sulfate) and the brushing of hulls that dislodges small paint chips. From a social marketing perspective, how would go about identifying the target audience for a campaign to address this problem? (For more background, see Johnson & Gonzalez, 2005.)

References

Bandura, A. (2002). Environmental sustainability by sociocognitive deceleration of population growth. In P. Schmuck & P. W. Schultz (Eds.), *Psychology of sustainable development*. New York: Kluwer.

Bewsell, D., Monaghan, R. M., & Kaine, G. (2007). Adoption of stream fencing among dairy farmers in four New Zealand catchments. *Environmental Management, 40*, 201–209.

Conway, G. R., & Pretty, J. N. (1991). *Unwelcome harvest: Agriculture and pollution*. London: Earthscan.

Dagron, A. G. (2001). *Making waves—Stories of participatory communication for social change*. New York: Rockefeller Foundation.

Environment Waikato. (2004). Clean streams: A guide to managing waterways on Waikato farms. Retrieved from http://www.ew.govt.nz/PageFiles/984/cleanstreams1.pdf

Escalada, M. M., Heong, K. L., Huan, N. H., & Chien, H. V. (2009). Changes in rice farmers' pest management beliefs and practices in Vietnam: An analytical review of survey data from 1992 to 2007. In K. L. Heong & B. Hardy (Eds.), *Planthoppers: New threats to the sustainability of intensive rice production systems in Asia* (pp. 447–456). Los Baños, Philippines: International Rice Research Institute. Retrieved from http://ricehoppers .net/wp-content/uploads/2010/04/Escalada-et-al-2009.pdf

Hamill, K. D., & McBride, G. B. (2003). River water quality trends and increasing dairying in Southland. *New Zealand Journal of Marine and Freshwater Research, 37*, 323–332.

Heong, K. L., & Escalada, M. M. (Eds.). (1997). *Pest management of rice farmers in Asia*. Los Baños, Philippines: International Rice Research Institute.

Heong, K. L., Escalada, M. M., Huan, N. H., Ky Ba, V. H., Quynh, P. V., Thiet, L. V., et al. (2008). Entertainment-education and rice pest management: A radio soap opera in Vietnam. *Crop Protection, 27*, 1392–1397. Retrieved from http://beta.irri.org/news/ bulletin/2009.06/PDFs/Heong_2008.pdf

Huelgas, Z., Templeton, D., & Castanar, P. (2008). *Three reductions, three gains technology in South Vietnam searching for evidence of economic impact.* Paper presented at the 52nd Annual Conference of the Australian Agricultural Resource Economic Society, Canberra.

Johnson, L. T., & Gonzalez, J. A. (2005). *Nontoxic antifouling: Demonstrating a solution to copper boat bottom paint pollution.* Proceedings of the 14th Biennial Coastal Zone Conference. Retrieved from http://www.csc.noaa.gov/cz/CZ05_Proceedings/pdf%20files/JohnsonL.pdf

New Zealand Ministry for the Environment. (2007). *Environment New Zealand, 2007.* Wellington, NZ: Author. Retrieved from http://www.mfe.govt.nz/publications/ser/enz07-dec07/environment-nz07-dec07.pdf

New Zealand Ministry for the Environment. (2008). *The dairying and clean streams accord: Snapshot of progress.* Wallington, NZ: Author. Retrieved from http://www.maf.govt.nz/mafnet/rural-nz/sustainable-resource-use/resource-management/dairy-clean-stream/dairycleanstream-06–07.pdf

Tabanico, J., & Nichols Kearns, J. (2009). *Behavior matters: Focused outreach to maximize behavior change.* Presented at the 2009 CASQA annual conference. Retrieved from http://stormwaterconference.com/LinkClick.aspx?fileticket=Ip0u60PxweY%3d&tabid=199

Think Blue. (n.d.). *About Think Blue.* Retrieved from http://www.thinkblue.org

United Nations. (2008). Vital water graphics: An overview of the state of the world's fresh and marine waters (2nd ed.). Retrieved from http://www.unep.org/dewa/vitalwater/

U.S. Environmental Protection Agency. (2009, January). *National water quality inventory: Report to congress, 2004 reporting cycle.* Retrieved from http://www.epa.gov/owow/305b/2004report/

U.S. Environmental Protection Agency. (2010). *Polluted runoff (nonpoint source pollution).* Retrieved from http://www.epa.gov/nps/

CHAPTER 10

Reducing Emissions

The Problem

While commercial sector emissions arise from a multitude of sources, in this chapter we will review programs to reduce emissions related to transportation (see Chapter 12 for information on reducing emissions related to commercial energy use, another significant source of emissions from this sector). The commercial sector accounts for a significant portion of global CO_2 emissions and air pollution. A report prepared by the Carbon Disclosure Project indicates that 98% of global transportation utilizes fuels made from oil and 13% of all CO_2 emissions come from transportation (Carbon Disclosure Project, 2010).

Potential Behavior Solutions

A diverse array of commercial behaviors affect emissions (Cairns et al., 2008). Below is a partial list of end-state behaviors that might be targeted to reduce commercial emission from transport.

Table 10.1	Commercial Behaviors to Reduce Transportation-Related Emissions
Area	**Examples of End-State Behaviors That Might Be Chosen for Adoption**
Fleet maintenance and purchase	• Maintain correct tire pressure. • Conduct regular engine maintenance. • Purchase fuel-efficient vehicles. • Purchase vehicles of appropriate size.

Area	Examples of End-State Behaviors That Might Be Chosen for Adoption
Fleet use	• Drive below the speed limit. • Turn engines off when parked. • Do not idle the vehicle to warm up engines in winter. • Do not quickly accelerate. • Use the most efficient travel routes. • Combine errands so that they can be done as one rather than several trips.
Commuting	• Ride a bike to work. • Walk to work. • Carpool to work. • Telecommute. • Use mass transit.

Two case studies are presented in this chapter that illustrate the remarkable results that can be achieved by agencies targeting transportation related behaviors. The first case reviews bike sharing programs that have been established in multiple locations around the globe, while the second looks at the implementation of telework at two large communications companies.

CASE #1   Bike Sharing Programs

Background

The first bike sharing program was launched in July 1965 in Amsterdam. The Witte Fiesten were standard bikes that had been painted white and made freely available for public use (DeMaio, 2009). The concept was simple. Someone who needed to travel a short distance could take one of the bikes, ride to their destination, and then leave the bike for someone else to use. However, within days of its inception Witte Fiesten was in disarray as vandals threw the bikes into canals or thieves appropriated them. Forty-five years later, bike sharing programs are faring better. There are approximately 100 bike sharing programs in 125 cities worldwide, with an additional 45 planned for introduction in 2010 alone (Shaheen, Guzman, & Zhang, 2010). Participation in these programs is staggering. For example, Velib in Paris has 23,600 bicycles in its program (DeMaio, 2009) and an average of 75,000 rentals a day (Erlanger, 2008). China's Hangzhou public bicycle system began with 10,000 bicycles in 2008 and has plans to expand to as many as 50,000 bikes (New York City Department of Planning, 2009). Indeed, approximately 139,000 bicycles are used in the various bike sharing programs worldwide.

The ill-fated Witte Fiesten program marked the first generation of bike sharing initiatives in which bikes were left around communities for public use.

Second-generation programs arose in Denmark in the 1990s (DeMaio, 2009), with the first large-scale implementation occurring in Copenhagen in 1995. Copenhagen's Bycyklen program involved solidly built bikes that could withstand abuse. These bikes could be picked up and dropped off at several locations in the downtown area and involved a coin deposit. While an improvement over the previous generation, DeMaio reports that these programs still suffered from theft due to the anonymity of the user. The third and present generation of bike sharing initiatives addresses anonymity through the use of smart cards, bike racks that lock electronically, onboard RTF of GPS for tracking of bicycles, and other enhancements (Shaheen et al., 2010). It was not until this third generation that bike sharing programs have experienced explosive growth.

Target Audience(s) and Desired Behaviors

Bike sharing programs have several target audiences. Perhaps the most important of these are last-mile commuters. One of the failings of mass transit is that it does not deliver commuters directly to their destination. Instead, users of light rail, subway, or other mass-transit options must walk or take a taxi from the closest mass transit stop to their final destination. Bike sharing stations that are located at these transit nodes provide commuters with a convenient way of bridging this last mile both at the beginning and end of their workdays. Bike sharing also targets commuters who may have driven to work but then use bikes for short trips within the downtown area. Finally, bike sharing targets tourists who utilize it along with—or separate from—mass transit. Significant revenue can be derived from tourists who primarily purchase day or week passes (New York City Department of Planning, 2009).

Bike sharing initiatives are normally designed to facilitate relatively short commutes in the central core of a city where the density of prospective users makes providing the service viable. Some universities have implemented programs where the bike is borrowed and then returned to the same location. In the United States, there are some 65 such programs with another 10 planned for introduction in 2010 (Shaheen et al., 2010).

Barriers and Benefits

There are a variety of barriers associated with the delivery of bike sharing programs. DeMaio and Gifford (2004) noted that there must be sufficient consumer demand for the program (e.g., bike sharing programs are not likely to work well in small communities), cyclists must be able to travel safely to their destination, the bike sharing program itself needs to be profitable, and theft and vandalism must be deterred. In addition, bikes must be maintained regularly and returned to bike stations to ensure that bikes are available when users want them (Shaheen et al., 2010). Perceived safety is a significant barrier to the use of bicycles (paradoxically, bike use has been demonstrated to decrease when helmets are made mandatory). While not a common perception, the health benefits of bicycling far outweigh the possibility of an accident (Pucher, Dill, & Handy, 2010). Further, the more people who bicycle the lower the risk

(Gardner, 2010). In Portland, Oregon, there was a 400% increase in cycling between 1991 and 2006, which was accompanied by a 69% decrease in accidents. Gardner noted that countries with the highest per capita cycling rates have the lowest percentage of traffic deaths. Weather is also a significant barrier to bike sharing programs and some, like Montreal's Bixi program, run seasonally given the severity of Montreal winters.

There are multiple benefits associated with bike sharing. DeMaio and Gifford (2004) noted that bike sharing programs can "reach underserved destinations, require less infrastructure, are relatively inexpensive to purchase and maintain, generally do not add to vehicular congestion, do not create pollution in their operation, and provide the user with the added benefit of exercise" (p. 2). Bike sharing programs differ markedly from other forms of transportation infrastructure regarding the speed with which they can be implemented (Shaheen et al., 2010). While light rail or subway systems might take a decade or more to put in place, bike sharing programs can be implemented in a fraction of that time. Indeed, the New York City Department of Planning (2009) reported that Paris's Velib initial deployment of 700 bike stations and 10,000 bicycles was performed in just 6 months and was doubled within a year of initial rollout. New bike stations that rely upon solar power, and therefore do not require excavation, dramatically speed up rollout (Shaheen et al., 2010). One such solar-powered program is Bixi in Montreal, which local managers suggest can have new stations installed in as little as 20 minutes (New York City Department of Planning, 2009). See Figure 10.1.

Description of the Program

With modern bike sharing programs cyclists normally sign up (place) for either a daily, weekly, or annual membership either online or at a bike station (Aceti, 2009). Once purchased, using a bike (product) is a simple as entering a code or swiping a membership card. The cyclist then rides to their destination and places the bike in a bike station close by (Shaheen et al., 2010). In many cases, these stations are no more than 300 yards apart (convenience), providing numerous locations where cyclists can return their bikes. Frequently, the first 30 minutes of a rental is not charged for (incentive), and a grace period of 15 minutes is provided if there are no open docks at a bike station. If a bike is not returned within 24 hours of its rental it is considered stolen and the renter's credit card is charged for the cost of the bike.

The majority of the existing bike share programs are run as franchise contracts in which a municipality allows a contractor to implement a bike sharing program in return for being able to sell advertising both on the bikes and at the bike stations. Some of the alternative models include municipalities running the programs themselves, having a transport agency deliver the program on behalf of the government, or having a nonprofit deliver the service (DeMaio, 2009).

To encourage cyclists to return bikes to less frequented stations, and therefore reduce the need for the company to do this, credits in terms of time or money are sometimes provided. These credits can have a substantial impact upon bikes being returned to less utilized stations (Shaheen et al., 2010).

Figure 10.1 Bixi Montreal Bike Sharing Station

Source: Graphic provided courtesy of Bixi Montreal.

DeMaio (2009) reported that bike sharing programs have led to a 1% to 1.5% increase in bicycle use in cities that have low levels of bike ridership. For instance, in Paris, bicycling rose from 1% in 2001 to 2.5% in 2007 and that 50 million trips were made on Velib bicycles in the first 2 years alone. Note that these increases are not due to the bike sharing programs alone as their introduction is often associated with enhancements in infrastructure that support biking.

Bike sharing provides an emission-free transportation option. The emission reductions, however, that are associated with bike sharing are challenging to estimate as the use of a bicycle does not mean that someone would have used a car instead. Nonetheless, the distance traveled on a daily basis is remarkable. For example, Velib users in Paris take an average of 78,000 trips per day for a total of 312,000 km (Shaheen et al., 2010). If these trips were completely displacing car travel, then an approximate 57,720 kg of CO_2 are averted each day. What percentage of these trips might be displacing personal automobile use? A survey of Washington, D.C., SmartBike users suggests that bike sharing displaced 16% of trips that would otherwise have been made by personal vehicle (Shaheen et al., 2010), while in several European cities roughly 8% of personal automobile trips were found to be displaced. If taxi hires are included as well this percentage increases to 13% in Paris (Gardner, 2010).

Bike sharing has several other positive impacts. Public health care costs are skyrocketing. Central to increasing health care costs is the burden that inactive lifestyles have upon the health care system. Gardner (2010) reported that in Minnesota, health care costs are significantly higher for those that are overweight or obese, 12% and 37% respectively. Further, the State of Minnesota expects that 31% of the increase in health care costs between 2005 and 2020 will be related to health problems associated with being overweight or obese. Bike sharing programs, granted that individuals who are overweight or obese use them, can contribute to an improved quality of life in addition to lessening the burden on the health care system.

In addition to reducing emissions, congestion through the displacement of trips, and enhancing health, bike sharing programs also are significantly cheaper to deliver than are infrastructure initiatives for automobiles (Shaheen et al., 2010). For example, providing parking for bicycles is 30 to 300 times less expensive than providing parking for vehicles (Gardner, 2010).

Critical Review

Bike sharing programs can be enhanced in several ways (Shaheen et al., 2010). Increasing the mobility of bike stations provides flexibility to respond to varying needs within a community, such as increasing the number of bikes that are available for travel between a subway stop and a sporting event. As noted previously, the Bixi system in Montreal makes use of solar powered bike stations that can be relatively easily moved from one location to another as needed. These solar powered stations do not require that electrical work be done prior to a station being installed. In addition, increasing the durability of bikes lessens the need for repairs, while enhancing the traceability of bikes not only deters theft but also provides necessary information that allows bike sharing coordinators to ensure that bikes are available where needed.

In addition to improving the delivery of the bike sharing programs, there are numerous actions that can be taken to increase the attractiveness and safety of bicycling. These actions increase the viability of bike sharing programs as well as bicycling in general. Bike lanes and separate bike paths, which visually or physically separate cyclists from motorists, have been found to be related to cycling frequency as has the distance to a bike path. Those who live closest to a path (within a half mile) are more likely to cycle than those who live just a short distance farther away (Vernez-Moudon et al., 2005). Some other initiatives that facilitate biking include traffic calming, bike parking, and shower facilities (Pucher et al., 2010).

CASE #2 ATT's & Nortel's Telework Programs (United States, Canada)

Background

Over 30 years ago, advances in telecommunications and computer technology led to informal arrangements where employees made personal provisions with their managers to work from home rather than the office (Atkyns, Blazek, & Roitz, 2002). These initial forays into off-site work led to large-scale implementation of telework by companies, governmental agencies, and institutions. Telework involves employees utilizing computers and telecommunications technology to work at settings other than a traditional workplace. Telework can occur in four different settings: the home, a satellite office that has been established by an employer, a telework center from which employees from multiple agencies work, or a combination of these and other locations (Transport Canada, 2010). The potential impact of telework programs is enormous—the U.S. Department of Transportation estimates that commutes are responsible for fully one third of all vehicle miles traveled (U.S. Office of Personnel Management, 2010).

Transport Canada notes that telework has multiple benefits for communities. These include

- reduced congestion;
- reduced transportation related emissions;
- enhanced viability of rural communities by eliminating or reducing the need to commute from these communities to larger centers; and
- enhanced resiliency for companies, governmental agencies, and institutions due to having a more dispersed workforce which can lessen the disruption caused by large-scale events such as severe weather, energy outages, and terrorist attacks.

Telework can, however, have unintended negative effects. For example, errands that might once have been conducted on a trip back from work are now done individually. Further, a vehicle that was once unavailable for other family members to use is now accessible. These "rebound" effects lessen the reduction in vehicle miles traveled (Sorrell, 2007). Further, telework may inadvertently encourage urban sprawl and longer commutes. Workers who are no longer traveling daily to a central location may feel more comfortable with purchasing a home in a more rural location, which may have the unintended effect of lengthening their commutes on the days in which they do travel to work as well as increasing their commutes for daily errands.

Target Audience(s) and Desired Behaviors

The traditional target audience of telework programs are employees who work in office settings who rely on computer equipment and telecommunications for many of their work-related tasks and who do not need to meet daily face-to-face with other staff or customers.

Telework programs target the daily commutes made by office employees. They replace or reduce these daily commutes to central offices with either shorter commutes to satellite locations or replace them with work that is done at home. Most telework is done at home rather than in satellite office spaces (Transport Canada, 2010).

Barriers and Benefits

Telework presents barriers and benefits for both employees and employers (Canadian Center for Occupational Health and Safety, 2010). For employees, the benefits include enhanced productivity, better balance between work and other demands, and more disposable time. Transport Canada estimates that employees who would normally commute daily 30 minutes in each direction save the equivalent of six work weeks a year by not commuting (Transport Canada, 2010). While there are several significant benefits for employees, telework also has some notable barriers for employees. These include reduced physical activity as most telework occurs in the home and consequently teleworkers are less likely to walk than if they were in an office. Further, there is a blurring of work and nonwork, greater family distractions, and less engagement with coworkers.

For employers, the benefits may include enhanced retention of employees, higher productivity and reduced absenteeism, fewer lost hours due to commute delays, larger potential employee pool due to removing the need to be geographically close, and financial savings due to a reduction in the office space needed. Barriers include safeguarding the security and confidentiality of office information; less control over workspaces and, therefore, higher liability for work-related accidents and injuries; and costs for setting up teleworking and management of employees who are not centralized (Canadian Center for Occupational Health and Safety, 2010; Transport Canada, 2010).

Description of the Program

The implementation of large-scale telework initiatives (product) requires planning on the part of an employer. Many organizations will begin this process with the creation of a planning committee that includes representation from human resources, unions, IT, and legal and management of the departments to be affected (U.S. Office of Personnel Management, 2010; Transport Canada 2010). This committee must decide what locations are appropriate for telework (e.g., home-based or satellite offices), who is eligible for telework, how teleworkers will be managed, and provide training and ongoing evaluation of telework initiatives. Further, the employer must market the program to their organization to encourage participation. Telework programs have now been implemented by a large variety of organizations, two of which are described next.

The U.S. telecommunications company AT&T has had telework programs in place since 1992. As of 2009, more than 10,000 employees have been approved for telework (AT&T, 2010). A recent survey of more than 9,000 telework employees indicated that work–life balance was the most important benefit of engaging in the program (incentive). The average round-trip commute of these employees was 113 minutes, which participants reported was now being spent on enriching their personal or family lives. In addition, fully 96% of respondents indicated that time saved from commuting was used toward being a more productive employee. This finding is mirrored in reports from managers who supervise teleworking employees. Ninety-eight percent of these managers report that teleworking had either a positive or neutral impact on employee productivity (AT&T, 2010). In 2009, AT&T's teleworkers eliminated 142 million miles that normally would have been commuted. Further, these reductions in commutes are associated with financial savings for employees in gasoline not purchased. AT&T estimates that their trip-reduction initiative is responsible for a reduction of 61,637 metric tons of CO_2 equivalents per year. Importantly, these effects are *after* accounting for the rebound effect of errands and other trips that would normally be part of daily commutes.

The Canadian telecommunications company, Nortel, has had telework programs in place for over a decade. In addition to reducing their environmental impact, a survey of Nortel teleworkers revealed that these employees reported improved productivity, less stress, and increased well-being as result of participating in the program. Fully 10% of Nortel employees are full-time teleworkers, and 85% of the workforce work away from the central offices at least occasionally (Nortel, 2010). The company provides workers with a secure connection to their intranet, as well as e-mail, software, and company directories (Transport Canada, 2010).

Critical Review

The success of telework programs is largely due to the benefits that accrue to both employers and the employees. In the environmental field, it is rare to find programs that have such clear benefits for all involved. However, as previously noted, there are barriers to its successful implementation. One of the most important barriers is that teleworking limits direct engagement with coworkers and management. This lack of engagement can be partially mitigated by making more frequent use of videoconferencing for meetings. With telework, face-to-face meetings are frequently replaced with teleconference calls. Teleconference calls forgo the richness that is part of face-to-face conversations. Further, it is often difficult to know who is speaking in a teleconference meeting. Consequently, staff who remotely join a meeting are at significant disadvantage.

Videoconferencing has progressed to the point that it is a viable alternative for meetings of several hours in duration. One of the most useful videoconferencing implementations mirrors the setup of a boardroom. Imagine a boardroom that contains only half of the normal boardroom table. Central office staff sit in a semicircle around their "half" of the boardroom table. Where the remainder of the table should be is a video screen that has projected on to it the participants who are joining the meeting remotely. For those who are joining remotely, on their computer screens they see the central office participants sitting around the table as well as the other staff who have joined the meeting remotely. Dedicated videoconferencing rooms such as this have several advantages over traditional teleconferences. They more closely approximate the interactions that occur in normal workspaces by allowing staff to not only hear a coworker but see that person as well. While not inexpensive to implement, the establishment of dedicated videoconferencing rooms can be offset through savings in air travel as these meeting rooms can also be used to replace shorter duration meetings that involve air travel.

Other Notable Programs

Go Boulder

Boulder, Colorado, has one of the most progressive mass transit programs in North America. In order to lessen traffic congestion and reduce air pollution, Boulder City Council initiated a far-reaching sustainable transportation program in the 1990s. This program was based upon community barrier research that identified impediments to the use of mass transit and other forms of sustainable transport. This research revealed a number of barriers to mass transit use. One of the most important transit barriers involved inconvenience. In short, residents were reluctant to ride the bus if they had to wait what they perceived to be a significant amount of time for the bus to arrive. In response, Boulder replaced a number of their larger buses with smaller buses that ran more frequently (product, convenience). As a consequence, riders could be insured that they could go show up at a bus stop and not have to wait longer than a few minutes for their bus to show up. In fact, the buses ran frequently enough that bus schedules were no longer necessary. These smaller buses fed into larger feeder lines that took commuters downtown. Boulder's research also revealed that residents were wary of using the bus if it meant that it would be difficult for them to get home quickly if a child were ill or some other family emergency arose. To address this barrier, Go Boulder bus passes include a guaranteed ride home (product). In the case of a family emergency, a transit user simply has to call the number on the back of their transit pass to be taken home by taxi. Boulder also increased ridership by selling bus passes to local companies and the University of Colorado in bulk. As a consequence, many employees and students who would not otherwise have a bus pass had one simply because they were an employee of a particular business or a student at the university. These and other changes that the City of Boulder put in place have resulted in increased mass transit usage along with increased walking and biking. Overall, there was a 6% modal shift away from single occupant vehicle trips toward more sustainable forms of transportation.

1-2-3 Campaign Against Global Warming

The First Unitarian Church in Portland, Oregon, initiated a campaign in 2001 to combat climate change (North, 2002). Following a presentation to the congregation on the threats posed by global warming (communication), parishioners were asked to make a commitment to reduce the temperature in their home by 1 degree, their driving speed by 2 miles per hour, and replace three incandescent lightbulbs with compact fluorescent lightbulbs (CFLs). Project organizers indicate that these three simple actions result in reductions in CO_2 of 1,300 pounds per year and average annual savings of $90 per household. Participants who signed the pledge forms received mailings from the church about the program, support from the church staff, and demonstrations of CFLs at the church.

A total of 412 households participated in the 1-2-3 program, resulting in an estimated 580,000 pound annual reduction in CO_2 emissions. Follow-up survey research documented that 98% of participating households carried out all (55%) or some of the actions (43%) they had pledged.

Summary

The case studies presented in this chapter underscore the dramatic impact that well-designed programs can have upon emissions from the commercial sector. They also underscore the importance of quickly diffusing these successes so that other organizations are able to benefit from the lessons learned in implementing their own programs. Many organizations are dealing with very similar behavioral changes that need to be addressed. When similar barriers and benefits exist across organizations, it is prudent to provide easy access to information and resources regarding successful programs to enhance their quick adoption. This same argument was made in the chapter on residential emissions (see Chapter 4), but it bears repeating as frequently organizations are attempting to create programs solely in-house simply because external resources do not exist that allow the quick adoption of programs that have been found to be successful elsewhere.

Questions for Discussion

1. How might the uncovering of barriers and benefits for a behavior to be targeted in an organization differ from uncovering barriers and benefits for a behavior to be targeted for a residential audience?

2. How can a company's desire to keep private information about their programs be reconciled with the need to quickly disseminate lessons learned across organizations?

References

Aceti, J. (2009). *Bike sharing programs*. Unpublished report.

AT&T. (2010). *Citizenship and sustainability*. Retrieved from http://www.att.com/gen/corpo rate-citizenship?pid=8506

Atkyns, R., Blazek, M., & Roitz, J. (2002). Measurement of environmental impacts of tele-work adoption amidst change in complex organizations: AT&T survey methodology and results. *Resources, Conservation and Recycling, 36*, 267–285.

Cairns, S., Sloman, L., Newson, C., Anable, J., Kirkbride, A., & Goodwin, P. (2008). Smarter choices: Assessing the potential to achieve traffic reduction using "Soft measures." *Transport Reviews, 28*(5), 593–618.

Canadian Center for Occupational Health and Safety. (2010). *Telework.* Retrieved from http://www.ccohs.ca/oshanswers/hsprograms/telework.html

Carbon Disclosure Project. (2010). *Carbon Disclosure Project transportation report.* Retrieved from https://www.cdproject.net/CDPResults/CDP-Transport-Report.pdf

DeMaio, P. (2009, May). Bike-sharing: History, impacts, models of provision, and future. *Journal of Public Transportation, 12*(4), 41–56.

DeMaio, P., & Gifford, J. (2004). Will smart bikes succeed as public transportation in the United States? *Journal of Public Transportation, 7*(2), 1–15.

Erlanger, S. (2008, July 13). A fashion catches on in Paris: Cheap bicycle rentals. *The New York Times.*

Gardner, G. (2010). *Power to the pedals.* World Watch report. Retrieved from www.worldwatch.org

New York City Department of City Planning. (2009). *Bike-share opportunities in New York.* New York, New York. Retrieved from http://www.nyc.gov/html/dcp/pdf/transportation/bike_share_complete.pdf

Nortel. (2010). *Nortel IT implementation steps for a comprehensive integrated work environment.* Retrieved from http://www.nortel.com/corporate/nortel_on_nortel/collateral/teleworking.pdf

North, R. (2002). *1-2-3 Campaign against global warming.* Retrieved from http://www.cbsm.com/cases/123+campaign+against+global+warming_138

Pucher, J., Dill, J., & Handy, S. (2010). Infrastructure, programs, and policies to increase bicycling: An international review. *Preventive Medicine,* S106-S125.

Shaheen, S., Guzman, S., & Zhang, H. (2010). *Bikesharing in Europe, the Americas, and Asia: Past, present, and future.* Retrieved from http://76.12.4.249/artman2/uploads/1/TRB10-Bikesharing.Final.pdf

Sorrell, S. (2007). *The rebound effect: An assessment of the evidence for economy-wide energy savings from improved energy efficiency.* UK Energy Research Centre Report.

Transport Canada. (2010). *Telework in Canada.* Retrieved from http://www.tc.gc.ca/eng/programs/environment-utsp-teleworkcanada-1052.htm

U.S. Office of Personnel Management. (2010). *A guide to telework in the federal government.* Retrieved from http://www.telework.gov/guidance_and_legislation/telework_guide/index.aspx

Vernez-Moudon, A. V., Lee, C., Cheadle, A. D., Collier, C. W., Johnson, D., Schmid, T. L., & Weather, R. D. (2005). Cycling and the built environment, a U.S. perspective. *Transportation Research Part D, 10,* 245–261.

CHAPTER 11

Reducing Water Use

The Problem

Many of us take water for granted. We turn on the faucet and out pours as much water as we want for drinking, cleaning, gardening, and other myriad uses of water. We assume that the water has been treated and fit for all these uses.

Yet much of the world's population suffers from a lack of sufficient water. Countries such as Yemen, Jordan, and others must husband the scarce water resources that they have. The water must be clean and usable whether for drinking or for industrial and agricultural uses.

But even closer to home in the United States, we experience water shortages. The State of California has wrestled for years with how to allocate their scarce water supplies. Should California grow rice given the water intensity required? Should California encourage residents and visitors to install water-saving devices, take fewer showers, flush the toilets less often, and take other measures to conserve on water usage?

Industry and agriculture are major users of water. Without water, companies such as Coca-Cola and Pepsi-Cola would not continue to exist. Automobile manufacturers need to supply water in their factories not only to meet employee drinking and washing needs but also to wash materials, clean floors, and perform other applications. Hotels need to supply water not only in their rooms but in their kitchens and laundries and for floor cleaning and other uses.

Clearly commercial users of water must be educated to use water carefully. We need to persuade commercial users of water to adopt water conservation practices.

Potential Behavior Solutions

Certain companies have been especially proactive in expanding and protecting their water supplies. For example, Coca-Cola knows that its future depends upon having access to good quality water. Coca-Cola has invested large sums of money to protect and enhance water sources around the world. It formed a partnership with the World Wildlife Fund (WWF) to work together to[1]

- measurably conserve seven key watersheds;
- improve the efficiency of the Coca-Cola system's water use;
- support more efficient water use in the company's agricultural supply chain, beginning with sugarcane;
- decrease the Coca-Cola system's carbon dioxide emissions and energy use; and
- inspire a global movement by uniting industries, conservation organizations, and others in the conservation and protection of freshwater resources around the world.

ITT is another company highly invested in promoting water conservation. ITT, which makes pumps and other equipment related to managing water systems, runs a very successful program called ITT Watermark. ITT helped establish the Stockholm Water Foundation, Stockholm Water Prize, and Stockholm Junior Water Prize. Bjorn Von Euler of ITT serves on the Board for Water Environment Federation and the IWA Strategic Council as well as on Water For People's Board.

Every commercial user of water needs to ask a set of questions related to their use of water:

- How much water do we consume annually, and what are the major uses of water in our operations?
- In each water use, is the amount being used efficiently? Is there any leakage? Are there any devices or equipment that would give us savings in the amount of water used? Can we justify the investments in the water savings to pay off in a reasonable period?
- Have we set up a person or group to monitor our water use and advise on improvements that we can make in water management?

Table 11.1 lists some end-state behaviors in commercial water usage that would help conserve water.

Table 11.1 Examples of End-State Behaviors	
Area of Focus	**Examples of End-State Behaviors That Might Be Chosen for Adoption**
Hotels	• Put signs in bathrooms suggesting guests leave towels on the rack unless they need exchanging. • Install faucet aerators or restrictors and low-flow showerheads.
Manufacturing/Industrial	• Upgrade process equipment such as washing machines and cooling towers. • Detect and repair leaks.
Agricultural	• Choose to grow crops that require less water consumption. • Improve the farm irrigation system to use water more efficiently.
Office buildings	• Replace older 3.5 gallons per flush (gpf) toilets with more modern 1.6 gpf models. • Install low-flow faucet aerators.

The real need in a city or a country is to identify those industries and applications where the largest water savings are possible. High users of water are hotels and farms among others. Therefore, we decided to feature two cases of commercial water conservation, the first dealing with the hotel industry, in this case in Seattle, Washington, and the second dealing with agriculture, in this case in the country of Jordan.

CASE #1   Conserving Water in Hotels (Seattle, Washington)[2]

Background

In 1999, Seattle Public Utilities (SPU) undertook a research project with its wholesale water partners to see what could be done to influence hotels in Seattle to reduce water consumption. The researchers on the project were Philip Paschke, Roger E. Van Gelder, and Heidi Siegelbaum.

Hotels are users of water in the following areas:

- Guest rooms are equipped for the use of water in sinks, showers, bathtubs, and toilets.
- Kitchens use water for serving water, using water in cooking, and washing dishes.
- Housekeepers use water for cleaning bathrooms and floors.
- Laundry areas use water and their equipment to wash linen, towels, and guest clothing submitted to them for cleaning.
- Water usage is affected by the hotel's decision on how many ice machines to locate in the hotel.
- Hotels with swimming pools need to replenish water in the swimming pool.

The purpose was to evaluate the effectiveness of combining an engineering with a behavioral, educational, and organizational analysis to reduce water consumption in the participating hotels and to provide a potential road map for other area hotels to utilize in their resource conservation efforts.

At the time, SPU provided water to over 1.3 million people and businesses in the greater Seattle area. Four reasons that SPU decided to target the hotel industry for water conservation included the following:

1. The lodging sector, representing less than 1% of commercial accounts, consumes approximately 5% of commercial water in SPU's service area.

2. The Pacific Northwest is a receptive market for emerging sustainable practices.

3. Hotels are very recognizable to the public and are sensitive to public perception.

4. A sector approach provides efficiencies by addressing many of the barriers that need to be uncovered.

The Seattle project team found that total water usage across a wide variety of hotels ranged from under 100 gallons per day per room (gpd/rm) to over 400 gpd/rm. Older, luxury hotels and hotels with full service restaurants and on-site laundry facilities typically exhibited the highest water usage per room. SPU estimated the savings potential to vary from between 0% and 45% of total usage, with between 10% and 20% taken as typical.

The hotel industry had already recognized the high cost savings that would result if they improved their water using equipment and if they encouraged their guests to conserve on water usage. A national survey of a sample of U.S. lodgings in 2000 showed that a majority of lodgings had adopted some combination of measures to reduce water consumption, including low-flow fixtures, towel–linen exchange programs, ozone laundry systems, and staff education and outreach. Several hotel chains, including La Quinta Inns, Holiday Inns, Hyatt, and boutique hotels such as the Boston Park Plaza and Colony Hotel had adopted water conservation policies. The SPU team wanted to implement similar strategies in the City of Seattle.

Target Audience(s) and Desired Behaviors

The Seattle project team knew that they wanted to develop a program to be used by all the hotels in the Seattle area. But to develop the program they needed to study a subsample of hotels who would agree to participate.

In sampling the participating Seattle hotels about their practices, the researchers found that a majority had installed some water conserving measures in the past five years.

- The most frequent step was to alert guests who stay multiple nights to have the option of not having towels and linens laundered daily.
- About 90% of the hotels had installed faucet aerators or restrictors and low-flow showerheads.
- Only 50% stated they had installed low-flow toilets.
- Air-cooled ice machines were used in 60% of the surveyed hotels.
- Only 5% had what they considered to be efficient commercial dishwashers.

The project team then developed a pilot program involving two hotels, the Westin and the West Coast Grand. The pilot program sought to investigate water conservation opportunities related both to "equipment measures" involving replacement or significant upgrades to existing equipment and "behavioral measures" related to equipment maintenance and to employee/guest education. Many commercial water conservation studies have focused primarily on equipment measures only. However, without adequate employee education and establishment of regular maintenance schedules, water savings projected for equipment replacements may easily be lost or overshadowed.

Overall water use patterns for the two study hotels prior to this effort fell within the expected range. The Westin, which is an older hotel complete with in-house laundry and a variety of banquet and restaurant facilities but with no site irrigation, consumed approximately 212 gpd/rm during the August study period. The West Coast Grand, which is a newer facility with low-flow toilet fixtures, banquet and restaurant facilities but no in-house laundry consumed 129 gpd/rm.

The amount of water consumed per room varied with each facility. The biggest users of water were kitchens and public areas, guest showers, guest toilets, and laundries. Relatively less water consumption occurred with guest floor ice and guest sinks.

For each of the two hotels audited, potential water savings were estimated to equal approximately one third of current water consumption. For the older Westin Hotel, close to 90% of the projected savings would come from equipment measures primarily related to upgrades to restrooms, ice machines, and laundry equipment. For the West Coast Grand Hotel, a converted office building, close to 90% would come from "behavioral" measures, primarily related to maintenance and operation of heating and cooling equipment.

To facilitate the partnership nature of this project, SPU drafted a participation agreement that the participating hotels were asked to sign. Factors considered to assess conservation potential included average gpd/rm, number of hotel rooms, investment criteria used by the parent corporation, and willingness to participate. Those hotels who participated agreed, among other things, to make every effort to

(i) implement water conserving hardware and educational programs and

(ii) implement at least one recommendation annually for the 3 years following the close of the project.

The project team needed to identify the main areas in hotel operations that played a role in water usage. They needed to know the amount of *actual water usage* as against the *potential water savings* and *payback period for recovering the investment cost* if water conservation were to be justified and successfully implemented. They distinguished between equipment-related measures and other behavioral measures. They selected the following as priority behaviors to influence:

Equipment-Related Measures: Considerable water conservation opportunities were identified through replacing or substantially upgrading older equipment. After utility incentives are factored in, most of these upgrades could be made with a simple payback of 2 years or less. The most significant equipment measures include the following:

- Guest Room Toilets: Replace older 3.5 gpf toilets with more modern 1.6 gpf models. In addition to excessive flush volumes, individual floor metering revealed significant water loss attributed to leaking flappers.
- Guest Showers: Replace older 3.5 gpm (gallons per minute) showerheads with models using 2.5 gpm or less.
- Faucet Flow Restrictors: Replace existing 2.5 gpm and 3.0 gpm faucet aerators with 1.5 gpm or lower aerators.

- Single Pass Water-Cooled Ice Machines: Replace existing water-cooled ice machines or connect to an existing cooling water recirculation system.
- Laundry: Install ozone systems and/or rinse water recycle system to reduce laundry water and associated water heating and chemical use.
- Dishwashers: Replace inefficient dishwashers with water conserving models. This measure may only be cost effective for dishwashers that are already nearing the end of their expected life.

Behavioral Measures: A number of measures were identified relating to maintenance and other behavioral changes. The most significant behavioral measures include the following:

- Toilet Leaks: Significant sources of leakage were discovered related to deteriorated toilet flappers. Implement a regular toilet flapper replacement schedule.
- Steam Heat Exchangers: Install sub-meters on cold water feed lines to all heat exchangers. Regularly log readings and make repairs to heat exchangers as necessary.
- Other Sub-Metering: Install sub-meters for other significant water consuming operations including dishwashers, pools and spas, laundry, irrigation, and kitchens. Log usage and perform maintenance as necessary to reduce waste.
- Towers: Cooling towers were not being operated at optimum levels.
- Conductivity Readings: These should be recorded at least weekly.
- Food and Beverage: Significant excess use was observed in kitchens where continuously running water, often for hours at a time, was used for thawing frozen food and washing rice. Educate kitchen staff regarding correct methods for thawing frozen food and rinsing rice. Frozen food may be thawed in a refrigeration unit, and sushi rice should be agitated in a colander. Additionally, sub-metering of kitchen use and back charging costs to the kitchens could help raise awareness among kitchen managers of wasteful practices.
- Housekeeping: Publicize towel–linen programs. Educate custodial staff to reduce number of times toilet is flushed during room cleaning.

Barriers and Benefits

Clearly each of these areas of concern needed a separate and well-thought-out program of how to convince the hotels and guests to change the behavior. There were many barriers to face. The barriers included the high cost of replacing equipment, work and noise that would inconvenience guests, guests who felt the level of service was reduced, risks to the hotel's image, risks to the hotel's profitability, and other barriers. Let's take some examples.

Replacing Guest Room Toilets. A study revealed that replacing old toilets with new toilets could save almost 2 gpf. However, replacing dozens of toilets in a hotel would face a number of barriers:

- Our cost of buying and installing more efficient toilets would exceed the discretionary funds available to this hotel.
- Our hotel would want to do it but corporate says no, given the other and often higher priorities begging for budget support.
- We calculated the payback period, and it is 4 years. We don't undertake investments unless they pay back in 1 or 2 years.
- Replacing so many toilets will present a nuisance to our guests in terms of making their room unavailable for some hours and the additional work noise that will be created in the hotel.

Ice Machines. Ice machines use a lot of water. In high priced hotels, they are usually found on every floor. In other hotels, they are usually found on every other floor. Wouldn't it make more sense to provide only one ice machine? The hotel would need fewer machines, and probably less water and ice would be consumed. However, the objections would include the following:

- Guests who use a lot of ice would regard this as an inconvenience and switch their future business to another hotel.
- This will increase the frequency of up-and-down elevator movement, which means the use of more electricity and slower elevator availability.

Towel–Linen Program. Much water can be saved if guests would agree to use their towels and linens again instead of having them renewed every evening. Many hotels have introduced this program, but many others have not. Even in the adopting hotels, the number of guests who retain their towels and linens may be in the 5% to 25% range. The hotel's objections to setting up such a program include the following:

- We are a luxury hotel, and the guests would be offended or largely ignore the program.
- There would be a fear that guests will complain or previous guests have already complained.
- Management interprets the towel–linen program as being "cheap."
- Housekeeping values daily washing as part of its excellence in service.
- The program was instituted in the past without proper accompanying materials explaining the basis for program adoption.
- Corporate policy is against towel–linen programs.
- There is a belief that daily linen service should be commensurate with room price.

The SPU believes that most hotel guests want to be part of the solution. If clear messaging is communicated in a positive way, the benefits to the hotel go far beyond just reducing their water and sewer and energy utilities bill. The hotel can provide a high quality experience that does not involve wasting resources and a clear link to the environmental benefits is in the hotel's best interest.

Regarding the barriers, the social marketer has to see what answers and motivations might address each barrier. Sometimes a barrier might be shown to be exaggerated. For example, many guests who are environmentally oriented might be upset in not finding a towel–linen program offered in a particular hotel. Sometimes the estimate of costs and savings and the payback period may be incorrect. Even if correct, there may be incentive money available from governmental grants to help pay for water conservation steps that a hotel can take.

Hotels must be persuaded of the benefits that they will achieve through water monitoring and conservation. The most persuasive benefit to hotels is cost savings where these cost savings do not affect the hotel's service quality or reputation. Beyond this is the benefit of doing the right thing and being seen as an environmentally caring hotel.

Description of the Program

Traditional methods of environmental education, outreach, and program activity predicate change based on providing information. The overwhelming body of behavioral science research suggests that information alone is rarely enough to change entrenched habits that have environmental impacts.

The SPU saw the necessity of going beyond disseminating information and using a marketing approach. SPU adopted the traditional 4P framework (product, price, place, and promotion) to convince hotels to carry out water conservation practices.

As for product, SPU had to show tangible evidence that conservation behavior would be feasible and profitable. Hotels were given the information needed to calculate the amount of investment needed, the amount of water saved, and the payback period, hoping that the hotels would move toward making the most profit-returning investments in water conservation. Hotels were also provided with information about other hotels that had managed water conservation and the subsequent savings.

As for price, SPU offers financial incentives that can be either straightforward rebates, a fixed amount per unit (e.g., toilets or custom incentives where the project is evaluated for estimated savings, project life, and estimated cost before an incentive is determined), but in no case would the incentive exceed 50% of the full project cost. The laundry water reclaim system would be an example of this. Either rebate or financial incentive will be paid after a project passes site inspection and the proper documentation is received. There may be other conditions required or payment options, but basically there are no payments until completion.

As for place, the project team distributed information to hotels on the importance of "going green." Materials were provided on how hotels could inform guests of the need to protect the environment and conserve water.

As for promotion, the project team supplied educational and outreach materials to hotels to encourage water conservation. This included presentations, articles, workshops, brown bag lunches, contests, internal training, videotape production, water and energy newsletters, posters, promotional gifts and prizes, sponsorship, external publicity, public relations, and support from local groups.

Besides the traditional 4Ps, SPU utilized two additional tools, norms and prompts:

- Staff and manager orientation materials aimed to get hotel management to adopt the norm of water conservation. The project team sponsored events that brought management to water treatment systems to increase their awareness of the importance of conservation.
- Prompts included posters reminding food and beverage (F&B) personnel to thaw in refrigerators, posters reminding associates and managers to report leaks, and paycheck stuffers to remind employees to use water carefully.

Each hotel had to decide how green it wanted to go. A hotel has a natural incentive to improve equipment and metering where there are clear cost savings. But each hotel had to decide whether it should understate its "going green" or make it a key positioning in its competitive strategy.

It turned out that the Westin applied a more or less systematic approach to implementing water conservation measures. The Westin had reduced their overall water use, as measured by gpd/rm, by about 25%. Some of the measures implemented were a total room toilet change out, all new 1.0 gallon aerators, new 2.5 gpm showerheads, a laundry water reclaim system, efficient kitchen equipment, and tracking the daily savings of a towel–linen exchange program. There were some other specific behavioral measures like reducing the rice washing in one of their restaurants, less toilet flushing by housekeeping, and reduced pressure washing on the loading dock.

SPU has paid incentives for many of the projects at the Westin. The Westin received incentives or rebates for toilets, ice machine replacements and other kitchen equipment, free aerators and prerinse spray heads, incentives for laundry water reclaim, and lots of free technical assistance and end use metering.

Evaluation

After the pilot implementation, the project team recommended that other hotels take the following steps:

- The water conservation effort needed adoption and support from upper management, including the CEO, CFO, and board of directors.
- A question-and-answer fact sheet needed to be distributed to every department, including national sales and reservations offices, setting forth the basis, benefits, and attributes of each program. This will ensure the entire staff and corporate offices are well informed and working from the same level of understanding.
- New staff orientation needed training materials, meetings, and employee manuals.

- All housekeeping and laundry staff needed to be retrained to ensure acceptance and understanding.
- Environmental criteria needed to be written into job descriptions and performance standards.
- The adoption of incentive systems was needed to promote conservation measures. Outreach to guests was also needed. Several hotels use cash bonus incentives to reduce water use.
- Reporting out to investors regarding adoption and progress, using performance measures and making programmatic adjustments, was needed every quarter. Communicating to the public through the hotel's websites, advertising and sales materials, and conversing with current and prospective guests about water and other conservation efforts was needed.

Substantial water conservation opportunities were identified. For each of the two hotels audited, potential water savings equaled approximately one third of current water consumption. However, for the Westin, which is an older facility, close to 90% of the projected savings were from equipment measures, while for the West Coast Grand, close to 90% were for "behavioral" measures, primarily related to operation of heating and cooling equipment.

The SPU provided the following basic guidelines in developing water conservation projects:

1. Identify both internal and external barriers to change and remove or minimize them.

   If the corporate office has a short return on investment (ROI) criteria that prohibits more expensive but highly effective retrofits, work with them to change those criteria. Discuss how sustainable practice is economically preferable and helps create a culture of opportunity and change.

2. Give people and the organizations they work in the tools to change: what's the issue, who to call, what to do. It can be as simple as giving out phone numbers and the authority to make change in each department, for each person's position.

3. Information must come from a credible source the receiving audience will listen to.

   Based on staff meetings, this might be the chief engineer, their peers, or the hotel magazines and periodicals read for current trends. Despite the trend in antigovernmental sentiment, local government is still considered a good source because it is relatively impartial and objective.

4. Use champions from the same industry. For the hotel sector, hotels will be more interested in what other lodging companies are doing. Accordingly, a case method approach would be useful in encouraging change.

5. Tailor information specifically to the sector, and use the types of persons characteristic of that industry in collateral development.

6. Provide immediate and regular feedback to support the desired behavior. Remote feedback is less effective.

7. The message should be frequent, positive, and the action framed such that the receiving audience believes it is losing something, as opposed to gaining something, as the result of not taking certain action (you lose by not practicing water conservation).

8. Use focus groups to ascertain whether "conservation" and "efficiency" impart the same meaning. Even though they are essentially the same, research findings suggest that the word *conservation* is viewed as having to sacrifice something of value and, therefore, people are resistant to the notion.

9. Design methods and tools in such a manner that persons and the organizations they work in can "pay attention" to water efficiency and water demands in the context of their daily experience.

10. Understand the audience's unique perspective and barriers to change.

11. Use existing social networks to diffuse information and use effective opinion leaders.

Critical Review

The most obvious shortcomings in the studies cited include a primary focus on upgrades to "domestic" fixtures (representing around one third of total use), with a corresponding lack of focus on process equipment or leaks. Additionally, there is a lack of follow-up data correlating actual savings with projected savings. Both of these shortcomings appear related to lack of sub-metering data to accurately test specific process equipment or to accurately measure results. Based on this, it is suggested that future studies use sub-metering where practical and that process upgrades and leak detection be given equal attention to upgrades of domestic fixtures.

Case Summary

SPU initiated a project in 1999 of informing and motivating Seattle hotels to think deeply about reducing water consumption. After researching what other hotels in the country did to address the problem of water conservation, SPU was ready to develop a social marketing plan for the Seattle area. Two hotels in Seattle agreed to serve as test sites. The plan called for encouraging these hotels to adopt equipment-related measures and behavior-related measures that would reduce water consumption. These measures related not only to water usage in the hotel's guest rooms but also in their kitchens and laundries. SPU implemented product, price, place, and promotion efforts to encourage the hotels' water conservation behavior. For each of the two hotels audited, potential water savings equaled approximately one third of current water consumption, and SPU regarded their efforts as a success to be expanded to all hotels in Seattle.

CASE #2   Fighting the Water Shortage Problem (Jordan)[3]

Background

A fact of modern life is that water is scarce. Some 80 countries, constituting 40% of the world's population, suffer from serious water shortages (Gleick, 2009). The three major factors causing increasing water demand over the past century are population growth, industrial development, and the expansion of irrigated agriculture (Collins/The World Bank, 2007).

The Hashemite Kingdom of Jordan is one of the world's water-poor nations. In 1999, Jordan was in the midst of its worst drought in more than a century. Because it was not possible to increase the supply of water, it was necessary to reduce demand. This would require not only investment in more efficient technology but also changes in people's behavior.

Many factors contributed to the continuation of Jordan's water shortage.

- Population growth from high birth rates coupled with unprecedented refugee immigration were placing intolerable pressure on water resources.
- Water had become a major national security issue with respect to Jordan's neighbors. The intense demand for water had reduced the Jordan River to a narrow stream.
- Millions of liters of water were being lost through antiquated plumbing systems and fixtures.
- Only 17% of the population knew about inexpensive water-saving devices.
- Jordanians felt a pervasive sense to powerlessness and inaction regarding the water shortage.
- Water was flowing into Jordanian households just 1 day per week, forcing many Jordanian families to buy extra water from expensive private suppliers.
- Farming technology lacked new irrigation methods and water was wasted.

Clearly one of the major areas needing help and improvement was Jordanian agriculture. The lack of water greatly reduced the productivity of Jordanian agriculture. To assist, the U.S. Agency for International Development (USAID) worked with the Ministry of Water and Irrigation (MWI) and the Jordan Valley Authority (JVA) and invited the Academy for Educational Development (AED) to apply social marketing to improve irrigation water use efficiency in Jordan. Other ministries and public sector organizations, such as the Ministry of Agriculture and the National Center for Agricultural Research and Technology Transfer, were also involved in land use planning, export marketing, and information outreach, as were private sector organizations, such as the Jordan Export Producers Association. This 3.5 year project began in July 2003 and continued through December 2006.

Target Audience(s) and Desired Behaviors

Table 11.2 summarizes the desired behaviors that the project team adopted for different target audiences involved in agriculture.

Table 11.2 Desired Behaviors for Target Audiences	
Target Audiences	**Desired Behaviors**
Landowners	• Develop and implement a concrete plan to save water on their farms.
Farm managers	• Implement the landowner's water conservation plan.
Agricultural laborers	• Spot irrigation leaks and fix them.
Extension agents	• Develop and implement a schedule for visiting farms and training them in modern water saving methods.
Government decision makers	• Set up incentives to encourage farms to implement water conservation methods.
Transporters and exporters	• Invest in better transportation modalities for domestic and foreign sales.

The task was to change the knowledge, attitudes, and behaviors of all of these target audiences. A baseline survey of on-farm water management on 800 farms was undertaken in early 2004. Findings indicated the following:

- More than a quarter of the farm units sampled were leased and managed by non-Jordanians, usually by Egyptians and Pakistanis, and this would require paying attention to cultural differences and practices.
- Farm laborers often made management decisions regarding timing and frequency of irrigation, fertilization, and pesticide application.
- Drip irrigation was primarily used, but farms did not use media filters or keep farm input/outputs records.
- Flow meters were seldom working properly, so it was impossible to accurately monitor on-farm water use, and irrigation was poor due to the layout of the drip irrigation system, lack of maintenance, and low water.
- The training of the public sector extension agents was found to be general and not up to date. There was no linkage between research and extension activities, and technical brochures and training manuals for farmers were almost nonexistent.
- Many of the poorer farmers relied on community-based organizations, producers associations, women's societies, and farm equipment and supply dealers for their agricultural technical information, but financial management capacity was deficient.

The project was organized to accomplish four changes that would yield measurable results:

1. Spreading of new attitudes and behavioral patterns

2. Creating community action programs in irrigation management and rainwater harvesting

3. Improving agricultural extension and technical support for farmers

4. Developing information campaigns for policy decision makers and the general public

More specifically, the project team defined these objectives:

- Promote more water-efficient crops (e.g., displace citrus and bananas with vegetables).
- Improve irrigation scheduling and irrigation system maintenance.
- Base fertilizer application rates on soil nutrient analysis.
- Develop a crop suitability map.
- Improve agricultural extension training and technical outreach to farmers.
- Upgrade the training of agricultural laborers.
- Issue revolving grants for farmer associations.
- Standardize farm code numbers in all data collection.
- Develop appropriate government legislation and policies for the agricultural sector.

A launching workshop, titled "Discovering Common Ground," was conducted for 92 stakeholders from government entities, donor organizations, nongovernmental organizations (NGOs), the private sector, and universities to share information and priorities, enhance coordination, and engage their participation. Fortunately, a consensus was reached among the multiple workgroups to cooperate in this effort to improve Jordanian agriculture.

Barriers and Benefits

What factors were impeding effective water conservation efforts in Jordan?

- Farmers didn't believe that much could be done to ameliorate the water shortage and tended to inaction.
- Farmers had little knowledge of up-to-date farming practices and technology.
- Access to efficient technologies was limited and expensive.
- Irrigation system was poorly planned and lacked measurement devices.

Clearly what was needed was trust on the part of the farming community that improvements were possible that would more than repay the investments that would have to be made. The food supply would grow and benefit the whole population.

Description of the Program

We can view the program through the 4P social marketing framework of product, price, place, and promotion.

As for product, the project team had to recommend the right equipment, supplies, and farm practices that would help the Jordanian farmers improve their water yield. To make this concrete, the project team established demonstration sites throughout the country to show farmers improved water management technologies and practices and to promote alternative cropping systems.

As to price, the project team had to figure out how to help Jordanian farmers pay for the various improvements in equipment and supplies. Because farm incomes were low, subsidies and grants had to be drawn from various government agencies and donors.

As for place, the project team hired, trained, and deployed a small cadre of recent university graduates to set up field demonstrations on improved irrigation and crop management, train farmers, and build confidence in government extension outreach. These extension agents focused on irrigation scheduling, promoting crops with lower water requirements, developing appropriate extension materials, keeping records, performing irrigation system maintenance, and liaising with other donor funded projects.

As for promotion, the project team knew they had to go beyond just delivering information and creating awareness among farmers. The team carried out a survey to identify farmer motivations, values, and perceptions on behavior change. The findings proved helpful in designing media campaigns to change farmer behavior. The project team used a variety of communication tools to improve farmer's information, attitudes, and behavior. They used fact sheets, posters, training manuals, radio, TV, CDs, and billboards. Messages were developed for different target audiences and delivered through multiple partners (e.g., schools, mosques, farmer cooperatives) and mass media, such as radio drama episodes, TV public service announcements, websites, and FAQS. These repetitive messages from multiple sources were used to saturate the entire farming community and were reinforced by field days, school clubs, farmer schools, field tours, journalist training, and other strategic initiatives. It was apparent at project outset that the social marketing campaign would be critical to achieving the anticipated results.

Evaluation

A final evaluation survey of 408 farms in November 2006 revealed the following achievements:

- There was a significant increase in the percentage of farmers using drip irrigation, in the quality of their irrigation management, including scheduling and system maintenance, and in the adoption of improved water management technologies, such as media filters and pressure gauges.

- The percentage of farmers aware of good agricultural practices for export marketing rose from an average of 8% to 25% during the last two cropping seasons.
- There was growth in the trust and confidence of farmers in the information received. These were enhanced by using demonstration sites, field days, and training workshops to certify extension service subject matter specialists and distributing technical information in print and mass media format.
- Improvements were made in the policy environment in water use allocation and irrigation.

On the other hand, farmer knowledge of cash crop alternatives, crops with lower water requirements, and the food safety standards in foreign markets were found to be low.

Critical Review

This case illustrates the power of social marketing and social action to alleviate a real problem—water scarcity—that adversely affected Jordanian agricultural productivity and Jordanian lives and well being. AED first needed to thoroughly understand the water shortage problem, which involved many economic, technological, cultural, social, and political issues. To improve agriculture, it was necessary to bring together many private and public bodies to agree on objectives and measurement standards. The different audiences had to be distinguished, and a baseline study was undertaken to find where each audience stood on knowledge, attitudes, and behavior. Then various programs were initiated and run over a 3-year period, and data was collected to measure the extent of improvements in agricultural productivity and farm attitudes and behavior. Significant improvements in irrigation, extension services, and audience knowledge, attitudes, and practices were achieved.

In all such projects, there is always a question of how many organizations to involve in the planning and implementation stages. Involving only one organization such as the Ministry of Agriculture is too little; involving several government and private organizations can be too many because each group presses for programs serving its own interests and often slows down progress. There is no easy answer to this question except that skills in consensus building and group norm development are essential.

A project such as this must recruit individuals who have the necessary skills. If they sense personal and professional gain from their involvement, they will perform well and remain active.

The project must develop clear and measurable goals. Subjective measurement parameters, such as "farmer satisfaction," "farmer understanding," and "gear production toward international markets" should be avoided. Basic terms like *farmer* should be clearly defined. In Jordan, many landowners live in

Amman, and their agricultural holdings may be multiple and scattered; this is a different meaning of farmer than a sole farmer with a small land holding.

This case illustrates the importance of making the right product decisions regarding irrigation equipment and agricultural supplies and the importance of developing field extension agents who become the channel for information, communication, and prompted and normative behavior change. All of this has to be supported by a steady stream of mass and specialized communications carried by the classic tools of communication with tailored messages going to each audience group.

Case Summary

The Hashemite Kingdom of Jordan is one of the world's water-poor nations. The government realized that increasing the water supply was not possible; therefore, it was necessary to reduce demand. They focused on several sectors, and we reviewed what steps they took to press for water conservation in the agricultural sector. The effort would call for making the right investments in efficient technology and changing the behavior of landowners, farm managers, agricultural laborers, extension agents, and transporters and exporters. The project team developed demonstration sites that showed how water could be used more efficiently; trained extension agents in the latest water saving measures; arranged for grants and subsidies to be given to deserving farms; and used a variety of communication tools to improve farmer's information, attitudes, and behavior. They delivered messages through fact sheets, posters, training manuals, radio, TV, CDs, billboards, and through schools, mosques, and farmer cooperatives. A final evaluation survey of 408 farms in November 2006 revealed a significant increase in the percentage of farmers using drip irrigation, the adoption of improved water management technologies, an impressive increase in the percentage of farmers aware of good agricultural practices for export marketing, and a growth in the trust and confidence of farmers in the information received. On the other hand, farmer knowledge of cash crop alternatives, crops with lower water requirements, and the food safety standards in foreign markets were still found to be low.

Summary

In reviewing these two cases of water conservation efforts, one involving an industry (hotels) and the other a nation (Jordan), we are alerted to the potential crises that could occur as water moves into short supply. In many areas of the world, a scarce water supply is being shared or contested by several affected parties. For example, seven U.S. states have claims to the water from Lake Mead in lower Colorado. Lake Mead's water level has been falling, and water managers have set a trigger point when they would have to introduce more drastic allocations that will affect the irrigating of lettuce, onions, and wheat; the watering of lawns and golf courses; and many other interests. This same problem of sharing a limited water resource is acute in many parts of the world. Often the population and agriculture in such areas has grown much faster than the availability of water. The inevitable result of not applying water conservation efforts today is the certainty of droughts and suffering tomorrow. We believe that marketing and demarketing theory and practice can be a source of much sound advice on how to discourage the wasteful consumption of water and how to sensibly allocate the remaining supply to contending parties.

Questions for Discussion

1. Table 11.1 listed some desirable end-state behaviors for hotels, manufacturing, agriculture, and offices. Add one or two more desirable end-state behaviors to each of the four sectors.

2. In the hotel case under price, there is a listing of price incentives that SPU offered to hotels that adopted the desired behaviors. Do you think that SPU was too generous or not generous enough? Can you think of other payments that SPU might offer to incentivize desirable behaviors of hotels?

3. How would you convince a hotel to invest in replacing low-flow toilets throughout the hotel when it would take 5 years to recover the costs?

4. Table 11.2 in the Jordanian agriculture case lists six different groups. One group is the agricultural laborers. What can you suggest that can influence poor agricultural laborers to try hard to save water and watch for any leaks?

5. Do you think that it would be feasible to develop a contest to award prizes to those farms that have saved the most water in one year? What could farms use as evidence to establish their water-saving claims? Do you think that this would be a good way to create publicity for water-saving behavior? Will it actually motivate water-saving behavior?

6. Marketers sometimes use fear appeals to motivate new behaviors. Should the project people fill the farm news media with water crisis talk (such as "no water will be available for Jordanian farmers within 3 years")? Will this work or actually hurt the cause?

Notes

1. For more information, please see http://www.environmentalleader.com/2010/03/22/world-water-day-roundup-coke-pepsi-nestle-nalco-epa-more/

2. This article is adapted from a study report prepared by O'Neill & Siegelbaum and the RICE Group on July 2002. The full report ran 127 pages. We have selected the main ideas and applied a social marketing framework to the material. We received permission to use part of the prose in the original report without using quotes. Our main purpose is to show an excellent example of applying a social marketing process to get hotels to apply better methods of water conservation.

3. This is a summary taken from two sources, "From Crisis to Consensus: A New Course for Water Efficiency in Jordan," published by AED, Center for Environmental Strategies, and the "AR-4.KAFA'A Final Report on Agriculture" supplied by Kristina Dunlevy of AED. This summary is published with permission from AED.

References

Collins/The World Bank. (2007). *Atlas of global development: A visual guide to the world's greatest challenges.* Washington, DC: Author.

Gleick, P. (2009). *The world's water 2008–2009: The biennial report on freshwater resources.* Washington: Island Press.

CHAPTER 12

Reducing Energy Use

usiness demands energy. Retail establishments want to maintain a comfortable temperature to attract customers. Office buildings need to provide adequate lighting to help maximize employee productivity. Office computers, printers, copiers, and other technologies are essential for running a competitive business. But all of these activities require energy, and business uses of energy—primarily electricity—have risen steadily over the past 25 years. Projections suggest that worldwide demand will increase by 1.5% per year through 2035 (International Energy Agency, 2010).

Energy use can be divided into four sectors: (1) residential, (2) industrial, (3) commercial, and (4) transportation. Our focus in this chapter is on electricity use in the commercial sector, including businesses, institutions, and organizations that provide services. Examples include schools, stores, restaurants, hotels, and office buildings, among others. Of all electricity consumed worldwide, most is used by the commercial sector (46%) followed by residential (34%) and industrial (20%). Note that while a considerable amount of energy is used for transportation, only a very small amount utilizes electricity (International Energy Agency, 2010).

The Problem

Energy stands at the forefront of many environmental problems. For the purposes of this chapter, we want to highlight the issue of global climate change and the important link between climate change and energy use. Worldwide, the overwhelming majority of electricity is produced by burning coal, oil, or natural gas. As an illustration, Figure 12.1 shows the breakdown of electricity generation by its sources in the United States. While each source of energy poses a unique set of environmental threats, it is carbon emissions that has attracted considerable attention in recent years.

Carbon Emissions and Global Warming. Despite the rhetoric, the available data are clear in showing that the earth is warming (National Academy of Sciences [NAS], 2010b). Over the past 100 years, the earth's temperature has increased by

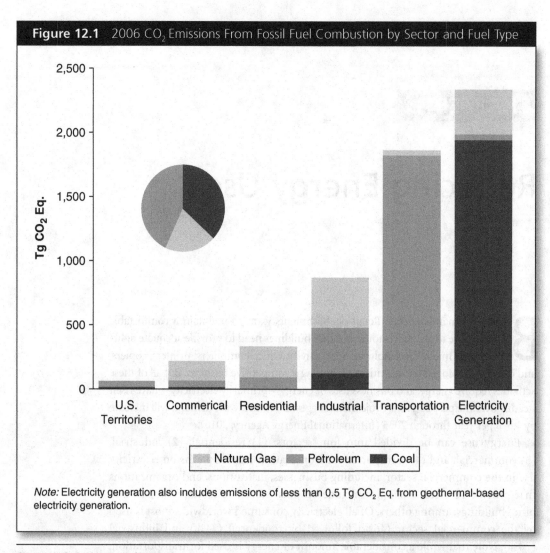

Figure 12.1 2006 CO₂ Emissions From Fossil Fuel Combustion by Sector and Fuel Type

Note: Electricity generation also includes emissions of less than 0.5 Tg CO₂ Eq. from geothermal-based electricity generation.

Source: U.S. Environmental Protection Agency, Inventory of U.S. Greenhouse Gas Emissions and Sinks: 1990–2008 (April 2010) U.S. EPA # 430-R-10-006

1.4°F (.8°C), with most of the warming occurring over the past three decades. While natural climate variability can result in large year-to-year and even decade-to-decade differences in temperature, these natural fluctuations cannot explain the longer-term trend. Global warming will result in a number of specific weather pattern changes, including increased rainfall, decreased snow cover, rising sea levels, and intense heat waves. The consequences of these changes can be dramatic, with decreases in the availability of freshwater, agricultural disruptions, negative effects on fisheries, and harmful consequences to human health (NAS, 2010a, 2010b).

Global warming is a direct consequence of human behavior and particularly our growing need for electricity. Burning fossil fuels like coal, oil, and natural gas releases a number of particulates into the air. Most notable among these emissions is CO₂, although there are a number of other gases that contribute to global warming. The carbon and other gases accumulate in the atmosphere, trapping heat that would otherwise escape from the earth's surface. This trapped heat creates a greenhouse effect, thereby warming the earth's surface temperature. The 2010 NAS (2010b) report concludes the following:

> Most of the warming over the last several decades can be attributed to human activities that release carbon dioxide (CO_2) and other heat-trapping greenhouse gases (GHGs) into the atmosphere. The burning of fossil fuel . . . for energy is the single largest human driver of climate change. (p. 2)

While fossil fuels are used to support a number of human activities, generating electricity is the largest. As shown in Figure 12.1, global electricity generation uses the most fossil fuels, particularly coal. Transportation is second, with a near-total reliance on petroleum. Finally come industrial uses, residential (primarily for space heating and cooking), and then commercial uses. So it seems clear that reducing electricity consumption, either through efficiency measures or conservation, can have a big impact on carbon emissions.

Given the dire predictions that unchecked carbon emissions can have on the planet, it seems clear that something must change. While there are a number of models for making human activity more sustainable, any solution will require changes in behavior.

Potential Behavior Solutions

Social marketing offers a promising tool for changing behavior. As we have seen throughout this book, social marketing programs draw on research findings with a target audience to identify specific barriers and benefits associated with specific behaviors. We then work to develop a product, modify the price, change the place, or develop promotional messaging to encourage individuals to change (the 4Ps of social marketing). In Chapter 6, we examined social marketing programs that targeted residential behaviors, such as home energy retrofits or installing solar hot water heaters. In this chapter, our focus is on behaviors that take place in commercial settings.

The commercial sector is the largest consumer of electricity—46% of all electricity consumption worldwide. This consumption occurs across a range of activities, including schools and educational facilities, retail locations, restaurants, hotels, and office buildings. While the electricity uses vary widely across these types of work environments, there are a number of specific behaviors that are associated with electricity use. As a starting point, we begin by classifying commercial energy use into broad categories of consumption. These are shown in Table 12.1. For each of these categories, we then identify specific behaviors that contribute to consumption.

For a social marketer, each of these behaviors provides a potential target. But selecting the specific behavior should be based on consideration of penetration, impact, and probability of change within the specific organization or target audience. For example, consider an office building with 20 floors. An energy audit of the building might show that a sizable percentage of electricity use is connected with the elevator. Encouraging workers and visitors to the office to take the stairs when they

Table 12.1   Commercial Uses of Energy in the United State

Use	Percentage of Total Energy Consumption	Examples of End-State Behaviors
Lighting	25%	• Install and use light emitting diodes (LEDs) or compact fluorescent lightbulbs (CFLs). • Use natural light from skylights and windows. • Install motion sensors to dim lights when room is not occupied. • Turn off the lights when leaving a room.
Space cooling	13%	• Use fans and natural ventilation, instead of electric air conditioners. • Plant trees outside to reduce sun exposure. • Close the blinds. • Turn off incandescent lights.
Space heating	12%	• In colder climates, use the turnstile when entering a building rather than a door. • Install added weather stripping and insulation to office buildings. • Heat only selected work areas. • Turn the heat down or off when leaving. • Discourage employees from using personal electric space heaters at their workstations. Wear a sweater or warm shoes instead.
Electronics	7%	• Install power strips and turning off electronics at the end of each work shift. • Purchase and use energy-efficient devices.
Ventilation	7%	• Add plants to the office environment. • Replace older ventilation systems with newer, more efficient ones.
Water heating	6%	• Install low-flow faucets. • Reduce the temperature setting on water heaters. • Install solar or geothermal water heating systems.
Refrigeration	4%	• Increase the temperature setting on refrigeration units. • Utilize shared refrigerator space rather than multiple individual units.
Computers	4%	• Turn off computers at night. • Reduce the brightness setting on monitors.
Cooking	2%	• Minimize food items that require cooking or refrigeration. Consider raw foods instead.
Other	20%	• Install photovoltaic solar system. • Unplug or power down equipment when not in use. • Install and program timers to disable equipment that uses "standby mode."

Source: U.S. Department of Energy. (2010). *Buildings energy data notebook*. Washington, DC: Author. Retrieved from http://buildingsdatabook.eren.doe.gov/TableView.aspx?table=3.1.4

arrive in the morning would provide a good behavioral target, in terms of impact. In addition, observational data might indicate a very low penetration rate (i.e., almost everyone uses the elevator). However, from a probability perspective, employees working on the upper floors face very different barriers than employees on the lower floors and, therefore, are less likely to change. These differential barriers need to be considered when selecting a target audience, and data should be utilized to inform the program.

We turn now to examples of social marketing programs that targeted behaviors within a commercial context. With these two examples, we focus on specific tools of changes—that is, promotional messages that were effective at producing change. Most of the previous cases discussed in this book have utilized multiple tools or simultaneously targeted several of the 4Ps of marketing. However, it's important to point out that social marketing efforts can take a variety of forms, and they do not necessarily require large budgets or multipronged programs. The essential elements are to utilize data about the target behavior, to focus on a specific target behavior (preferably nondivisible and end-state), and to develop a strategy to induce change that specifically targets the barriers or benefits associated with the behavior.

CASE #1   Using Prompts to Encourage People to Turn Off Lights (Madrid, Spain)

Background

For this case, we focus on the use of prompts to change behavior. Prompts have been used to promote changes in many environmental behaviors, and they are widely used in the energy domain. Essentially, prompts serve as a reminder, but they can also help to convey a social norm about what other people value. Here, we examine the use of prompts to encourage individuals to turn off lights when they leave a room.

When asked what actions individuals can take to conserve energy, turning off lights is one of the most frequently mentioned. The behavior is readily visible and globally applicable. For many businesses, lighting accounts for a substantial percentage of electricity use, and small reductions in consumption can have large environmental benefits. However, it is important to point out that relative to other behaviors turning off lights when leaving a room is likely to have a low impact. As discussed in Chapter 6, often one-time behaviors like installing more efficient lightbulbs or using timers to control lights can have a larger aggregated effect. But one advantage of prompting is its relatively low cost and the possibility of coupling prompts with other social marketing techniques.

Target Audience(s) and Desired Behaviors

The data for the current case come from Oceja and Berenguer (2009). Their project was designed to test the impact of prompts in different contexts and to compare the relative impact of different prompt wordings. The studies were conducted in Madrid, Spain, in the washrooms at the Universidad Autónoma and in a fast-food restaurant. The public washrooms at the university serviced students, faculty, and staff, and they studied both the men's and women's washrooms.

The washroom was a windowless space with a manual light switch on the side of the entry doorway. The behavior of individuals was recorded after they vacated the washroom, and only data from single occupants was used.

The behavior of interest was whether the person turned off the lights when they left the washroom. This is a nondivisible, end-state behavior. To establish a baseline, observations were conducted in the washrooms at the university and also in a local fast-food restaurant. Across all the observations, individuals were more likely to leave the lights on than to turn them off. However, individuals were far more likely to turn the light off if it was already off when they entered. That is, if the person had to turn the light on upon entering the space, they were nearly twice as likely to turn it off upon exiting.

Barriers and Benefits

No new audience research was conducted. However, the authors conducted a thorough literature review, noting prior studies that had used prompts and the importance of social norms in determining behavior.

Description of the Program

The focus of the project was on the use of prompts as a reminder to turn off lights when leaving the washroom. The project also examined the impact of different prompt wordings on behavior, along with perceptions about the local norm associated with turning off the lights. In this context, the norm refers to a person's beliefs about the extent to which other people leave the lights on. While such a norm could convey lack of concern about energy conservation, it could also convey a politeness or concern for safety.

Implementation. Several variations of the prompt were implemented. For our purposes here, we focus on observations of 200 users in the public washrooms. Half were male, and half were female. Most (85%) were university students, and the remainder were faculty or staff.

The authors assessed four different prompts, each placed in a different washroom (all prompts were in Spanish; the English translation is shown here):

- Cost–benefit: "You pay for the electricity that you waste." ("La electricidad que derrochas la pagas tú.")
- Common good: "Save electricity for the benefit of all." ("Es un bien de todos, ahorra electricidad.")
- Social disapproval: "Don't let the side down! Save electricity." ("No quedes en mal lugar, ahorra electricidad.")
- Correct behavior: "Before leaving, turn the light off." ("Al salir, apaga la luz.")

A fifth washroom was used as a control, and no prompt was posted.

Evaluation

The results from the behavioral observations showed several interesting effects. First, there was a basic trend for people to leave the lights on when leaving the room. On average, only 42% turned out the lights upon exiting. There was no gender difference, and men and women were equally likely to turn the lights off when leaving. Second, as with the pilot study, individuals were more likely to turn off the lights if they were already off when entering. In this case, 54% turned out the lights if they were already out when entering; 31% turned out the lights if they were on upon entering.

The evaluation also showed an interesting pattern for the prompts, and not all prompts were equally influential. In the control condition, 39% of individuals turned out the lights. Of the four different prompts, only the one that emphasized the correct behavior produced a significant change in behavior (65% turned the lights off) compared to the control. The cost–benefit (35%), common good (40%), and social disapproval (35%) did not differ significantly from the control (39%).

Critical Review

The results from this case highlight the potential for prompts to affect behavior. Particularly noteworthy is the emphasis on observed behavior rather than self-report or intentions.

The results show that prompts can have an effect on behavior, but importantly, the wording on the prompt can dramatically alter its impact. In this case, three of the prompts did not produce any change in turning off the lights. The only prompt that did have a significant effect was the one emphasizing correct behavior: Before leaving, turn the light off. This finding is in line with other behavioral research on the influence of prompts (Geller, Winett, & Everett, 1982; Werner, Rhodes, & Partain, 1998).

In summarizing the existing research on prompts, we offer the following recommendations for maximizing the impact. In general, prompts work best when

1. ... *they target a relatively simple behavior.* Across a number of studies that have tested prompts, it appears that they are most effective for behaviors that require very few steps or little effort on the part on the person. In this regard, prompts have been found to effectively prevent litter, increase recycling, and encourage specific energy conservation behaviors.

2. ... *the behavior is repetitive.* Given the nature of prompts, they apply most clearly to behaviors that occur with frequency.

3. ... *the person is already inclined to perform the behavior.* That is, prompts serve as reminders rather than persuasive elements. So in order for them to be effective, the person must have an existing motivation to do it. These motivations can be internal—for example, feeling a personal obligation to conserve energy—or external, such as a desire to avoid social disapproval.

4. ... *they are placed in close proximity to the behavior.* Because prompts are most effective for simple behaviors, placing them in close proximity increases their effectiveness. In part, this may be due to a saliency effect whereby the prompted behavior is on the person's mind at the time of

the behavior, but it may also be due to the complexity of more distant behaviors. This quality of prompts also limits the generalizability of a prompt. So, for example, prompting someone to turn off the lights when leaving the washroom is unlikely to also prompt them to turn off the office lights at the end of the day.

5. ... *they emphasize the correct behavior.* In the case just discussed, Oceja and Berenguer (2009) found that the prompt to "turn the light off" was most effective. This highlights the importance of messages that target the correct behavior rather than a prompt that reads, "DON'T LEAVE THE LIGHT ON."

6. ... *when worded politely.* Studies have shown that including "PLEASE" in a prompt can increase its effectiveness.

In addition to these specific recommendations, there is also some evidence that prompts can interact with characteristics of the surroundings—for example, prompting a behavior when it is clear that no one else is doing it can backfire. Consider the case of cigarette butt disposal. Placing a sign in an area that is highly littered encouraging smokers to use an ashtray is unlikely to induce proper disposal. In fact, such a prompt may serve to make salient the social norm in favor of littering and thereby increase littering rates (cf., Schultz & Tabanico, 2009).

CASE #2   Norms-Based Messaging to Promote Hotel Towel Reuse (California)

Background

With the growing concern about the resource and environmental issues posed by consumption, many businesses have begun implementing environmental programs and policies. In part, these efforts can be seen as an attempt to brand themselves as a green business and to retain or even attract new customers. But environmental programs can also have a positive financial impact by reducing the company's operating budget—for example, through cost savings on energy bills or reductions in waste. One business sector that was quick to recognize the potential cost savings of environmental programs was the hospitality industry, and today messages encouraging hotel guests to engage in conservation behaviors are nearly ubiquitous.

Our second case focuses on recent research examining the impact of towel reuse programs adopted by hotels.

Target Audience(s) and Desired Behaviors

The data for the current case come from a series of studies by Schultz, Khazian, and Zaleski (2008). The target audiences for the studies were guests staying one week at a time-share resort in Southern California. These guests were generally couples and families on vacation, and as with most time-shares, the guests were "owners" of time at the resort. Additional social marketing projects were conducted with guests staying at an adjacent hotel and with guests at a large hotel chain in Arizona (see Goldstein, Cialdini, & Griskevicius, 2008; Goldstein, Griskevicius, & Cialdini, 2007).

The project aimed to increase the percentage of guests who reused their bath towels. The targeted behavior was to hang the bath towel on the provided rack. Prior to the program, hotel staff replaced all the used bath towels each time the room was cleaned. For hotels, bath and linen replacement costs are substantial, including labor, equipment, energy, chemicals, and overhead (Fitzmorris, 2003). Motivating guests to reuse their towels can have a direct bottom line impact, in addition to the environmental benefits.

Barriers and Benefits

Prior to developing the program, the research team interviewed resort staff, including the general manager, director of operations, and housekeeping staff in order to learn about the day-to-day experiences associated with towel replacement. The research team also conducted interviews with resort guests, asking them about their willingness to participate in a towel reuse program.

Description of the Program

The project focused on normative messages and the role of social norms in promoting conservation behavior. Social norms refer to an individual's beliefs about the common and accepted behavior within a group. Research by behavioral scientists has distinguished between these types of social norms: injunctive and descriptive (Cialdini & Trost, 1998). Injunctive norms refer to a person's beliefs about what other people approve of doing. Descriptive norms refer to a person's beliefs about what other people actually do—that is, how widespread the behavior is among group members. Prior research has been clear in showing that social norms can strongly affect a person's behavior and that there is a strong tendency for individuals to follow the norm (Nolan, Schultz, Cialdini, Griskevicius, & Goldstein, 2008). Studies have also shown that normative messages are most influential when the injunctive and descriptive elements are aligned—that is, other people approve of this behavior, and other people do it (Cialdini, 2003; Göckeritz et al., 2010).

The principles of normative social influence were applied to create a new in-room display encouraging guests to reuse their towels. Two versions of the message were created. The first simply described the program and encouraged guests to "please reuse the towels." The second—the social norms message—included basic program information, along with an injunctive and descriptive norm. The full message read as follows:

> Many of our resort guests have expressed to us the importance of conserving energy. When given the opportunity, nearly 75% of our guests choose to reuse their towels each day. Because so many guests value conservation

and want to conserve, this resort has initiated a conservation program. Washing towels every day uses a lot of energy, so reusing towels is one way you can conserve. If you would like your towels replaced, please leave your used towels on the bathroom floor. Towels left hanging on the towel rack tell us that you want to reuse them.... PLEASE REUSE YOUR TOWELS.

A picture of the bathroom and placard is shown in Figure 12.2.

Figure 12.2   Two Images of a Hotel Bathroom

Source: The photographs were provided by the authors.

Implementation. The messages were printed on rigid plastic in-room displays and placed on the bathroom counter near the towel rack. There were a total of 132 time-share units, of which 100 were randomly selected to receive the normative message and the remaining 32 received the control message with a basic description of the program. The imbalance in room assignment was at the request at the resort management, who wanted to maximize the potential program savings.

The research team worked closely with the housekeeping staff to ensure proper placement of the placards. The team also attended several of the morning staff meetings and worked with the cleaning staff to ensure that towels left on the racks were not inadvertently replaced.

The impact of the in-room placards was evaluated over a 6-month period, resulting in a total of 794 unique "stays." Each guest stay was defined as a 7-day period, and for each round of cleaning, the team counted the number of towels replaced in each room (from 0 to 4) along with the percentage of rooms where at least one towel was reused (coded as 0 = no, 1 = yes).

Evaluation

The program design allowed for a direct comparison of the norms-based message and the control message. In the control condition, an average of 57% of the rooms reused at least one towel on the first cleaning day, and the average room replaced 2.32 towels. For the rooms that had the norms-based message, 62% of the rooms reused at least one towel and the average room replaced 1.74 towels. The difference in the number of towels replaced in each room corresponds to a 25% reduction. This effect was replicated in the hotel portion of the resort and also in a separate hotel in Arizona (Goldstein et al., 2008).

Following the study, the hotel staff implemented the norms-based messages in all the time-share and hotel rooms. Based on cost data provided by the resort, the research team estimated a cost savings of 20.5 cents per towel, excluding staff time (which could not be easily estimated but is quite substantial). Cumulatively, this resulted in an estimated annual cost of $18,300 for materials, energy, and equipment to change every towel on every cleaning day across both the time-share and hotel (assuming a replacement of four towels per unit as baseline). With the existence of a generic towel reuse program, the number of towels changed in each room dropped to 2.32. This results in a cost savings of 42% ($7,686). The added use of the norms message resulted in an additional reduction to 1.74 towels per room, for an added cost savings of 25% ($2,654). This resulted in a combined savings of $10,340 per year. Given that the printing of 200 placards for the study cost only $370, the cost savings are clear.

Critical Review

The results from this case illustrate the potential for norms-based messages to promote changes in behavior. The results from an experimental test showed a 25% reduction in towel use for a social norms message versus a generic message. However, there are several important considerations in creating social norms messaging.

First, it is important to note that the norm in this case was in favor of the target behavior. The message indicated that 75% of guests choose to reuse their towels when given the opportunity. Importantly, this was a factual number, derived from initial observations and piloting with the resort. But in instances where the norm is not in line with the target behavior, using a norms-based message can backfire. For example, informing employees that only 20% of the staff in an office turn off their computers when leaving for the night is unlikely to encourage someone to turn off their computer. In fact, while such messages are commonly used to "raise awareness" about the severity of an issue, they are likely to undermine efforts to promote conservation.

A second consideration in creating a norms-based message is the referent group. That is, what source is used to derive the norm? In the time-share example, the referent group was other guests who have stayed at the resort. But would a more specific referent have provided a stronger effect? For example, some of these might include "Other families with children . . ." or "Other guests who have stayed in this room. . . ." The existing research on this topic suggests that more focused referents can be slightly more effective, but even a generic referent can have a strong effect (Schultz, Tabanico, & Rendón, 2008).

The important consideration is not to use an out-group as a referent. Studies have shown that providing normative information about individuals from an out-group (e.g., a business competitor, a rival school, a neighboring city) can backfire (Abrams, Wetherell, Cochrane, Hogg, & Turner, 1990).

Finally, a third consideration in utilizing normative messages is that they are generally viewed as not influential. That is, when asked about the impact of normative messages, individuals—particularly individuals from individualistic cultures like those in North America and Western Europe—tend to underestimate their effect. To illustrate, a study by Nolan et al. (2008) found that normative messages produced a 10% reduction in household energy use (see Chapter 6). However, when residents were asked how much the message motivated them to conserve, the norms-based message was viewed as the least influential; in aggregate, the environmental message was seen as the most motivation, despite the fact that observational data showed that it did not induce conservation. The bottom line from these findings is that program managers should not rely solely on self-reports about what will induce change. With regard to social norms, despite the tendency for people in the United States and other individualistic cultures to deny that they are influenced by what other people think and do, social norms provide a powerful tool for effecting change.

Other Notable Programs

The two cases that were presented provide good examples of social marketing tools that can be used to induce change. Both examples were focused on energy conservation, and both of the cases were small-scale examples that emphasized the development and testing of a behavior change tool rather than a large-scale application. However, in the commercial energy arena, there have been a number of larger-scale programs. In this short section, we briefly highlight a few of the many successful cases.

Energy-Efficiency Industry Partnership, Mexico

Between 1995 and 2003, the Alliance to Save Energy conducted a social marketing program to promote energy efficiency among businesses in Mexico (Auer, 2004). The workshops were originally connected with the Mexico Sustainable Cities Program, with financial support from a number of Mexican and international organizations. The goals of the program were to raise awareness, increase access to technology for Mexican businesses, increase capacity, and promote policies and programs that encouraged energy efficiency. Initially, the program consisted of a series of public workshops and business seminars, containing presentations by vendors of energy-efficient products and services. Through feedback and formative program evaluation, the team refined the program to involve roundtable meetings, web materials, and a circulated weekly news bulletin about energy-efficient commerce and policy.

Over the 9-year span, the program administered 27 sessions featuring more than 200 presentations and was attended by more than 2,000 participants. Surveys were conducted with participants immediately following the sessions, and follow-up interviews were conducted with a sample of participants. The surveys immediately following the sessions showed a high level of engagement, generally positive ratings of the sessions, and an increase in awareness about the importance of energy efficiency. Among participants, the longer-term evaluations showed an increase in knowledge about the available energy-efficiency technologies and financing options. Among the presenters, there was strong agreement that product sales resulted directly from the seminars. Based on follow-up interviews, the team estimates that $2.8 million in sales resulted directly from the seminars, and these sales resulted in 20 million kWh of electricity saved and 152 billion Btu's saved in natural gas per year. The story of one seminar participant is presented in Box 12.1.

Box 12.1   The Impact of Community Workshops

Consider the case of Diego Castillo (a pseudonym is used here to maintain the anonymity of interviewees), a senior manager at a large tool manufacturing company in Puebla, Mexico, who attended a seminar in 2002. Castillo recognized that with a combination of good housekeeping and low cost interventions, his company could substantially reduce its electrical demand. The seminar inspired him and other company employees to sign up for a short course at Puebla's Canacintra (state industry association) to explore, in greater depth, how to reduce demand for electrical power. After the 15-hour course, instructors made site visits to the company to discuss specific energy-saving measures and devise an implementation protocol. One of the instructors was Marco Peña (again, a pseudonym), who was also a presenter at a Puebla seminar.

After several site visits by Peña, Castillo decided to purchase programmable logic control (PLC) devices to identify and monitor the sources of peak power demand in the plant. (Castillo is in the final stages of installing this equipment). The seminar led indirectly to sales for Peña. But, that transaction (with a value of around US $4,000) was not added to the data in Appendix D or E because it resulted directly from Castillo's experience at the Canacintra course and the subsequent site visits. The PLC will probably reduce the tool manufacturer's power demand by around 10 percent thanks to lower base and peak load demand. (Auer, 2004, pp. 22–23)

The Energy-Efficiency Industry Partnership illustrates the use of community-based workshops and seminars as a channel for reaching a target audience. The approach has been applied successfully in a number of other environmental domains, where representatives from a target audience (e.g., local business owners, residents, boaters, restaurant managers) come together to discuss an issue. The workshops are best when they are interactive and where each person is allowed to make a meaningful contribution. The workshops are also best when facilitated by a person who helps move the group toward consensus and who uses the group discussions to foster a social norm of concern and action. For a good example of this guided group discussion technique, see Werner (Werner, Byerly, & Sansone, 2004; Werner & Stanley, 2006). In these examples, Werner used the approach to promote the use of nontoxic household products.

Green Knights at CB Richard Ellis— Designating an Office Champion for Conservation

CB Richard Ellis (CBRE) is a multinational real estate services firm. It is the largest such firm in the world, managing more than 2 billion square feet of building space worldwide. CBRE has made a firm commitment to sustainability and has adopted environmental protection as one of its corporate priorities (see www.cbre .com). While boardroom decisions clearly affect the environmental impact of a business, CBRE also recognized the need for environmental consideration across its many daily activities. To this end, CBRE developed a "Green Knights" program. Within several of its corporate offices, one member is identified as a Green Knight. This person is charged to act as an advocate for sustainability, to provide assistance to CBRE employees to ensure compliance with sustainability standards and programs, to assist in creating new programs and products, to serve as a resource within the organization, and to engage in sustainability activities within the larger community. To date, there are 113 knights across the United States. While no evaluation data is available on the Green Knights program, it represents a coordinated effort to establish and promote sustainable practices in the operations and management of CBRE's client properties.

ENERGY STAR-Labeled Office Buildings

For many businesses, the decision to embrace environmental sustainability can have a positive impact on both sales and cost. From a sales perspective, sustainability can become an element of the brand, helping to attract new customers and increasing the value of the products and services they offer. In addition, conservation activities—especially energy conservation—can help to reduce operating costs. One good example of these positive outcomes can be found in initiatives to promote green buildings. While the behavior of the individuals that utilize a built space can dramatically affect energy consumption, it is also the case that the efficiency of the space itself can moderate consumption. Buildings from classrooms to corporate office space utilize lighting, temperature regulation, and water heating and chilling. And more efficient design, building materials, and technology can help to reduce the building load.

To encourage builders and property owners to create more energy-efficient buildings, the U.S. Environmental Protection Agency (EPA) developed its ENERGY STAR Benchmarking Program. The program utilizes a portfolio manager, which provides a standardized method for calculating a building's energy performance rating and to compare the energy performance of one building to similar others. Buildings are scored from 1 to 100, and buildings with a score of 75 and above qualify for the ENERGY STAR. The program offers participating buildings free technical assessment and recommendations for improving energy efficiency. Since the program launched in 1999, nearly 9,000 buildings in the United States have earned the ENERGY STAR. A recent evaluation of the program showed that after receiving the benchmark score and recommendation, building owners adopted 44% of the recommended upgrades and repairs, including both low-cost and capital outlay measures (Nexus Market Research, 2009). This resulted in a sizable reduction in the consumption of electricity and natural gas. Additional analyses by Miller and Pogue (2009) suggest that ENERGY STAR buildings are cheaper to operate, compared to similarly sized buildings without the label; that tenants find energy-efficient spaces more productive; and that green management practices are increasingly important to tenants.

The U.S. EPA's ENERGY STAR benchmarking program is one of many building rating programs across the globe, and there is growing interest in standardizing the scoring methods. Other examples include the Building Research Establishment Environmental Assessment Method (BREEAM) in the United Kingdom; Green Star in Australia; and Leadership in Energy and Environmental Design (LEED), among others. As businesses look to reduce their operating costs and to embrace a more environmentally sustainable business model, benchmarking programs offer a very useful mechanism for facilitating improved energy efficiency.

Change-a-Light, Change the World

In 1999, the U.S. EPA launched a campaign to encourage individuals and organizations across the country to switch to more energy-efficient forms of lighting, including CFLs and (more recently) LEDs. Compared to traditional incandescent lightbulbs, CFLs use 75% less energy and last 10 times longer; LEDs are estimated to be 80% more efficient than incandescents and can last 40 times longer. The Change-a-Light, Change the World campaign focused on a single behavior and utilized a pledge commitment (U.S. EPA, 2010). The campaign involved media relations (not ad buys), advertisements by retailers and utilities, corporate partnerships, and visibility at community events. The campaign was oriented around the pledge and generating commitments on the part of organizations and individuals. In taking the pledge, organizations committed to replace at least one light with an ENERGY STAR qualified one. The program has garnered considerable support from corporations, and in 2005, more than 70,000 individuals pledged to change at least one light.

Summary

Energy stands at the forefront of many environmental problems. Generating electricity is one of the largest areas of energy consumption and one of the leading sources of GHG emissions. The majority of electricity is generated from coal and natural gas, which result in large quantities of particulates emitted into the atmosphere, most notably CO_2. The aggregated effect of carbon emissions world-wide has played a central role in the greenhouse effect and global warming. This chapter began with a discussion of the various sources of carbon emissions and then focused on commercial uses of electricity.

The chapter presented two detailed cases that illustrated effective tools for promoting conservation in a commercial environment. In the first example, we summarized results from a study by Oceja and Berenguer (2009) of individuals turning off lights when leaving a room. Their results showed that using a prompt, placed in close proximity to the light switch, and emphasizing the correct behavior resulted in a 26% increase in the percentage of time that lights were turned off (from 39% in the control condition to 65% when prompted with the correct behavior). In a second case, we examined a norms-based message used to promote towel reuse among hotel guests. Results showed that compared with a control message, the norms-based approach generated a 25% reduction in the number of towels replaced in each room. These examples—and other cases discussed in the chapter—illustrate the role that social marketing can have in creating programs and crafting messages to promote conservation.

Questions for Discussion

1. Using the data and material presented in this chapter, how does using electricity contribute to global warming?

2. Alyssa works in a university administrative office. Based on a typical office environment in your area, generate a list of 10 nondivisible, end-state behaviors that contribute to Alyssa's electricity consumption. From your list, which behavior would you choose as a target for a social marketing campaign? Why?

3. For the behaviors you identified, do you think that a prompt or social norms approach would provide an effective tool for promoting change? Why or why not?

References

Abrams, D., Wetherell, M., Cochrane, S., Hogg, M. A., & Turner, J. C. (1990). Knowing what to think by knowing who you are: Self-categorization and the nature of norm formation, conformity and group polarization. *British Journal of Social Psychology, 29*, 97–119.

Auer, M. (2004). *Evaluating the energy efficiency industry partnership in Mexico: A report for the Alliance to Save Energy.* Retrieved from http://ase.org/files/611_file_Mexico_EEIP_Evaluation_2004_04_Full.pdf

Cialdini, R. B. (2003). Crafting normative messages to protect the environment. *Current Directions in Psychological Science, 12*, 105–109.

Cialdini, R. B., & Trost, M. R. (1998). Social influence: Social norms, conformity, and compliance. In D. Gilbert, S. Fiske, & G. Lindzey (Eds.), *Handbook of social psychology* (4th ed., Vol. 2, pp. 151–192). Boston: McGraw-Hill.

Fitzmorris, R. (2003). Hotel and motel laundry cost factors. Retrieved from http://www.laundrytoday.com/

Geller, E. S., Winett, R. A., & Everett, P. B. (1982). *Preserving the environment: New strategies for behavior change.* Elmsford, NY: Pergamon.

Göckeritz, S., Schultz, P. W., Rendón, T., Cialdini, R. B., Goldstein, N., & Griskevicius, V. (2010). Descriptive normative beliefs and conservation behavior: The moderating role of personal involvement and injunctive normative beliefs. *European Journal of Social Psychology, 40,* 514–523.

Goldstein, N., Cialdini, R., & Griskevicius, V. (2008). A room with a viewpoint: Using social norms to motivate environmental conservation in hotels. *Journal of Consumer Research, 35,* 472–482. Retrieved from http://www.carlsonschool.umn.edu/assets/118359.pdf

Goldstein, N. J., Griskevicius, V., & Cialdini, R. (2007). Invoking social norms: A social psychological perspective on improving hotels' linen-reuse program. *Cornell Hotel and Restaurant Administration Quarterly, 48,* 145–150. Retrieved from http://www.influenceatwork.com/Media/RBC/Cornell%20Quarterly%20-%20Norms.pdf

International Energy Agency. (2010). *World energy outlook.* Bedfordshire, England. Retrieved from http://www.worldenergyoutlook.org/docs/we02009/WE02009_es_english.pdf

Miller, N., & Pogue, D. (2009). *Do green buildings make dollars and sense?* USD-BMC Working Paper 09–11. Retrieved from http://catcher.sandiego.edu/items/business/Do_Green_Buildings_Make_Dollars_and_Sense_draft_Nov_6_2009.pdf

National Academy of Sciences. (2010a). *America's climate choices. Volume 2: Adapting to the impacts of climate change.* Washington DC: National Academies Press. Retrieved from http://books.nap.edu/

National Academy of Sciences. (2010b). *America's climate choices. Volume 1: Advancing the science of climate change.* Washington DC: National Academies Press. Retrieved from http://books.nap.edu/

Nexus Market Research. (2009). *Evaluation of the National Grid and NSTAR ENERGY STAR® benchmarking programs.* Cambridge, MA. Retrieved from http://www.env.state.ma.us/dpu/docs/electric/09–64/12409nstrd2ah.pdf

Nolan, J., Schultz, P. W., Cialdini, R. B., Griskevicius, V., & Goldstein, N. (2008). Normative social influence is underdetected. *Personality and Social Psychology Bulletin, 34,* 913–923.

Oceja, L., & Berenguer, J. (2009). Putting text in context: The conflict between pro-ecological messages and anti-ecological descriptive norms. *Spanish Journal of Psychology, 12,* 657–666.

Schultz, P. W., Khazian, A., & Zaleski, A. (2008). Using normative social influence to promote conservation among hotel guests. *Social Influence, 3,* 4–23.

Schultz, P. W., & Tabanico, J. T. (2009). Criminal beware: A social norms perspective on posting public warning signs. *Criminology, 47,* 1201–1222.

Schultz, P. W., Tabanico, J., & Rendón, T. (2008). Normative beliefs as agents of influence: Basic processes and real-world applications. In R. Prislin & W. Crano (Eds.), *Attitudes and attitude change* (pp. 385–409). New York: Psychology Press.

U.S. Environmental Protection Agency. (2010). *About the ENERGY STAR Change a Light Campaign.* Retrieved from http://www.energystar.gov/index.cfm?c=change_light.changealight_about.

Werner, C., Byerly, S., & Sansone, C. (2004). Changing intentions to use toxic household products through guided group discussion. [Special issue.] *18th IAPS Conference,* 147–156.

Werner, C. M., Rhodes, M. U., & Partain, K. K. (1998). Designing effective instructional signs with schema theory: Case studies of polystyrene recycling. *Environment and Behavior, 30,* 709–735.

Werner, C., & Stanley, C. (2006). *Guided group discussion: A strategy for changing behavior.* Presentation at the EPA Community Involvement Conference and Training. Milwaukee, WI. Retrieved from http://www.epa.gov/ciconference/previous/2006/download/presen tations/opt_guided.pdf

SECTION IV

Going Forward

CHAPTER 13

Concluding Thoughts and Recommendations[1]

I n this concluding chapter, we provide a series of recommendations that can spur the utilization of community-based social marketing (CBSM). Further, we also address the importance of calculating return on investments (ROIs) and the use of social media. Our recommendations are organized around the five steps of CBSM, which lend themselves well to a clear division of labor between federal/state/provincial (FSP) agencies and those working at the municipal level. More specifically, it is suggested that FSP agencies take primary responsibility for the first two steps (selecting behaviors and uncovering barriers and benefits), provide social marketing assistance with the third step (developing strategies), and utilize two-stage funding for pilots and broadscale implementation. Finally, it is suggested that FSP agencies have an important role to serve as a clearinghouse for effective programs.

Selecting Behaviors

Program planners are hampered in developing effective behavior change strategies by a lack of reliable information regarding which behaviors are most important to tackle. To address this challenge, it is recommended that FSP agencies *tier* behaviors. That is, for each domain (e.g., water, waste, energy) these agencies should identify which behaviors are most worthwhile to promote. Tiering would involve determining which set of behaviors had the best combination of impact, probability, and penetration (see Chapter 1 for further information on selecting behaviors). Why have agencies at the FSP level taken on this task? Most agencies working at the municipal level simply do not have the resources to rigorously select behaviors. It is suggested that FSP agencies create three tiers for each domain and sector (e.g., residential waste reduction versus commercial waste reduction). Tier 1 would include those behaviors that have the best combinations of high impact, low penetration, and high probability. Tier 2 would include those behaviors that, while still important to promote, do not have the combinations of impact, penetration, and probability found with Tier 1. Finally, Tier 3 would include behaviors that might be targeted once Tier 1 and Tier 2 behaviors have been adequately addressed.

Information collected by FSP agencies should be periodically updated to ensure that changes in penetration and probability are captured. Further, national web-based resources that allow municipal program planners to quickly identify which behaviors for a particular domain, sector, and region are most useful to foster would be immensely beneficial.

Uncovering Barriers and Benefits

As with selecting behaviors, it is challenging for municipal program planners to collect accurate information on barriers and benefits for specific end-state, non-divisible behaviors. With the exception of the largest municipalities, the time, expertise, and money required to rigorously identify barriers and benefits ensures that most municipalities will not collect this information. Further, it makes little sense to have numerous municipalities collecting this information rather than coordinating its collection at the FSP level.

Because barriers and benefits may differ by region, this research will need to be done in such a manner that regional variations in barriers and benefits can be identified. Research conducted at the national or state/provincial level that is regionally specific is far less expensive than having multiple regions attempt to identify barriers and benefits independently.

Developing Strategies

Presently, the task of developing behavior change programs falls almost exclusively to municipal agencies. Sadly, the lack of a central repository of knowledge regarding the development of effective behavior change programs means that each municipality must develop its own initiatives to address the environmental problems it faces. FSP agencies have several roles to play regarding the development of effective programs. Most FSP agencies do not deliver behavioral change programs directly. Instead, they rely upon municipal governments and nonprofit agencies to deliver programs that they fund. The fact that FSP agencies fund these programs provides enormous leverage to influence the quality of programs delivered at the municipal level. This leverage can be used to ensure that municipal programs target the most beneficial behaviors (e.g., high impact, low penetration, high probability). Further, this influence can be used to ensure that only programs that address identified barriers and benefits receive funding. It makes little sense to fund programs that are not anchored in a clear understanding of what precludes and motivates a target audience to act.

One of the most useful actions that FSP agencies can undertake is to begin to hire social marketers. Social marketers have played an active role in the development of health programs for decades, but their contributions have been largely absent from the environmental field until recently. These individuals can oversee the selection of behaviors, the conducting of barrier and benefit research, and its effective dissemination to municipal agencies. Further, they can assist municipal agencies in developing and evaluating their programs.

Conducting Pilots and Broadscale Implementation

It is suggested that FSP funding is provided in a two-stage process. More specifically, funding would initially be available only for the developing, conducting, and evaluating of a pilot. Only when a program was shown to be effective could funding be obtained for broadscale implementation. In addition, for large-scale programs, where considerable sums of money may be involved, it is prudent to have pilots be independently evaluated.

In addition to providing two-stage funding, FSP agencies should consider creating national repositories of effective behavioral change programs. The anti-idling program described in Chapter 4 indicates just how useful turnkey programs can be for municipal agencies. This program, which was initially pilot tested in Toronto, is now being utilized in over 200 Canadian communities. Development of turnkey programs is predicated upon there being a relatively consistent set of barriers and benefits (or providing several variants on programs that address differing barriers and benefits). Nonetheless, the provision of turnkey programs has the potential to dramatically improve the quality of programs that are delivered.

Summary of Recommendations

1. FSP agencies collect information on the impact, probability, and penetration of behaviors and use that information to tier behaviors.

2. FSP agencies periodically update this information to ensure that changes in impact, probability, and penetration are captured.

3. Information regarding which behaviors to target is pooled into a national database that is searchable based upon domain (e.g., water, waste, energy), sector (e.g., residential, commercial, agricultural), and region.

4. FSP agencies identify regionally specific barrier and benefit information. Priority is given to collecting this information first for Tier 1, Tier 2, and then, finally, Tier 3 behaviors.

5. FSP agencies collate information on barriers and benefits into a national database that can be searched by behavior, sector, and region.

6. FSP agencies structure their grants to ensure that municipal agencies target behaviors that have the best combination of impact, probability, and penetration.

7. FSP agencies selectively fund those programs where there is a clear correspondence between the strategies utilized and the barriers and benefits identified for a behavior.

8. FSP agencies hire social marketers who assist municipal agencies in the development of CBSM programs.

9. FSP agencies provide two-stage funding for programs. Pilots are funded initially, with additional funds being contingent upon successful pilots.

10. FSP agencies create national repositories of effective turnkey programs.

Return on Investment

Environmental programs are frequently evaluated based on the percentage of a target audience that adopts a sustainable behavior following a campaign. This is an important metric, but it needs to be compared to the program delivery costs to be truly meaningful. More specifically, when CBSM pilots are conducted we want to know what the ROI is for a program prior to delivering a program broadly. In a recent article, Lee (2010) set out the following guidelines for calculating ROI:

1. *Dollars Spent.* This figure should include all costs associated with the project. From a CBSM perspective, this would include all expenditures involved in selecting behaviors, identifying barriers and benefits, and developing and pilot testing the strategy.

2. *Behaviors Influenced.* Evaluation of the pilot should provide reliable information on the number of people who adopted the targeted behavior.

3. *Cost Per Behavior Influenced.* Divide Dollars Spent (#1) by Behaviors Influenced (#2).

4. *Benefit Per Behavior.* Benefit per behavior refers to costs avoided by the adoption of a sustainable behavior. These costs might involve the expenditures involved in building a new landfill if waste cannot be diverted through waste reduction activities or a new water treatment plant if water-efficiency gains cannot be secured.

To calculate ROI, do the following:

Step 1: Behaviors Influenced (#2) Times Benefit per Behavior (#4) Equals Gross Economic Benefit

Step 2: Gross Economic Benefit Minus Dollars Spent Equals Net Benefit

Step 3: Net Benefit Divided by Dollars Spent Times 100 Equals ROI

It is very useful to test several strategies against one another to determine their relative ROI. That is, one strategy might result in 60% of a target audience adopting a sustainable behavior, while another strategy, which costs significantly less, results in 50% adopting the same behavior. Depending on the behavior, many agencies would be willing to accept a slightly lower level of adoption if the cost was substantially less. Finally, note that the ROI for fully researching and implementing a CBSM strategy will be significantly higher than it will be for an agency that adopts an already well-researched campaign and simply implements it.

Social Media

The advent of social media, such as Facebook, Twitter, blogs, and Web 2.0 technologies, has led to considerable interest in how social media might be used to promote sustainable behaviors. Indeed, requests for proposals (RFPs) now frequently state that applicants must be well versed in the use of these approaches. Further, it is common for agencies to spend considerable time and money in the development of these resources. However, these new technologies should not be seen as a panacea. Instead they should be viewed from the perspective of how well, if at all, they can be utilized to address the barriers and benefits associated with a behavioral change. In the first chapter, it was explained that CBSM involves first carefully selecting a behavior based upon information regarding impact, penetration, and probability, and then identifying the barriers and benefits for this behavior prior to developing a strategy. From a CBSM perspective, these new technologies should only be employed if they address known barriers and benefits. If they do not contribute to addressing barriers and benefits, they are likely of little worth.

It also follows that agencies need to be strategic in considering just which behaviors they wish to foster via a website. It is common for agency websites to encourage visitors to engage in a wide assortment of behaviors. However, for many agencies, these websites are the *only* engagement that they have with a target audience. Consequently, if the website does not adequately address the barriers and benefits to a behavior, the likelihood of the action being adopted is very small. By implication, if agencies are attempting to foster changes in behavior solely through a website, they should limit themselves to just those behaviors for which the barriers and benefits can be adequately addressed online.

Conclusion

This book demonstrates the utility of applying CBSM to the delivery of environmental programs. Given the severity of the environmental threats humanity faces, it is critical that we begin to rigorously apply social science knowledge to the delivery of these programs as doing so can dramatically improve their quality. We believe that the delivery of successful programs can be furthered through the quick adoption of this chapter's recommendations. Further, we recommend that not only should programs be carefully evaluated but that these evaluations focus on ROI. By calculating ROI, we can determine the relative effectiveness of various strategies and make more informed decisions regarding which pilot programs warrant broadscale implementation.

Note

1. Recommendations in this chapter are covered in more depth in McKenzie-Mohr, D. (2011). *Fostering sustainable behavior: An introduction to community-based social marketing* (3rd ed.). Gabriola Island, BC: New Society.

Reference

Lee, N. (2010). Where's the beef? Social marketing in tough times. *Journal of Social Marketing, 1*(1).

Appendix

Additional Resources

Websites

Action Research, Inc.: http://www.action3630.com
AED, Social Marketing and Behavior Change: http://www.aed.org/Approaches/Social Marketing/index.cfm
Community-Based Social Marketing Training: https://register.cbsm.com/workshops/workshop-schedule
Fostering Sustainable Behavior: http://www.cbsm.com
Social Marketing Services, Inc.: http://www.socialmarketingservice.com
Tools of Change: http://www.toolsofchange.com

Discussion Forums/List Serves

Fostering Sustainable Behavior Forums

To subscribe, visit www.cbsm.com

Georgetown Social Marketing Listserv

To subscribe, send an e-mail message to LISTPROC2LISTPROC.GEORGETOWN.
EDU. In the body of the message, write "subscribe SOC-MKTG (your name)."
Type your actual name in place of "your name."

Index

About the Authors

 **Doug McKenzie-Mohr** has been working to incorporate scientific knowledge on behavior change into the design and delivery of community programs for over two decades. He is the founder of community-based social marketing (CBSM), and his book *Fostering Sustainable Behavior: An Introduction to Community-Based Social Marketing* has become requisite reading for those who deliver programs to promote sustainable behavior.

Dr. McKenzie-Mohr has worked with a diverse array of governmental and nongovernmental agencies, assisting them in identifying the barriers to behavior change and in developing and evaluating CBSM initiatives to overcome those barriers. More than 50,000 environmental program managers have attended workshops on CBSM that Dr. McKenzie-Mohr has delivered internationally. He has served as an advisor for Canada's public education efforts on climate change, as the coordinator of the international organization Holis: The Society for a Sustainable Future, and as a member of Canada's National Round Table on the Environment and the Economy. He is a former professor of psychology at St. Thomas University in New Brunswick, Canada, where he co-coordinated the Environment and Society program.

 **Nancy R. Lee** has more than 25 years of professional marketing experience, with special expertise in social marketing. She is an adjunct faculty member at the University of Washington and the University of South Florida and owns a small consulting firm in Seattle, Washington: Social Marketing Services, Inc. She conducts seminars and workshops on social marketing and marketing in the public sector and has participated in the development of more than 100 social marketing campaigns.

She has been a guest lecturer at the University of Cape Town in South Africa; the Health Promotion Board in Singapore; Victoria University in Melbourne, Australia; National University of Ireland in Galway; Yale University; and Oxford University. She has conducted social marketing workshops for more than 2,000 public sector employees involved in developing public behavior change campaigns, including most recently for US AID in Jordan. She has been a keynote speaker on social marketing at conferences including ones addressing public health, injury prevention, and environmental protection.

Nancy has coauthored six other books with Philip Kotler, including most recently *Social Marketing in Public Health, UP and OUT of Poverty: The Social Marketing Solution, and Social Marketing: Influencing Behaviors for Good.*

Nancy is a member of Rotary and is a volunteer member of the Monterey Bay Aquarium's Seafood Watch Advisory Committee, the City of Mercer Island's Green Ribbon Commission, and the Mercer Island School District's Advisory Committee.

P. Wesley Schultz is professor of psychology at California State University, San Marcos. His research interests are in applied social psychology, particularly in the area of sustainable behavior. Recent books include *Social Psychology: An Applied Perspective, Psychology of Sustainable Development,* and *Attitudes and Opinions.* His current work focuses on social norms and the importance of social norms in fostering sustainable behavior. He has worked on projects for a variety of organizations, including the U.S. Environmental Protection Agency (EPA), National Institute of General Medical Science, National Institute of Justice, and the California Integrated Waste Management Board.

As a social marketer, Professor Schultz has been engaged in program design, strategy, and evaluation for more than 20 years. Recent projects include work on the Think Blue San Diego storm water pollution prevention program, Energy Upgrade California to promote residential energy retrofits, StopWaste.Org's recycling program, the Fish Consumption Education Collaborative to reduce exposure to contaminated fish, and work with the California Environmental Protection Agency to promote proper disposal of household hazardous waste.

Philip Kotler is the S.C. Johnson Distinguished Professor of International Marketing at the Kellogg School of Management at Northwestern University in Evanston, Illinois. His *Marketing Management* (13th ed.) is one of the world's leading textbooks on marketing, and he has published 50 other books and over 150 articles in leading journals. His research spans strategic marketing, consumer marketing, business marketing, services marketing, and e-marketing. He has been a consultant to IBM, Bank of America, Merck, General Electric, Honeywell, and many other companies. He has received honorary doctorate degrees from 12 major universities in the United States and other countries. He initiated the development of the field of social marketing that deals with environmental, health, educational, and other issues.

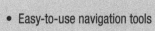

Printed in the United States
By Bookmasters